Living From Hand to Mouth

My Memoir

---

by Jerry Adler

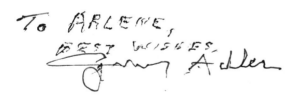

author**HOUSE**™

1663 LIBERTY DRIVE, SUITE 200
BLOOMINGTON, INDIANA 47403
(800) 839-8640
WWW.AUTHORHOUSE.COM

First published by AuthorHouse 08/09/05

ISBN: 1-4208-6122-0 (sc)

Library of Congress Control Number: 2005904892

Printed in the United States of America
Bloomington, Indiana

This book is printed on acid-free paper.

With gratitude, to
my wife, Jean,
my son, Michael,
my daughter, Susan,
and to the blessed memory
*   of my first wife, Sylvia.*

Contents

Acknowledgements

I wish to thank the following for their support, encouragement, and ideas in making this book possible: My devoted wife Jean, Dorothy Ringer, Dr. Frank C. Binkley, Marilyn Cooper, and Sally Brand; to my two children, Michael and Susan, for the special love that a son and daughter can give their Dad.

A special acknowledgement to my brother, Larry: he was an original in the realm of classical music, who proved to a world-wide audience that a simple instrument, the harmonica, in the sensitive hands of a true artist, gets the kind of respect and admiration accorded such musical giants as Vladimir Horowitz and Isaac Stern.

I vividly recall an afternoon rehearsal at the Hollywood Bowl as they were preparing for an evening benefit concert featuring the artistry of Horowitz, Stern, and Adler, plus the Los Angeles Philharmonic. Larry, who played the piano with equal virtuosity as the harmonica, had the *chutzpa* to sit at the piano and began to play in the presence of musical royalty while the orchestra was on a break. Horowitz walked up to Larry, and said, "Larry, why do you continue to play that silly little instrument, the harmonica? THIS is your instrument!"

Larry's instrument was the harmonica. He gave me the love, understanding, and encouragement to make the harmonica my instrument as well, and establish my own mark as a solo performer.

Last but certainly not least, a grateful thank you to my dear friend and editor, Kathi Futornick, who managed to shuffle a chaotic manuscript, sprinkle it with her professional magic and turn my anecdotal contributions into readable order. I could not have done it without her.

Prologue

The inspiration for this book began with my first wife, Sylvia. She was convinced that I had an exciting story to tell. Having been married to her for forty-five years, she had the insight to see the potential. The rest was up to me. Unfortunately, I am a procrastinator. "Yes, dear. I'll begin the book tomorrow."

Tomorrow never came for her. Sylvia died of cancer in August 1990.

During the many months that followed her death, I was advised by her oncologist, who was also a close friend, to return to work as quickly as possible. The advice was put into practice, and in due time, I made the difficult adjustment.

The purchase of my computer was the key that opened the door to my mind and my heart. My emotions overflowed with the grateful realization that I had the energy and the desire to bring this exciting story to fruition.

The book is divided into two parts which reflect the two phases of my life: *The Early Years* - the years before I retired from traditional show business, and *Life After Fifty* - the later years, entertaining passengers on cruise ships. The stories on celebrities are short and center on individuals with whom I worked and for many of you, are household names. Yes, I am a name dropper but the stories are genuine and show the human side of these very famous people. When the "Hollywood" style of my career ended, another door opened. Today it's not unheard of for people to begin a second career after 50. Like so many of these people, I enjoyed every minute of my second career and have included a series of stories to which many of you cruise-going readers can relate.

The Early Years

As Luck Would Have It

It was more than just a train-ride from Baltimore to Broadway. I was saying good-bye to my family. I was going from Baltimore to someplace else. The harmonica I held in my pocket was my ticket to somewhere bigger and better. I had just won the Baltimore Sun Harmonica Contest and nothing could stop me from setting my sites on show business. I was confident and had made up my mind to leave the things I had known and go off to something much bigger.

I was fifteen, the year was 1933, and the Great Depression was in full swing. But when you are at that time in your life when you want to knock the world on it's heels, you go after those things that make you determined to cover as much territory as possible. I began marching up and down Broadway attempting to make it past stage doormen, without any luck. The first day was a washout. I was confronted with discouraging remarks like, "Hey kid, getoutahere! I ain't got no time to listen to no harmonica." On the second day I became more brazen. Paul Whiteman was appearing at the Paramount Theater with his orchestra. I walked through the stage door and stated to the doorman, "I'm Jerry Adler and I have an appointment with Mr. Whiteman." He smiled at me and told me to be seated. He told Whiteman about the "pushy" kid at the stage door. I can only assume that Mr. Whiteman was in a generous mood when he told the doorman to send me back to his dressing room.

> ..."*I introduced myself as the youngest harmonica virtuoso in the worls!*"...

I managed to get an audition with Paul Whiteman, one of the most popular orchestra conductors of the day. I entered his dressing room and introduced myself as "the youngest harmonica virtuoso in the world!" Virtuoso? A nondescript gentleman was sitting at the far end of the room reading a newspaper. Whiteman smiled at me with amusement. "OK, kid, Let me hear you do your stuff. What are you going to play?" One of the big hits at the time was a pleasant lilting tune called, *Button Up Your Overcoat* and, it was the only song I knew by heart. I literally tore into it like a wild animal attacking raw meat. I tried to play it so fancy that even I didn't recognize it! I finally settled down long enough to finish it. Surprisingly, Whiteman seemed pleased. He said, "That's pretty good, kid. What else do you know?" Throwing caution to the wind, I said, "I can play anything. You name it, I'll play it!" Whiteman nearly broke into open laughter, but somehow managed to keep his amusement under control. Instead, he decided to challenge me. "Do you know Gershwin's, *Rhapsody In Blue*?" Keep in mind that I was fifteen and had yet to make my first professional appearance. Of course I was familiar with *Rhapsody In Blue* but was years away from being competent enough to attempt it. I panicked for a brief moment but was not about to have this golden opportunity slip through my fingers. I said, "Yes, I know *Rhapsody In Blue*. . . .but I don't like it." Caught off guard. He said, "You WHAT?"

"That's right, Mr. Whiteman. I don't like it."

Whiteman turned to the man reading the newspaper. "Did you hear that, George? This kid doesn't like the Rhapsody."

♫

George Gershwin

That was my introduction to George Gershwin. I wanted to fall through the nearest available hole but Gershwin was kind and understanding. This dapper, quiet gentleman smiled at me and said, "You play very well, young man. I'll tell you what I'll do. I will teach it to you and hope that you will learn to like it."

Looking back, I did not appreciate the offer. Although I feel badly now, at that time, my youthful arrogance convinced me that I didn't need anyone to teach me how to play. I was determined to learn *Rhapsody In Blue* myself. What that moment did, was confirm for me the belief that I really was a musical "virtuoso", appreciated by the best in the business. Whiteman gave me his card and told me to contact him in about a year and he promised to include me in his next variety show. Several months later, George Gershwin wrote a special arrangement of *Rhapsody In Blue* for me, which I use to this day.

When I returned to Baltimore I sensed that I was now on my way to something very big. I now had the confidence to leave my family, friends and places I had known, and go off into the unknown. My mind was made up and nothing could stop me. Gershwin and Whiteman acknowledged that I had much to offer. The rest was now up to me.

♫

What I felt after leaving Whiteman's dressing room reinforced my long-held belief that I was preordained to be in show business. It's a strange feeling when you are young and trying to connect the dots to fore-tell your future. The year I was born, 1918, was the year of the worst influenza epidemic in U.S. history. It literally snuffed out thousands of lives. Mothers and their newborn babies were dying in frightening numbers. Of those afflicted, few survived. When I was two months old, my mother and I came down with this rampant killer. We were counted among the few mother and baby survivors. Just as we have "Cancer Survivor" lists today, our names are engraved on a bronze plaque that lists the influenza survivors in alphabetical order. It still hangs in the City Hall of Baltimore, Maryland. Looking back on an event totally out of my control, I can't help but wonder if someone up there was sending me a message that I would receive top-billing - that is what my future would bring.

My father was a tradesman – a hard working plumber who did more ditch-digging than plumbing. Things were very rough in those days. Money was scarce and the work hours were long. Dad went to work at 5:00 A.M. and returned home at 8:00 P.M. As children, my brother Larry and I saw very little of him, so the responsibility for raising two boys fell onto my mother's shoulders.

Mother was the proverbial rock with a very generous dose of warmth. She was a beautiful woman who went about her daily life without much fanfare. That's how she liked it. She held the family together on pennies a day. My father would serve the cabbage, latkes, (potato pancakes), matzo balls and ladle out the chicken broth. There was such an aroma with that soup! I can sense it now. Just waiting for the smell to hit me was enough to make me feel warm and safe. As much as I loved the smell of mom's stuffed cabbage and broth, I loved even more the eating of it. It all comes back to me. The peaceful smell of home. There was little talk at the dinner table. We held with Jewish tradition - conversation always took second-place to the eating of good food.

> *Happiness does have a smell and I know it stole into*
> *every corner of our home in those early years.*

My mother was always on the run from the moment she lifted herself out of bed, to the stove, to the broom, to the desk where I did my home work. She worked with a purpose so the results of my father's meager funds would not be wasted. She saw a future for Larry and me and by getting us to read one book a week from the library, she saw education as the key to our future.

As a child, I was weak and sickly. Our doctor prescribed cod liver extract to build up my resistance. This came in powder form and had to be mixed with water. I flatly refused to drink this "toxic brew" and mother had to arrange for the pharmacist to place the powder in individual capsules. A very costly process but caring mothers did these things for their children even during the Great Depression. I swallowed twelve capsules every morning for two years. It seemed to do the trick.

Although my mother continued to motivate me in school, I remained only a fair student. Passing grades were a chronic struggle. To my family's surprise, we learned from the school nurse that I had dyslexia This was later confirmed by our family doctor. The diagnosis came at a time when dyslexia was not a commonly recognized or accepted affliction. Over the years I learned to compensate. Another difficulty was a lack of concentration. This is the real reason for receiving poor grades. Music constantly went through my head and brightened my spirits. It was not to be stopped, and I welcomed it. So, instead of focusing on the class assignments, I was nervously finger-tapping out tunes on my desk. One day, my home room teacher approached me from the rear of the room. I was so involved with the Lucky Strike Hit Parade, the most popular radio show of the thirties, that I didn't notice her. She asked, "Would you please tell me what you are doing?" Without thinking, I looked up and said, *Stardust*, which happened to be number one on the Hit Parade list. Music dominated my thoughts as a child and throughout all of my adult life. Not conducive for school lessons but in the end, it worked out just fine.

The flu I had contracted as an infant left me frail and weak, and without much self-confidence. So I never cared for sports or activities that were physically demanding. Instead, I sold subscriptions to Liberty Magazine. Compensation came in the form of prizes. I sold enough subscriptions to earn a dream bicycle. Winning the bike made me mobile enough to explore our section of Baltimore. I was only nine years old and as I became a proficient rider, my self-esteem began to grow. I wanted to explore the different areas of our neighborhood. But my parents ordered me to remain in our neighborhood. Not always listening, my treks brought me into racially segregated sections. This was the first time that I became aware of socially-defined differences between whites and blacks. I discovered, for example that blacks lived in their own section and also attended separate schools. This puzzled more than shocked me because I was never consciously aware of color "differences". This would not be my last experience with racial prejudice. My liberal attitude was ingrained in me. I believed then as I do today that it is natural for blacks and whites to play and work together, so why not live in the same neighborhood?

My father barely earned enough to make ends meet...

Dad seemed to be more attentive to Larry than to Mother and me. I don't know why. We knew that he worked hard at a job he hated. When he finally managed to own his own business, he arranged to have "Adler's Plumbing Shop On Wheels" painted on each side of his truck. He was terribly proud of that. As with many Jewish parents, he was devoted to his family. One day my father informed us that he was sending Larry to a boy's camp due to his fine school grades. He was sending him to Camp Cody, an exclusive camp in the mountains of New Hampshire. My father barely earned enough to make ends meet and I was puzzled by the expensive gesture. However, after Larry was there for two weeks, my parents arranged for us to visit him. I had never been anywhere other than the five or six block area of our neighborhood. The sights of fresh greenery, majestic mountains and the thrill of the open road was too much to absorb. I found myself staring open-mouthed at things that others take for granted. We passed many neatly organized farms with cattle. My God, it was my first view of real cows!

When we reached Camp Cody I thought it was the closest thing to heaven on earth. I drank in the luxury of camp life with its crystal clear lake, sleeping cabins and the glorious aroma of burning wood from a bonfire. How I yearned to be part of it.

We spent five days in a guest cabin and enjoyed the fruits of camp life, which made me more eager than ever to have the opportunity to participate. How does one earn such a prize? I knew that earning it scholastically was out of the question. Tapping out *Stardust* was not going to do it. I would have to create something far more inventive.

Two years later, my father announced that he had set aside enough money to send me to Camp Airy. This was a boy's camp sponsored by our local synagogue. It was located in the Blue Ridge Mountains of Maryland. I was speechless! What had I done to deserve such a wonderful gift? Dad put his arm around my shoulder and said, "Mother and I are so proud of what you did to earn a new bicycle plus the wonderful things that you are doing for the young mothers in the neighborhood." I burst into tears of joy! I was always a sucker around babies so I decided to offer my services as a baby sitter for the monumental sum of 10 cents per hour. My efforts had been recognized.

Preparing the list of items that I was instructed to bring is one of the major highlights of my life at that time. I cannot ever recall being so happy. Needless to say I did not get much sleep for the two weeks prior to my departure. I had been teaching myself the harmonica, and Mother urged me to take it along. My parents and I had a great celebration dinner on the night before I was scheduled to leave for camp.

I was on my way to a new adventure and was determined to fulfill every dream that I had ever had about camp life. I was terribly thin, wore glasses and was constantly walking out of my tennis shoes. I was a physical mess and was very conscious of that fact. We assembled in front of the synagogue to board a large, comfortable bus. We were all anxious to leave and it seemed like hours before we finally departed. All of us had our faces glued to the windows, waving our good-byes. This was my first experience at being away from home and family. The thrill of independence and personal responsibility gave me a wonderful feeling of euphoria. My spirits were at an all-time high and the comradeship between the boys and the counselors was an electrifying experience. The counselors taught us the camp songs as we made our way into the Maryland countryside.

> *When I started to learn the harmonica, I found that I had a natural flair for learning quickly.*

When we finally arrived at Camp Airy, I was overwhelmed by its beauty. It was my second experience in mountainous country and I could not get enough of it. We were quickly assigned cabins and ordered to unpack our things neatly within ten minutes, and then meet our counselor in front of the cabin. He introduced himself and warmly shook hands with each of us. His name was Victor Emanuel and we were to be his responsibility for the next three weeks. He impressed me as being a very generous, kindly individual and within minutes, we all felt as if we had known him for years.

Mr. Emanuel, was well-tanned and muscular. He took us on a guided tour of the camp. Each step was even more exciting than the last. An Olympic-sized swimming pool as well as lake swimming, horseback riding, campfires, movie, basketball court, hayrides, softball diamond and canoeing. It was more than a dream come true.

I was able to bunk with my close friends and we talked constantly about what our favorite pastimes would be. Most of us looked forward to horseback riding and canoeing. I had never been on a horse nor paddled a canoe.

When I began to learn the harmonica I discovered that I had a natural flair for learning quickly. I'm sure that my brother's influence had a good deal to do with that. I had been playing harmonica for about two months prior to going to camp, so I felt that I was at least one step above being a novice. The harmonica made me an immediate celebrity with the other boys. I was asked to play at the bonfire weenie roasts plus the hayrides. Whenever we went on bus rides, I was asked to bring my harmonica. One day we were told that we would be visiting Camp Louise, a girl's camp, also sponsored by our synagogue. We all piled into our buses and drove the three miles to Camp Louise. All of the girls were waiting at the entrance to "give us the once over". Children at that age can be extremely cruel and insensitive. I was bombarded with remarks, such as "four-eyed monkey, skinny, ugly and puny".

I managed to sneak away from the "wonderful" day at Camp Louise and I spent most of the time sitting in the bus playing my harmonica. Nobody was happier to return to Camp Airy. The Camp Louise experience was a bitter one and I promised myself that it would not happen again.

I began to take the harmonica seriously when I was thirteen. The reasons were twofold: to make my brother Larry proud of me and, social survival. I previously mentioned that I was a scrawny, unattractive boy and did not share the kind of social activities that most of my peers took for granted. I envied the kids who already had girlfriends. I did know a few girls, but none of them took me seriously.

It suddenly occurred to me, that if I applied myself to the harmonica it would magically provide a passport to happiness. I could get girls to like me. Fortunately, I learned to play well enough to be invited to parties. It was at that point that girls began to accept dates with me. In retrospect, I had discovered that my proficiency with the harmonica had developed in me a sense of self-esteem. I realized that I finally had something to offer.

> *...my proficiency with the harmonica had developed in me a sense of self esteem.*

A couple of my friends had parents wealthy enough to buy them cars. At thirteen, they could obtain driver licenses in Virginia. Their parents permitted them to use phony Virginia addresses and return to Maryland with official licenses. I became aggressive enough to cultivate the boys who had cars with rumble seats in order to be invited to double date. For those of you too young to know about rumble seats, they are folding seats in the back of the car where the trunk is located but not covered by the top. I had visions of spending an evening of kissing, groping and squeezing. Instead, the couple inside the car insisted that I play the harmonica!

Picture in your mind's eye this bizarre scene. The car is parked in a dark, secluded area. The couple up front is "making out", and my date and I are in the rumble seat. She is huddled in the corner trying to keep warm, and I sit there like an idiot blowing a harmonica and freezing my ass off! It is physically impossible to "make out" when one needs two hands to play the harmonica! I often wondered what my brother did under similar circumstances.

♬

Eddie Michelson

At thirteen, my best friend was Eddie Michelson. We were the same age, but Eddie was tall and massive and passed for someone much older. We were inseparable and spent many hours together playing records, with me playing the harmonica while Eddie beat out a rhythm with his hands on the table. Eddie eventually became a better than average drummer. My forte was my God-given ability for remembering as well as playing special arrangements to the sounds of Goodman, Dorsey, Lunceford and others.

My long awaited Bar Mitzvah (Confirmation) had finally arrived. This is an important ceremony in which, by Jewish tradition, a young man enters manhood. It is the culmination of many hours of memorization and practice by a thirteen year old boy who has learned a special section of the Torah in Hebrew. I read it aloud in front of family, close friends, and assembled congregation and was then considered "a man."

> *...the best Bar Mitzvah gift he could give me would be a trip to a whore house.*

My friend Eddie took everything literally, so he decided that, "being a man", the best Bar Mitzvah gift that he could give me would be a free trip to a whore house! He did have a considerable edge on me in sexual activity. When the Bar Mitzvah ended, we arranged to go to the whore house the next day, which was Sunday. I was very excited and damned nervous. I had a preconceived idea of what a whore house would be like. We arrived at a small, run-down house located in a depressed section of Baltimore. Eddie knocked and a huge woman in her early forties opened the door. She had thick, blond hair that obviously needed washing, and she wore a filthy, food-stained apron. She looked at me with a smile that was missing two front teeth. She turned to Eddie and said, "Hi, Ed. Didja bring us some new business?"

"Hi, Mrs. Slade. This is my friend, Jerry Adler."

She shook my hand vigorously, nearly pulling my scrawny arm out of its socket. This was not what I had pictured in my fertile mind. We entered a dark, foul-smelling room. The furniture had gaping rips, was discolored and, in general, looked as if it had never been cleaned. There was a round wood table in the center with a huge lamp and an open bulb hanging from the ceiling that was covered with cobwebs. I was ready to leave immediately, but Eddie pushed me into a chair. I did not anticipate anything like this. I pictured a bevy of stunning girls lounging on exquisite upholstered furniture waiting to be the lucky ones to be chosen. Instead, I was sitting opposite a fat, ugly old lady. The only whore was the lady's seventeen-year-old daughter. She came out of the bedroom and was larger than her mother and looked like Buster Keaton. Eddie assumed (correctly) that I would be too nervous to go first, so when he went into the bedroom with this "vision", the mother and I sat in silence.

This lasted for about a minute and then she asked, "Do you play pick up sticks?"

I had no idea what she was talking about.

"It's a game. You play it with different colored sticks."

With this, she tossed a can of brightly colored red, blue, yellow and green sticks all over the table. She volunteered to teach me and before long, we were involved in this fascinating game to the accompaniment of a violently bouncing bed spring coming from the bedroom. Eddie finally came out with a stupid grin on his face. "OK, Jer, you're next."

I said, "I can't. I'm right in the middle of a game."

He looked at me as if I had lost my mind. "To hell with the game! She's in there waiting for you!"

"I'm sorry, but I never quit in the middle of a game."

The mother said, "That's OK, honey. The game can wait."

I replied, "No, it can't. I've got to see how this ends."

Eddie began pacing nervously, gesturing toward the bedroom. When we finally finished the game, I said, "I'm tired, Eddie. Let's go home."

He cried, "Are you crazy! I just paid Mrs. Slade a buck for you!"

I replied, "It's OK, I'll give you the buck out of my allowance."

> *The harmonica...has a total of 48 notes...can produce any type of music...*

My fascination with show business was overwhelming. I was impatient to show what I could do. The harmonica that I played was a Hohner #270, made in Germany, measuring 5 ½ inches long with a range of three octaves. It is called a Hohner Chromatic, meaning that it has a slide under the mouthpiece that, when pressed with your index finger, changes to half notes similar to playing the black keys on the piano. It has a total of 48 notes and theoretically, can produce any type of music from country-western, to popular, to jazz as well as classical, depending on the skill of the player.

When I first started to play, I was following my brother Larry's lead and quickly developed into a respectable player. At my brother's suggestion, I entered the Baltimore Sun Harmonica Contest. He had entered the same contest five years earlier, and won first prize. I asked his advice as to what I should play.

"Play Beethoven's Minuet in G, as I did. You can't miss."

I was familiar with the melody and knew it to be a simple melody to play. I was disappointed, because I felt that I should play something flashy to really impress the judges. Larry said, "Jerry, they will all be playing things like that. Be different. Show them that the harmonica, in the right hands, can be applied to classical music. That will impress them."

I did have a problem unrelated to the contest. I had developed an abscessed tooth and my right jaw was quite swollen. I suggested to Larry that perhaps I should wait until the following year.

He fluffed it off. "I know you. If you wait, you will never do it. Forget about the tooth and just think about the music and show them what you can do."

After I rehearsed in private, Larry asked me to play it for him. I thought that I had played it well and looked at him for approval.

He said, "So far, so good. Play it again. You left out the middle section."

"What middle section?"

He took my harmonica and played a very fast and technically difficult section that I had never heard!

"I've never heard that part and even if I had, I wouldn't be able to play it!"

"Sure you can.. Just apply yourself."

He kept me awake until three-thirty in the morning learning the damned thing. My tooth was killing me and I was running a fever but I did learn the middle section.

The following day Larry went with me to the contest, but my jaw was now twice its normal size. Several harmonica players preceded me while I sat there moaning with pain. When my name was called, I suddenly developed a surge of energy and walked on stage with a new determination. I announced my selection. I received a nod from the main judge and then proceeded to play. Just as I reached the middle section which was so difficult, the judge raised his arm and said, "Thank you young man. We have heard enough."

I left the stage totally dejected. I felt that I had loused up everything. I had to sit there and wait for three other contestants to perform before they agreed on the first prize winner. When I heard my name called, I was thrilled and angry at the same time. I walked on stage and was presented a silver-plated loving cup and a medal plus a week's paid engagement of $150 at the Hippodrome, the most popular vaudeville theater in Baltimore. Larry threw his arms around me to offer congratulations. I gratefully smiled but remember, I was up all night learning a difficult part that I didn't get a chance to play!

Larry and I have had many parallels in our respective careers. We were both self-taught. Larry began his career at the age of thirteen. Five years later, with his encouragement. I also began at thirteen. We both won first prize playing the same number. Although there were many parallels, we were also complete opposites in temperament. From early-on in his childhood, he realized he was going to be someone special. He had the intellect and talent that allowed him to cultivate the "right" people. From the age of 17, he associated with people such as Franklin P. Adams, a writer for the New Yorker magazine, James Thurber, Elsa Maxwell, S.J. Perlman, Professor Hiakawa, Isaac Stern, Vladimir Horowitz, Jack Benny, Fred Allen, Charlie Chaplin, Itzak Perlman, and the list goes on. Larry was a virtuoso musician on the harmonica as well as the piano. He was a brilliant scholar, arriving at his senior year in high school at the unprecedented age of 14 while I was struggling to receive passing grades. He also became a junior cantor at our synagogue at the age of 12 and surprised all of us with his ultra-religious lifestyle.

On Sabbath, Larry would not allow mother to do any work around the house. The Sabbath started at sundown on Friday and ended at sundown on Saturday. This meant that we were not permitted to turn on lights, carry coins in our pockets, etc. Larry saw that we adhered to the Jewish traditions whenever he was around. On the other hand, when Larry entered show business at the age of 15, he quit high school because he was convinced that they could not teach him anything more.

Larry's chutzpah and genius mesmerized our family and by the age of 18 he was an established harmonica virtuoso. There was one drawback to all of this. His religion was a hindrance to his chosen lifestyle. While on the road, the only food that he ate was cornflakes to maintain his kosher traditions. He ate cornflakes for breakfast, lunch and dinner. It only took a short time before he realized that this would not work. Overnight, he changed his eating habits, rejected his religion and everything it represented.

> *He (Larry) was also blunt in telling me to create my own style rather than copy his.*

Along with this incredible change in lifestyle, he developed a monumental ego. Glowing press releases were considered normal and he felt that he was well on his way to becoming an international star. Larry and I were extremely fond of each other and he took a strong interest in my future. He encouraged me to practice the harmonica just as he did, and be self-taught, just as he was. He was also blunt in telling me to create my own style rather than copy his.

♫

Red Skelton

It was now time for one of my harmonica contest prizes, a week's engagement at the Hippodrome. I discovered that I was going to be on the same bill with the great Red Skelton! My first professional engagement and I was sharing it with a super star! Of course I was excited about meeting him in person as well as watch a polished entertainer perform his artistry close-up. In those days, we performed five shows a day with a first run movie in between. The film was "One Night of Love," starring the great opera star, Grace Moore. The film was a national smash hit and it was being held over for the third week. However, the stage shows were changed every week due to previous commitments by the performers. I was nervous about going in with a film that was being held over. However, Red packed them in at every performance.

As the week progressed, I was puzzled that none of my friends or relatives had come backstage to congratulate me. I finally realized that the price of admission was fifty cents until 5:00 P.M. and seventy-five cents in the evening. They had all seen the movie and were not about to pay to see it again. I was devastated.

Skelton was every inch the professional performer. I watched him closely in an attempt to pick up bits and pieces that I could apply to my act. He spotted me in the wings while he was on stage and came to me later and said, "Jerry, why don't you come to my dressing room and let me show you a few things to make you feel more comfortable on stage." He showed me how to stand when addressing an audience, what to do with my arms, using the proper body language to make a point, and last but not least . . . timing. A particular bit of advice I have never forgotten. Skelton said, "When you finish a number and the audience applauds, don't interrupt them. Let them finish the applause before you continue. Most acts have a tendency to talk while the audience is still applauding, and that's wrong." I practiced his advice and noticed a tremendous difference in the response.

Despite his uncanny timing and impeccable delivery he was always successful in wrapping his fans in his arms and each performance became a love affair between artist and audience. However, sad to say, Red was an alcoholic. So much so that it was a miracle that he was able to stay on his feet during a performance. One night I watched closely when he came off-stage. The moment he was out of sight of the audience, he collapsed in a drunken stupor. To my knowledge he never looked for help and continued drinking until his death. Red was a kind person, drunk or sober and he was adored by every employee in the theater.

Ten years had passed when I suddenly came face to face with Red on a shooting stage at MGM, where he was under contract. He was chatting with studio mogul, Louis B. Mayer. He spotted me immediately and walked over and embraced me in a huge bear hug. It was so good to see him again and he looked ten years younger. He became a huge success in films until finally he returned to his old roots, live comedy in a theater. One of his other great talents was with an artist's brush. His forte was painting clowns and it eventually made him an independently wealthy man. What a gentleman.

> *It was ...at the Hippodrome that an incident occurred that was to change my future dramatically.*

It was during my engagement at the Hippodrome that an incident occurred that was to change my future dramatically. A British agent happened to attend one of the evening shows and, after the show, came backstage to see me. He asked if I would be interested in going to England and perform at the London Palladium. I had no idea what the London Palladium was but it sounded important. I was never more excited! My answer was an unqualified, "Yes". But, because of my age, I would have to get permission from my parents.

It took less than thirty seconds to watch my career collapse in a ruinous heap. My Mom and Dad attempted to handle this delicately with as much compassion and understanding as befits loving parents.

"We're sorry, son," my father said. "We cannot allow you to quit school. There will be plenty of time to think about show business after you graduate."

I performed the time-honored ritual of raving and ranting, including unwarranted accusations that they didn't care about me and were ruining my one and only opportunity! I failed to win my case. Well, almost.

I entered high school but my heart wasn't in it. Show business stubbornly blocked my thinking process.

One day, I went to my room, found the British agent's business card and wrote to him that I was now ready. Within one month I received an answer including a Palladium contract for five hundred dollars a week! I was bouncing all over the house with excitement and rushed to show the contract to my father. He read it in disbelief. I knew what he was thinking. He didn't earn that much in two months. After two hours of arguing and debating, I finally won them over.

My mother was the oldest of four girls in her family, a strikingly beautiful woman with raven hair pulled back in an exotic bun. But Mother had always been an introvert. She completed high school at a time when most girls had to leave school to support their families. Despite her education, she had no interests outside of family life. Nothing else interested her or influenced her, except my father. He was a relatively pleasant looking man who was also the oldest of four brothers and four sisters who had an inordinate affection for his family - brothers, sisters, father, mother nephews, aunts, and uncles. He showered them with much love and affection and Mother seemed to take a backseat and accept this narrow view of life. Apparently, my father came from the old orthodox school of Jewish tradition where "family" deserved top priority. Not having the incentive to pursue other interests, Mother adjusted and eventually found the arrangement acceptable. I could be wrong but I do not recall their taking simple walks together, going to the movies, or any other form of relaxation as husband and wife. Everything in the world was family, and nothing else mattered.

So there I was, on the brink of taking my first step to something "big" and to do so, meant creating a major upheaval in our family structure. Although Larry had broken the ice several years before and was off being famous, I was the last one at home and my parents were not going to ship me off to London alone, not at sixteen. As I looked at Dad, I suddenly realized that he was as excited about the future as I was. Here was an opportunity to dump his miserable, back-breaking job, go to Europe, and assume the responsibilities of managing Larry while taking care of me. For the record, Larry was not made aware of these changes. As for my father, it appeared to be a foregone conclusion that this is what would happen.

It was also decided that Mother would travel with me. Dad and I were so caught up in the excitement of our new venture that we didn't notice the immediate strain on Mother. My mother was a sensitive, insecure woman who dreaded any changes in her life. This change of lifestyle so overwhelmed her that it turned to panic. Mother was a dear, loving and tender flower that was about to be transplanted into a world totally foreign to her.

> *How quickly Dad's priorities had changed.*

Dad had saved enough money to purchase tourist class tickets for Mother and me to sail to England aboard the Queen Mary. Unlike the cruise ships of today, the Queen Mary was built as a luxury liner designed to transport passengers and oftentimes families, on very long journeys. Mother and I proceeded first while Dad stayed behind to tie up the loose ends of our lives. How quickly Dad's priorities had changed!

♫

Dr. Giovanni

Mother and I arrived at the dock in New York. I was excited but mother was in a state of terror. She had not been to New York in years and was paralyzed by the hustle and bustle of such a fast moving world. Mother succumbed to exhaustion while I quickly learned the procedures to get us on board. I managed to make friends with one of the security guards who recognized that this was all new to us. He led us through the process and we were finally aboard and safely settled in our stateroom. Mother was mentally and physically traumatized. She rested in the stateroom while I went up on deck to enjoy the excitement. So many passengers and visitors! As luck would have it, I recognized an old acquaintance, a delightful gentleman named Dr. Giovanni. He was not a real doctor. He was also in show business and did a superb pickpocket act by calling people up from the audience and then proceeded to remove items like wallets, rings, watches and even suspenders without their knowledge. I had met him when he was on the bill with Larry in Baltimore. I introduced myself, reminding him that I was Larry's brother and that we had met in Baltimore. He too was delighted to meet someone he knew from show business, and asked about my plans. After explaining my Palladium contract, he asked, "Where is your stateroom?" I said that we were in tourist class. He smiled and said, "Come with me and don't say a word. Let me do all of the talking." We went to the Chief Purser's office and Giovanni introduced me as follows. "I would like you to meet one of the youngest international stars in show business. This young man is Jerry Adler, the finest young harmonica player in the world. He will be performing at the London Palladium. He would be delighted to entertain the passengers on behalf of the Seamen's Aid Society." The Purser looked at me. "Would you really do that, Mr. Adler?" I nodded in agreement but was baffled. He reached over his desk to shake my hand. When we returned to the outside deck, I said, "What was that all about?"

He smiled and replied, "You'll see."

I was very curious but did not press the matter. I excused myself to check on Mother. As I turned to leave, Giovanni called to me. "Jerry, you forgot something." I turned and he handed me my wrist watch and wallet! He had removed them while speaking to the Purser. I was so startled that I began to laugh. He said, "You can now check on your momma." I laughed all the way to the stateroom.

In those days, there was no such thing as cruise ships. Ocean liners were forms of transportation and did not provide lavish shows such as they do now. Most of the entertainment was recruited by tracking down celebrity passengers to perform. Oftentimes donations would be collected in a "hat" for the benefit of the Seamen's Aid Society.

When I returned to the stateroom, Mother was resting. A short time later, there was a knock on the door. A young man in a bright, attractive uniform and wearing a pill box hat said, "Excuse me sir. Are you Mr. Adler?" I nodded and he asked my mother and me to please follow him. We were puzzled but assumed that this was something that we had to do. We followed as instructed and walked to the First Class section of the ship where he led us to an exquisite suite with two huge beds, a sitting room, and a large bathroom with shower, bathtub and what appeared to be two toilets! The young man grinned and said, "This is your new suite, sir."

Arrangements were made to have all of our belongings transferred to the suite but mother and I were still in shock as to what was happening. In a short time, Giovanni came to visit. I introduced him to Mother and he sat down to explain. "Whenever an entertainer comes aboard, they are approached by the Chief Purser and he requests that they perform for the passengers. In return, the entertainer is automatically bumped up to First Class but eats in the Tourist dining room. In your case, they were not aware that you were an entertainer so I acted as your spokesman. I hope that it was OK with you?"

I said, "Are you kidding! It's great! Thank you very much."

"I'm sure that you and your mother will be much more comfortable here," Giovanni responded.

I said, "By the way, can you explain something to us? Why do they have two toilets in the bathroom?"

Giovanni began to laugh and looked at mother slyly. "The other one is a bidet."

Neither Mother nor I knew the meaning of the word but we decided that it had to do with something that involved mother. We elected to wait and ask the stewardess.

Our performance was a huge success and as it turned out, Giovanni and I were the only entertainers aboard. We became instant celebrities and during the crossing, all of us, including Mother, were invited to many cocktail parties. Mother and I drank Cokes.

Life aboard the Queen Mary was both exciting and overwhelming. Never having been exposed to such luxury, I remember the first time we had lunch on deck. We finished eating, picked up our dishes and began looking for the kitchen to wash them! We quickly found out that this was a no-no. The exquisite food, and the lifestyle that was once unreachable, became a reality. How to adjust? Mother and I had difficulty at first, but slowly eased into our once-in-a-life-time experience.

When we arrived in Southampton, Larry met the ship and traveled with us to London by train. He had booked a medium priced hotel where we waited until my father arrived.

From the moment of Dad's arrival, he and Mother spent every waking hour looking for a decent home to rent that was within our budget. Keep in mind that the only one earning any money at that time was Larry, so we had to be extremely frugal. We finally found a nice house in Golders Green, a residential suburb of London that seemed appropriate for our needs.

> *I gained...self-confidence and show business savvy for the most important engagement of my career.*

The British agent who booked me at the Palladium suggested that I work the many music halls that peppered London and its surrounding hamlets before tackling the finest music hall in England. That way, my name would increase in popularity and the experience would better prepare me for my Palladium debut. I worked for one year before he would allow me to take the Palladium plunge. I gained a great deal of self-confidence and show business savvy for the most important engagement of my career.

Larry had met and fallen in love with a lovely English model. Within three months, they married and were off on their own. At sixteen, I was old enough to assume family responsibilities while Dad was managing Larry's career. I was starting to fit in like a native, absorbing much of the characteristics and general demeanor of the British. While I blended in with surprising ease, it was far more difficult for Mother. She continued to fear being left alone and would not venture out of the house, even to shop at the grocery, which was only a block away. She always waited for Dad or me to return home.

♪

Max Miller

A year had passed and it was now time for my Palladium engagement. Our house was buzzing with excitement. I was beginning what I hoped would be my big-time career at the most prestigious music hall in Great Britain. It was a dream come true and I lay awake for many nights in anticipation.

The headliner was British comedian, Max Miller. I had heard his name and knew that he was considered a super star. On the morning of rehearsal, I was jumping out of my skin with excitement. My first priority was to view the marquee at the front of the theater . There it was! "JERRY ADLER - America's youngest mouth organ virtuoso". I rushed backstage and gasped in astonishment at the myriad of activity taking place. A large orchestra was in the orchestra pit and stage hands were moving props into position. It was all so glamorous!

The stage manager spotted me and walked over to introduce himself and welcome me to the Palladium. He said, "Young man, I must caution you about one thing. Max Miller is a lovely and talented gentleman but he does have a dreadful habit which we can't get him to break. Max is going to be the compere of the show and . . ."

I interrupted. "He's going to be what?"

The stage manager laughed. "I beg your pardon. I believe you call them M.C.'s in America. Anyway, when he introduces an act, he has this awful habit of endlessly rambling on, despite the fact that he has not seen or heard the act before. The only way to stop him is to walk on stage even though he is still introducing you. When he sees you, he then announces your name and then you are on your own."

I thought of that as being strange, but in the excitement of the moment, I had forgotten his advice. Miller never showed up for rehearsal so I never had the chance to meet him until later.

On opening night, I was flying pretty high. Here is a seventeen-year-old making his entrance into the big time at the fabulous London Palladium! I planted myself in the wings from the opening of the show for fear of missing my cue. My historical moment was about to arrive. Miller began his introduction and I hung on every word. "Ladies and gentleman, it now gives me great pleasure to introduce a young lad just over from America. He is considered to be the youngest mouth organ virtuoso in the world. You are really in for a treat. He makes this simple instrument sound like an entire orchestra! His virtuosity is remarkable! The tones that he achieves . . ." Max continued to talk. The stage manager appeared next to me as he was pushing me on stage. "Ferchrisake, didn't you listen to one word that I said to you this morning?"

I replied, "Wait a minute. Let the man talk."

My ego went sky high and I was enthralled with the wonderful things that he was saying about me, completely forgetting the stage manager's sage advice. Ego can be a deadly thing, especially to a fledgling performer. In total frustration, he gave me a hard shove again, propelling me on to the stage. Max did not see me as he continued to extol on my musical genius. When I reached a point approximately an arm's length away, he suddenly flung his arm toward stage right, shouting my name. He wore a huge gold ring which caught me flush on the mouth as the back of his hand struck my face. The audience went into gales of laughter, thinking that it was part of the act until they realized that Max had opened a huge gash on my upper lip and I was squirting blood all over the stage! I rushed off, holding my lip as I ran to my dressing room to grab a towel to stop the bleeding. A doctor was quickly summoned and he had to sew six stitches into my upper lip! Max rushed to my dressing room, apologizing profusely, urging me to sue him!

So much for my Palladium debut.

Between sobs, I tried to tell him that it was an unfortunate accident. So much for my Palladium debut. However, Max insisted on paying my salary plus all expenses as long as I was unable to perform. I accepted his generous offer.

I was totally dejected. I felt my career was over and I would never play the harmonica or the Palladium again. Mother tried to console me and did everything to raise my spirits including cooking my favorite dishes. Unfortunately, it was impossible to chew anything in my condition. During the first two weeks following the unfortunate incident, I could only consume liquids through a straw. The time dragged slowly. My lip took one month to heal and for a while, the press played it up.

> *...I recieved a cablegram from my New York agent.*

Eight weeks after the Palladium fiasco, I received a cablegram from my New York agent saying that he had booked me into the Orpheum Theater in Montreal with Fats Waller and his Orchestra. My spirits soared and I immediately sent a cablegram accepting the date. My lip had healed and the stitches had been removed. My mother was concerned that I was returning to work too soon. I assured her that I was in perfect shape and looking forward to the Montreal date.

Mother and I boarded the Cunard Berengaria bound for New York. Unfortunately, Mother was not a good sailor. On this particular crossing, we experienced one of the worst Atlantic storms of the year requiring an extra day for the crossing. Mother ate only one apple and a few crackers during the entire trip! When we arrived in New York, she was weak from lack of food and nervous exhaustion, so she welcomed my suggestion to return to Baltimore where she could regain her strength and be nurtured back to health by her loving sisters.

Fats Waller

One of my aunts met Mother at the train station while I boarded the train to Montreal. Upon arrival I was the first one off, and took a cab directly to the theater. There is nothing quite like looking up and seeing one's name on a marquee. The first thing that I did was to take a picture of it I then entered the stage door and there he was, Fats Waller in the flesh, seated at the piano. He and his band were rehearsing a number so I quietly took a seat in the theater, enjoying the music and waited for my name to be called for my own rehearsal. When I heard, "Jerry Adler next," I sprinted onto the stage and introduced myself to Waller. We then got down to business and had a flawless rehearsal.

The manager came to my dressing room and said, "We always present a flash finale in our shows. This week, we are featuring the song, *Smoke Gets In Your Eyes*. Do you know it?" "Yes," I replied.

He said, "That's fine. We'd like to feature you so please get together with Mr. Waller and rehearse the number. You will be standing in the center of a graduated pyramid with four chorus girls on either side of you."

Wow! Chorus girls!! To a young kid, it doesn't get any better. We rehearsed the number and we were ready.

A rehearsal for the finale was called for 1:00 P.M. I took my position on the pyramid with the girls on either side. The rehearsal came off without a hitch. The first show opened at 3:00 P.M. to a packed house. I was too nervous to watch the show from the wings so I remained in my dressing room and listened to it until it was time for my act. My performance was received with tremendous enthusiasm and I returned to my dressing room feeling like I was king of the hill.

A runner was sent to warn the acts of the time and minutes remaining before the finale. A comic was working in front of the curtain, enabling the stage hands to set up the finale extravaganza. I changed into a white flannel suit, white shoes, black shirt and white tie.

> *...my agent had booked me into a high class burlesque house!*

Everyone took their specified positions and when the girls took their places on the pyramid, I went into a state of shock! All of the girls were naked from the waist up! It never occurred to me until that moment that my agent had booked me into a high class burlesque house! The band struck up a fanfare, the curtain went up . . . and so did I! There I stood, surrounded on either side by eight pairs of the greatest looking boobs that I had ever seen! Admittedly, I had not seen that many at my age. However, it failed to halt the magical chemistry that was surging through my body, when the inevitable happened. I tried desperately to ward it off, including clamping my knees together. Nothing helped.

The girls and the audience were thrown into fits of laughter as I made a feeble attempt to play *Smoke Gets In Your Eyes*. My mouth was becoming more dry each second and to compound the problem, the girls' laughter caused their boobs to bounce uncontrollably. I silently prayed for an immediate heart attack. Needless to say, the Manager replaced me in the finale with someone more mature.

The girls teased me unmercifully but fortunately I was compensated by a new and more exciting experience. After the novelty had worn thin, I became well-acquainted with two of the girls who involved me in serious sex. It was a great learning experience and I feel that this taught me more about the subtle points of sex in one week than most teenagers learn from puberty to at least the age of twenty.

On Stage

Al Jolson
Nicholas Brothers

I appeared at the Palace Theater in New York. The headliner was the inimitable, Al Jolson. In addition to Jolson and myself, there were two other acts, one being the fabulous Nicholas Brothers. This was their first engagement in an all white theater and they were obviously nervous. They were headliners in black theaters and nightclubs, and white patrons could see them at any time at those places, but blacks were not allowed to see them at the Palace. Remember, this was 1935 and discrimination against people of color was the norm. The Nicholas Brothers had good reason to be nervous.

Once again I became aware of color "differences" and was appalled at the ugliness.

Jolson was an exciting and dynamic performer and was generally considered, "the greatest entertainer of all time". Unfortunately, the general public was not aware that he was also the most "difficult entertainer of all time". As brilliant as he was professionally, he was blatantly cruel to his fellow performers. He possessed the magic formula to generate wild excitement from every audience. The huge irony was that his forte was doing his show in black face. I'm sure that he would not be allowed on the stage today as a "blackfaced" singer.

My dressing room was one flight above his. The Nicholas Brothers' dressing room was next to mine. One night, Jolson called out, "Hey, Nicholas Kids! Come on down here. I want my shoes shined." As they started to pass my room, I stepped out in front of them and blocked their way. I shouted, "Mr. Jolson, if you want your shoes shined, shine them yourself!" Jolson came out of his room and looked up. He said, "Adler, mind your own Goddamned business."

"I'm sorry, Mr. Jolson, but these young men are artists, not shoe-shine boys." Jolson was furious. "Listen, you little bastard, you come down here right now!"

I was pretty new to the business but refused to be intimidated by his order. Jolson lost control. "You'd better damned well come down here or you're fired!"

> *...Jolson grabbed me by my shirt and pulled me out into the stage door alley.*

I stood my ground. He didn't hire me and couldn't fire me. By this time, the owner had heard the argument and came running. I was steaming but kept my anger in check. When I saw the owner, I walked down the stairs. As I reached the bottom, Jolson grabbed me by my shirt and pulled me out into the stage door alley. By that time, we were swinging at each other. The owner quickly separated us. Thank God, he took my side. He let Jolson know that he was way out of line and should be ashamed of himself for picking on a young kid. Jolson was ready to quit and sue but found out that he could not get out of his contract. Everything finally settled down but most importantly, the Nicholas Brothers never shined his shoes!

I have always been a maverick, but at the same time sensitive to the injustices heaped on any minority. I didn't just feel the injustice, I often acted out my resentment. I believe that I learned much of my liberal attitude concerning equal rights from my brother Larry, and with his help and his example, put much of it into practice. Neither of us deliberately looked for trouble but we stood our ground. We grew up with blacks and believed we were all equal. That strong feeling has always stuck with me which was, in those days, an open invitation for at least a bloody nose. By standing our ground or coming to the defense of those unfairly maligned, my brother and I managed to become entangled in many minor brawls. Most of the injustices were obvious to us in the entertainment business with the majority having to do with racial bias, a subject that was taboo in the 1930s.

A few years later in Atlanta, Georgia, a bunch of us decided to play a game of soft ball in the stage door alley in-between shows. Two of the group were black. Neighborhood kids noticed the black kids playing with us and began shouting abusive, disgusting anti-black remarks threatening physical harm if they didn't stop. The two black boys sadly left the alley and returned to the theater. Three boys joined me in an attempt to reason with these ruffians. The neighborhood kids reaction was to start a fight by yelling, "You nigger-lovin kikes!"

Without giving it much thought, we proceeded to beat the hell out of every one of them until they ran off. I ended up with - you guessed it, a split lip. I didn't dare tell the stage manager what had happened to me so I applied pressure to my lip until it stopped bleeding and played the rest of the engagement in great pain.

♪

Ritz Brothers
Ray & Grace McDonald
Ethel Shepherd

Between engagements, I always returned home to Baltimore. One day, I received a call from my agent asking if I would be interested in going on a vaudeville tour with Ed Sullivan. This was prior to TV so I was not familiar with his name. He told me that Sullivan was a famous gossip columnist with the New York Daily News. The show consisted of Sullivan as M.C., and featured the popular comedy team, The Ritz Brothers. To round out the bill, there was Ray and Grace McDonald, a brother and sister song and dance team, Ethel Shepherd, a fine pop singer, and me. The tour was scheduled for eight weeks and during that period, Ray and I became very close friends. Years later, he was signed as a contract player with MGM and we both worked on several Mickey Rooney-Judy Garland films. Ten years later, we both found ourselves in the Air Corps, eventually ending up together in the Air Corps show, "Winged Victory".

♫

Ed Sullivan

Ed Sullivan was a marvelous man to work for. He did everything possible to get our names in the papers including constant plugs in his daily column. As much as I admired Ed, I was completely baffled by his popularity as an M.C. His mannerisms were, to say the least, very strange and it was difficult to understand what he was saying. Despite all of those handicaps as a performer, he was extremely popular. When he introduced each act, it sounded as if he didn't know what he was talking about! From my point of view, he sadly lacked the charisma and professional know-how to be a successful M.C. It just proved how little I knew about show business.

My association with Ed lasted for a number of years. Long after the tour was over he would call me from time to time to invite me to perform with him at various V.I.P. functions. One of his pet projects was a yearly event in New York, called "The Harvest Moon Ball" at Madison Square Garden. It was a mammoth benefit show to raise money for the needy and homeless children in New York.

Ed Sullivan was a power to be reckoned with. When performers were asked to appear, they rarely refused unless it was for a good reason. When Ed called and asked me to appear, I was flattered. The show consisted of headliners from stage, screen and radio and it felt wonderful to know that he thought enough of my talent to include me in such a line-up of great stars.

Several weeks after the benefit, a large wooden crate arrived at our home from Ed Sullivan. My father and I carefully opened it to discover twelve bottles of 1926 Cordon Rouge champagne! No one in our family drank and it did seem strange to send such a gift to a young kid. A card was enclosed thanking me for my contribution to the success of the show. We assumed the same gift was sent to every performer. My Dad came up with an excellent suggestion. "Why don't we save it for when you get married?" That seemed pretty logical so Dad called a good friend who knew about wines and how to properly store them. They remained in our basement for seven years.

♫

Clark Gable

Everyone was screaming to get a look at the King!

The following months were filled with bookings in most of the major night clubs, hotels, and theaters throughout the U.S. Two special tours stand out in my mind. The first was with Clark Gable, and the second tour was with W.C. Fields. David O Selznick planned a promotional tour for Gable after the gala premier of "Gone With The Wind", in Atlanta. At each city, lines of people waited to get into the theater, blocking traffic for miles! It was a nightmare for the police and other crowd control personnel. Everyone screaming to get a close look at The King!

On the day that we arrived in Atlanta, the airport was jammed with gawkers and we also had a long motorcade led by the mayor and Margaret Mitchell, the author of the famous "Gone With The Wind". We eventually arrived at our hotel and the theater was on the same block. There were lines of people as far as the eye could see waiting to buy tickets.

I met Clark Gable during our first week of the tour which was scheduled for the Orpheum Theater in Atlanta, where "Gone with the Wind" was born. Clark was very reluctant to tour in this project. It was shortly after the film had been completed and as he explained to me, "I was exhausted by the shooting schedule and was ready for a long, extended vacation." David O. Selznick, the producer was eager to squeeze every ounce of promotion out of Clark. He had invested his whole life into the success of this film and he needed Gable's cooperation to make it all happen. Originally, Selznick had planned on Gable and Vivian Leigh to tour together. However, that was not to be. Vivian's agent had stipulated up front that she would not be available for public appearances and planned to return to England at the completion of the shoot.

As Clark described it, "I knew that it was going to be a huge extravaganza and that David had poured his heart and soul into the project. I wasn't about to let him down." The studio had engaged a choreographer to teach Clark how to tap dance. They had also booked six beautiful, young dancers to join him in the routine. Clark was not a dancer but he was surprisingly light on his feet.

I was curious as to what Clark had planned as an act. He told me that other than the dance routine, he thought that he would simply stand on stage and open his part of the show by throwing it open to his audience with a friendly question and answer session. I had never heard of such a novel idea and thought it to be brilliant! It worked beautifully. He kept it to forty minutes and obviously satisfied his many fans.

Clark Gable was a wonderful person to work with. Not the slightest bit of temperament. Always cool and collected and frankly, was bewildered by the enormity of it all. He said, "Jerry, I can't figure out what all the fuss is about!" He obviously loved the attention and seemed to enjoy every moment on stage. We became good friends and I soon discovered that he was a gin rummy fan. Whenever he was not scheduled for press interviews, we managed to get in one or two nights of gin rummy at the hotel. The tour lasted six weeks and it was enjoyable from beginning to end.

W.C. Fields

W.C. Fields was another story. I must preface my remarks by saying that he was always kind and considerate to me. Perhaps he sensed that I never felt intimidated by him. With others, he was extremely difficult to work with. I once asked him, while traveling on a train with him to Boston, "Bill, why do you give so many people such a hard time?" His immediate reply was, "Because they are all assholes!" He drove stage managers crazy and treated other performers like sub-humans.

Bill and I worked together for the entire tour but we picked up different acts at each weekly engagement. One particular week was a colossal disaster. We had arrived in Detroit and, as usual, took a cab directly to the theater . Facing us on the marquee in bold, white letters was, IN PERSON! W.C. FIELDS. Special added attraction, OUR GANG KIDS!

He clutched his chest and I thought that he was having a coronary. It was 9:00 A.M. with plenty of traffic on the streets. He walked out into the middle of the traffic, waving his cane and screaming, "Who in the hell booked those little sons of bitches on my show?" I tried to calm him down, constantly tugging on his arm so that he would not be hit by a car.

The poor, hapless stage doorman was the first to be subjected to the awful tirade of curses and accusations, as if the old guy was personally responsible for the whole thing. I had to physically pull Bill away and push him into his dressing room. Without my presence, he would have crushed the poor man's skull with his famous ivory-tipped cane.

Needless to say, tensions were at fever pitch and the Kids had yet to arrive. Rehearsal was called for 10:00 A.M. because the theater had to open at 1:00 P.M. Bill could be heard all over the backstage area, screaming at nobody in particular. The orchestra was setting up in the pit in preparation for the rehearsal. We now come to the moment of truth. The Our Gang Kids arrived, accompanied by two, stern female chaperones. I could tell by the Kids' expressions that they were excited about working with W.C. Fields. Bill was still yelling incoherently. The manager quickly took charge and, gently but firmly told Bill to calm down. Bill mumbled something under his breath and proceeded to rehearse. The Kids were warned to give Mr. Fields a wide berth. All things considered, I thought that the rehearsal went reasonably well.

> *"This child has the measles! We must quarantine the theater immediately!"*

We were two days into the engagement when one of the Kids, Spanky McFarland became ill. A doctor was called and after examining Spanky, he said, "This child has the measles! We must quarantine the theater immediately!"

When Bill heard the news, his whole body blew up like a balloon. His face turned purple and I thought that he was going to physically explode and disappear! I had never witnessed a human being go totally berserk before. It was not a pretty sight.

♫

Spanky McFarland

Spanky was feeling rotten and the ladies were doing everything possible to make him comfortable. I walked into his room and asked if there was anything that I could do. Without warning, Spanky's door flew open and this raging bull loomed menacingly at everyone. His eyes finally fixed on poor Spanky. Bill actually charged at this sick child with his lethal cane. It took the ladies and me to keep him out of striking distance. Bill was raving obscenities at Spanky which, of course, caused him to cry in fear. The ladies demanded that he leave the room immediately! Bill began waving his cane around like a baseball bat and I actually had to duck to avoid being struck! I grabbed the cane and ripped it out of his grasp. It was never my lot in life to be the guardian of W.C. Fields, as glamorous as that might sound. I tried to remain calm under very difficult circumstances. I said, "Bill, are you out of your mind? Do you realize that this is a lethal weapon and someone could be seriously injured or killed! Now, please stop making an ass of yourself and go back to your dressing room." My God, I was sending a grown man to his room! I was not sure what his reaction would be. Amazingly, he just sagged in despair. His entire body seemed to deflate. He turned to Spanky. "I'm sorry, kid. This just ain't my day." He quietly left.

> *My God, I was sending a grown man to his room.*

Food was ordered for all of us for two weeks! Our clothing was brought from the hotel including sleeping cots. Living conditions in the theater were less than desirable but we did the best that we could. It was a nightmare that I prefer not to repeat. Our other dates had to be rearranged due to the quarantine.

♪

Milton Berle

I worked with Milton Berle in vaudeville since the age of 17 and he was a huge star, even in 1935. His forte was the baggy pants, broad comedy of burlesque and the audiences adored him. However, I must confess that I was not one of his myriad of loyal fans. I never considered him "funny" in the generic sense. Berle was never a stand-up comedian which called for a quick wit and a comedic sense attributed to comedians such as Jack Benny, Fred Allen, Buddy Hackett, Johnny Carson, etc. Yes, he told jokes but those jokes were written by second-rate comedy writers and his jokes usually fell pretty flat as told by him. He was never capable of delivering comedy material as written by such geniuses of Woody Allen, Mel Brooks and Carl Reiner.

Milton was in his element in slapstick comedy situations that emphasized the ridiculous such as coming on stage "in drag" or involving himself with physical comedy with his own "stooges" who worked as foils for the bawdy slapstick material.

Berle was born for television. It came upon him as a gift from heaven. In a very short period of time he was the darling of TV and soon gained the amazing title of Mr. Television! As far as I know, he did not make friends easily. He had an aggressive and argumentative personality and became exceedingly difficult to work with. He had a zillion fans but very few friends. I always "got along" with Berle but we were never close. We respected each other's talent but that was as far as it went.

♫

Stan Fisher

I recall an incident at the Palmer House in Chicago. A harmonica player and former pupil of mine, Stan Fisher was appearing with Berle. Stan had an ego that equaled Berle's and that is probably why they were "meant for each other" professionally. I was in Chicago on business and when I read that Stan was appearing with Berle, I called him to let him know that I was in town. Stan became quite excited and pleaded with me to come to see the show. He said, "PLEASE bring your friends with you, and I will order a ringside table for you tonight." I agreed and, true to his word, he did reserve a perfect table.

The show was marvelous and Berle was truly in his element. Stan played brilliantly and was the perfect second banana for Berle in one of his favorite comedy bits. To give you a general idea of the extent of Stan's ego, he came running to our table after the show and announced to all seated at our table, "How'd you like the show? Wasn't I GREAT!" How does one deal with a line like that? I answered by waving my hand back and forth and replied, "Yeah, I thought you were pretty good." He was momentarily taken aback but soon realized that I was kidding and went right back to being Mr. Ego. "Jer, have you ever met Miltie?" I couldn't resist. I replied, "No, I've never met him. Is there any chance that I could actually meet him?" Stan excitedly replied, "Of COURSE! I hope your friends will excuse you for a few minutes." He grabbed my hand and off we went to Berle's dressing room. Stan knocked on the door and Berle called out, "Come in!" Stan entered ahead of me and excitedly announced, "Miltie, I want you to meet my best friend……….." And before he could announce my name, Berle looked at me and said, "JERRY ADLER! Where in the hell have you been? I looked all over the country for you and then I had to hire this schmuck in your place!" Stan was devastated but soon regained his composure. We had a nice visit and I returned to my table.

Milton Berle was a genius in his own element and deserved every accolade he ever received.

♪

Jimmy Durante

Jimmy Durante and I go back to when he was part of a comedy trio, Jackson, Clayton and Durante. They were an incredible comedy team with Jimmy the featured element. I appeared on the bill with them several times at some of the leading vaudeville houses. Jimmy was a charming and generous man and well-liked by everyone in the business. When I appeared with the threesome, I was a novice in show business. I was a seventeen-year-old kid who was eager to learn, and I must say that I had a sincere mentor in Jimmy Durante. I was always surprised that he took such an interest in my performances. Jimmy pointed out incidental professional mistakes such as body posture on stage, talking to my audience correctly, etc., very similar to the advice given by Red Skelton. I learned much from these comedy icons and I will be eternally grateful for their help.

Needless to say, the trio was a consistent show-stopper and always in the next-to-closing spot in every show. It is unfortunate that at the height of their career Jackson became seriously ill and had to drop from the act. Durante and Clayton tried to carry on as a duo but somehow the magic was gone and they soon realized that they would have to split up. Durante continued as a single and became an overnight sensation.

I admired Jimmy not just for his talent, but because he had little or no formal education. However, he had an inbred sense of what constituted a one-on-one relationship with his audience. He was definitely a crowd-pleaser and the audiences loved him. He could do no wrong as a performer and it did not take long before Hollywood recognized his talent and he was soon signed by MGM as a regular on their roster of popular stars. He remained with MGM for many years until retirement.

Working in nightclubs and theaters was great training for anyone who had not been in the business very long. There were so many places to play where one could hone his or her craft. All of that is now gone and today's talent seems to confirm my feelings of a lost era. To have the opportunity to work with show business giants such as Red Skelton, Bert Lahr, Eddie Cantor, W.C. Fields, Jimmy Durante, Jack Benny and so many more, was a free ticket to a remarkable education.

♪

Benny Goodman

My next tour was with clarinet genius, Benny Goodman. Benny was, in many ways, an introvert. However, being the consummate musician, he demanded nothing less from the men in his orchestra. Many times this created shouting matches between Benny and his musicians. There were always the underlying threats of quitting. These outbursts were usually settled amicably. However, Ziggy Ellman, one of Benny's top trumpet players had heard a rumor and was determined to have it clarified. He walked into Goodman's dressing room and said, "What's this I hear about adding strings to the band?"

Benny said, "That's right. I think that it is time to expand the orchestra."

Ziggy replied, "If that's the case, I quit."

Benny looked at him. "Why? Don't you like violins?"

He replied, "They sound like mice."

Ziggy did quit and it was a tragic decision. He was such an integral part of the brass section but he refused to change his mind. He was replaced by another trumpet virtuoso, Bunny Berrigan.

I gained priceless training by simply watching and listening to Benny play his clarinet. Each sound, each tone, each interpretation was magnificent. It was awe-inspiring. Benny practiced every day for hours. I love my work and certainly enjoy performing. However, I have never had the fierce dedication that produces a Benny Goodman.

♫

I was informed by my British agent that he had booked a number of exciting engagements for me in Europe. Mother was in a state of fear regarding the Atlantic crossing. I cannot say that I blamed her. On the other hand, she did not wish to be left behind in Baltimore, away from Dad and me. We boarded the French liner, Ile de France. I thank God for providing us with near perfect weather. For the first time, Mother enjoyed the crossing. We disembarked in Southampton and took the train to London's Waterloo Station where we were met by my father. We drove straight to our home in Golders Green.

I was booked into the Palladium once again, this time with much better marquee billing plus a considerable increase in my fee. The publicity man for the Palladium took advantage of the fiasco debut concerning the bloody lip and was able to get considerable press mileage out of the story, creating additional interest in my appearance.

The engagement was highly successful for me and it helped to elevate my stature as a performer. After the two week engagement, people began recognizing me on the street and some approached me for my autograph. Although it was a great boost to my ego, I kept my emotions at a responsible level.

The Palladium was followed by a series of bookings throughout Great Britain. I played in most of the townships of England, Ireland, Scotland and Wales. Ninety percent of the dates were in music halls and the other ten percent in nightclubs. The audiences were astonishingly receptive and I found myself confronted by hordes of people of all ages, waiting for me outside the stage door for autographs. The "fans" after the Palladium performance were not just a fluke. I was now crossing that line into legitimate recognition.. I had read about such happenings and wondered if it would ever happen to me.

The tour was educational as well as enjoyable. I took advantage of my free time to visit the great historical castles throughout the British Isles, but especially in Wales. One could spend weeks in Wales going from one castle to another. Each had its own history as well as personality and I wish I had visited every castle. But I could only steal time now and then from a very busy schedule.

♬

> *...the London Palladium for the third time...*

I was booked to play the London Palladium for the third time with one very important difference. It was to be a Royal Command Performance before their Majesties, King George V and Queen Mary. I was seventeen, going on eighteen at the time.

♬

King George V and Queen Mary

The rehearsal was handled in a much more formal manner with several government officials in attendance. The official Emissary to their Majesties instructed everyone on British protocol. We were to be presented individually to the Royal Family in their box after the performance. The women were instructed to curtsy and the men were to bow. I was standing off to one side and without thinking blurted out, "I'm not going to bow to anyone!" All eyes were riveted on me. Sully, our stage manager assured the Emissary that I would comply with his instructions, glaring at me as he spoke. The Emissary was not assured.

He said, "Look here, if this young man is going to create an embarrassment to their Majesties, I insist that he not be allowed to perform." Once again, he was assured that I would do as instructed. When the Emissary left the theater, Sully came towards me as if to run a sword through my heart!

"How dare you make such a rude and stupid remark! Let me remind you, young man that you are the guest of Great Britain, and as such, you will abide by the rules as well as the protocol. Have I made myself clear?" I lowered my head sheepishly, nodded yes and went to my dressing room. I knew that I had behaved in a rude and shameful manner, and I felt terrible. I am appalled at how cocky I was. I attributed cockiness to self-assurance. A big mistake! I was determined to do my best to represent my country honorably.

The Royal Command Performance went beautifully and when we all took our bows at the finale from the stage, we turned slightly towards the Royal Box and the ladies curtsied and the men bowed. The audience stood up and cheered wildly. The orchestra then struck up, "God Save the King" and everyone in the audience rose to their feet and sang along. We were then escorted to the Royal Box and were presented to their Majesties. When it became my turn, I honestly cannot account for what I did. It was not deliberate nor was it a challenge to British protocol. It was simply force of habit. Whenever I met important dignitaries in America, I automatically reached out to shake their hand. As I bowed, I shook hands with the King and bowed to the Queen! The photographers had a field day shooting pictures of the handshake. King George was very gracious and completely composed. He smiled and gripped my hand firmly.

The following morning, I was summoned to the American Embassy and was escorted to the office of U.S. Ambassador, Joseph Kennedy. He was seated at his desk and when he looked up and saw me, he leaped to his feet, came around to the front of the desk and ordered me to sit down. He scowled menacingly. "Do you have any idea of what you have done?" I meekly nodded, yes.

"Well, for God sake, young man, what is your explanation?"

I tried my best to explain that it was not deliberate and the reasons for doing it. He was not buying it.

> "...you will officially be barred from entering the United Kingdom again."

He said, "We are going to deal with this one step at a time. First, you are to remain here in my office and hope to God that it all blows over. However, if we receive one phone call from a British subject protesting your disgusting behavior, I suggest that you be prepared to leave on the first available ship back to the United States. If that happens, you will officially be barred from entering the United Kingdom again."

I sat in a chair against the wall for four hours waiting for the ax to fall, but nothing happened!

The Ambassador finally said, "I can only assume that the crisis has passed. You are free to go. However, make yourself available to me for the rest of the week." I thanked him and got the hell out of there as quickly as possible.

My brother was furious with me but my parents were obviously not aware of the seriousness of my offense. They simply dismissed it and attributed it to my youth.

♫

Danny Kaye

In all my years in show business, I have never seen a performer as perfect in every aspect of virtuosity as Danny Kaye. The first time that I saw him on stage, I stood with a group of other entertainers in the wings of the Capitol Theater in New York. We watched his performance in open-mouthed amazement. He sang like an angel, danced amazingly well, performed a brilliant bit of comedy monologue, and did prat-fall acrobatics. Prat-fall refers to comics who take "falls" on stage making it appear as if it was accidental. When he conducted the orchestra, he had the audience rolling in the aisles! He had blonde hair, stood six feet four and was nothing less than pure genius.

Danny and I got along beautifully and he usually kept me in fits of laughter with little or no effort. He was a charming, decent person without a trace of temperament. He was as congenial as anyone could possibly be. He even clownishly helped the stage hands with the opening and closing of the curtains plus setting up stage props. None of it was "put-on." He did it because he loved doing it. Even the heads of the stage hands union, usually a group with a no-nonsense mentality, allowed him this freedom.

Ninety percent of his material and his original comedic songs were written by his talented wife, Sylvia Fine. She seemed to be the driving force that kept this human wind-up toy in perpetual motion. So. . . .this was the remarkable dynamo known as Danny Kaye.

As talented as he was, he was equally graced with a loving charm. Everyone in the theater from the audience to those working backstage worshipped him. It was not long before he was grabbed up by movie producer Samuel Goldwyn and practically shot to the West Coast by rocket!

Goldwyn pulled out all the stops to get this brilliant performer on film. His first movie was "The Goldwyn Follies," a colorful, breezy fluff of a film with very little plot but loaded with gorgeous girls and plenty of music. Danny was finally in his element. He was given carte blanche to do anything that he wished on screen and the audiences ate him up.

Danny was a one-in-a-million multi-talented actor, singer, dancer and comedian and we have never seen anything like him since.

Nawabzada Igbal Muhammed Kahn, "James"

I was booked into the Club Lido in London for two weeks. It was the most elegant club in town. The audiences were quite vocal with their approval of my performances. As their enthusiasm spread, everyone sprang to their feet with even more wild applause. I was not accustomed to such a response. Seated front row center on opening night I became aware of a group of turbaned Hindus who appeared to be responsible for this extraordinary outburst of cheers. I thanked everyone and finally left the stage.

I had moved to the Mount Royal Hotel in Marble Arch because of its convenient location to the club. At 11:00 A.M. the following morning, I received a call from the desk clerk telling me that I had a guest in the lobby. I asked who it was and the clerk said that it was an Indian gentleman. I assumed that it was one of the turbaned men at last night's performance. It's a bit difficult to miss a group of men wearing turbans in a nightclub. I told the clerk to send him up. Shortly, there was a light knock on the door. I opened it to find a tall gentleman wearing a beautifully tailored silk suit and a white turban. He was also carrying a small silver tray containing an envelope. I invited him in and he moved the tray toward me. "For you, Mr. Adler," I opened it and read, "Please look out your front window."

My first reaction was that I was dealing with someone unbalanced. "What does it mean?" I asked.

He seemed to sense my apprehension as he smiled, and walked to the window and opened it. "Please, sir, look down at the entrance to the hotel."

I was living on the fourteenth floor and I was not about to follow the orders of some nut wearing a turban whom I had never met before, telling me to look down to the street! He stepped away from the window and gestured with his hand.

I timidly moved forward and said, "What am I supposed to be looking for?"

Still smiling, he replied, "You will see soon enough."

> *My first reaction was that I was dealing with someone unbalanced.*

I was quite skeptical, but I did it. I looked down and saw another Hindu standing at the hotel entrance. "OK, I see one of your friends standing there. Now what?" I said.

"Please, sir. The automobile parked at the curb."

I looked down again and noticed that the other Hindu was standing in front of a magnificent, gold, two-door Mercedes-Benz with a metal covered spare tire on each front fender. "OK, I see the car. What about it?"

"It is yours, sir."

"I don't understand. What do you mean, it's mine?"

"The Maharajah thoroughly enjoyed your performance last night, as we all did, and wants you to accept this small token of his appreciation for your delightful program."

I was completely tongue-tied. I was a young kid who had never been exposed to lavish gifts of this magnitude. I found it difficult to say anything that made much sense. I finally said, "I am overwhelmed by his generosity, but please explain to the Maharajah that I cannot accept such a gift."

He was upset at my response. "Oh, dear. The Maharajah will be most distraught at your refusal."

"Kindly ask him to call me at the club this evening and I will explain." He bowed and quietly left.

I called Larry to tell him of this wild incident. After listening to the story, his one word reply was, "Schmuck!"

"What do you mean, schmuck? What was I supposed to do?"

Larry said, "A gift like that from a Maharajah is the equivalent of your sending him a birthday card. Why did you refuse?"

"I simply felt that it was not the proper thing to do!"

"SCHMUCK!" Larry responded.

The same party came to the club that evening. A note was delivered to my dressing room from the Maharajah. "If you have not made previous plans, we would be honored to have you join us at our table." I was surprised to find that the Maharajah and I were about the same age. He was a bit taller than me, strikingly handsome with a huge walrus mustache. He stood up and shook my hand. He quickly gestured me to be seated. "Mr. Adler, it is so good to meet you in person. I sincerely apologize for making you feel uncomfortable. Can you find it in your heart to forgive me?"

"There is no need to apologize," I said. I did not wish to put him on the spot, but I knew that I had to say something. "Forgive you! On the contrary, I was highly flattered that anyone would think enough of my performance to present me with a gift!"

We became immediate friends. He insisted that if I was ever in Bombay, that I would be a guest at his Palace. "And please, call me James."

I found out later that his full name was Nawabzada Igbal Muhammed Khan. James was fine with me.

I thanked him for the invitation and added, "Please call me Jerry."

Two months later, I was booked into the leading hotel in Bombay. I suspected that James had had a hand in it. Bombay is not exactly on the regular hotel tour.

When I arrived, I checked into the hotel and was about to unpack, when I was interrupted by a knock on the door. There stood two identically dressed Hindus in spectacular red uniforms. I sensed what was about to happen. The spokesman came forward and said, "You, sir are Mr. Jerry Adler?"

"Yes, what can I do for you?"

"We are here to take you to the Palace of James!"

He grinned a mouth full of gold teeth and said, "Please, sir, be good enough to follow us." They quickly picked up my luggage and I followed them to the entrance. I knew that I was going to witness something spectacular but I was not prepared for this! Parked in front, was a classic Rolls Royce. In the front and back of the car were eight identically clad gentlemen in bright green uniforms, wearing black turbans, all mounted on magnificent white horses. The spokesman placed a stool at the passenger entrance and opened the door, gesturing for me to enter. He proudly said, "We are here to take you to the Palace of James!"

I gave him the appropriate surprised look which is, I am sure, what he was waiting for. I entered the car and we were slowly on our way. Four horsemen in front and four in the rear. All of the windows were smoked glass for privacy. I had terrible pangs of guilt as we passed unbelievable squalor, homeless people sleeping on the sidewalks plus thousands of beggars who looked as if they had not eaten in weeks! I was shocked to notice that none of them looked at our entourage as we passed. We finally arrived. I have never seen the Taj Mahal but this is what went through my mind as I viewed the Palace. The spokesman rode with the driver. We came to a stop in front of a long flight of marble steps. As I reached for the door handle, he said, "Please sir, allow me." He exited the car and opened my door. Suddenly, a huge red carpet was pushed by two men at the top of the stairway which unraveled and came bouncing down the steps and stopped directly in front of the door. I stepped out on to the carpet.

James was standing at the top with his entourage awaiting my arrival. I kept expecting to see Cecil B. DeMille seated on a camera boom yelling, "That's a take!"

I climbed the stairs and we greeted each other warmly. I was assigned a private butler, personal maid, footman, a private secretary and a car and driver at my disposal for the duration of my stay.

James suggested that I go to my quarters and freshen up a bit before tea. My "quarters" was twice the size of our home in Golders Green I quickly joined James in the tea room and questioned him about my hotel engagement. He admitted that he had suggested my appearance to the hotel owner, but assured me that he did not apply undue pressure. He simple gave him my agent's name and address. I don't know where James got it because I had not given it to him, and I did not ask.

The decor within the Palace was breathtaking. Beautiful furniture with elaborate gold inlay, huge paintings of family, (past and present) plus gallery type paintings by well known artists on the walls in the dining room. The dining table seated forty two. The wood was a highly polished ebony and many huge, thick Indian rugs adorned the floor -- all were art treasures.

There were servants standing at attention in practically every room! Nothing less than a scene out of "The Arabian Nights." For a while we chatted about the great times we had in London but then he insisted on showing me around. I accepted his invitation to act as my guide and confessed that I had never been to India and was enjoying the opulence of my surroundings. I explained I had a rehearsal scheduled for the following morning which would take about two hours. After that, I would be free. He became quite excited. "Please, may I attend your rehearsal?"

I said, "Of course! Why not?"

He was like a little kid and his enthusiasm about such a simple thing was amusing. He then asked if I had ever been on an elephant. I said I had not, but was eager to try. He ordered one of his servants to prepare the elephants. We finished our tea, walked to the entrance, and there they were -- four elephants! Two were beautifully decorated with brightly colored stones imbedded in huge leather harnesses scrolled in gold designs. I climbed a ladder into a leather chair strapped to the elephant. James chose to be hoisted up on his elephant's trunk. Both of us were protected from the blazing sun by large canopies. The other two elephants were not decorated and carried two men each. One of the two was armed with a high-powered rifle. The other two men were mahouts, men who sat behind the head of the elephants to guide them.

> *James had his elephants brought alongside mine and he handed me a rifle.*

Off we went into the forest. My first surprise was the comfortable ride. I was equally surprised at the speed of these pachyderms. We went from forest to high-growth jungle in a matter of thirty minutes. James had his elephant brought alongside mine and he handed me a rifle.

I asked, "Why, the rifle?"

"It's for hunting tigers. Haven't you ever hunted?"

"No, and I do not intend to start now."

He looked startled. "Don't you approve of hunting?"

"I'm sorry, James but I cannot share your enthusiasm. I am seriously disturbed by the deliberate killing of animals."

He appeared to be shaken. "Oh, dear. I have offended you for a second time!"

I quickly replied, "No, you did not offend me. You may hunt as much as you wish. I just don't wish to take an active part in it."

James ordered everyone to turn back. When we reached the Palace and had dismounted, I said, "James, you should not have canceled your hunt on my account." He graciously responded, "Please, Jerry. I can go hunting anytime."

I eased his mind by mentioning the thrill of riding an elephant for the first time.

I had been booked into the Imperial Palace Hotel for one week, but business was so great that the manager asked if I could remain for an additional week, which I did. I cannot accept all of the credit for the good business. I'm certain that James had much to do with calling hundreds of his friends to see my show.

We spent an incredible two weeks together and I saw everything in Bombay. James was a great host. But one day he said something that struck me funny. He said, "By the way, Jerry, during your stay, you will have your own private elephant." (Well, doesn't everyone?).

Although I was impressed with the luxuries within the Palace, the one thing that impressed me the most was having my own car and driver. The chauffeur drove me to the hotel every evening and waited until I was ready to leave. He took me wherever I wished to go but he had a quaint habit. Whenever we conversed, he would salute me before responding to questions or comments! James' servants and his friends all appeared to step out of fantasy land. I met many of his interesting, fascinating friends. They were charming, bright and very entertaining. But I couldn't indulge their desire to entertain me at dinner before a performance, explaining that I never eat just before going on stage.

I completed my contract and was ready to return to London. James pleaded with me to stay longer but I had contracts to honor so I had to refuse. In the two weeks I remained his guest, we had established a strong bond. I thanked him for his unforgettable hospitality and insisted that we get together on his next trip to London. Not much time passed before James made another appearance.

James arrived in London on a business trip, two weeks later. He called and insisted that we have dinner. Fortunately, I was free so we met at Olivelli's, one of my favorite Italian restaurants. Larry had introduced me to its exquisite cuisine months before. James and I had a wonderful dinner and evening but as we were about to leave, we found ourselves surrounded by uniformed and plain clothes police. All of the customers were asked to remain seated and show identification. We were not detained for long but soon found out that the second floor of the restaurant was a whore house—the most notorious in London. To my sorrow, it was also discovered that Mr. Olivelli was the owner of both businesses. He was arrested and the entire building was closed down. I have yet to find an Italian restaurant to compare with Olivelli's.

I received an offer for an extended tour of France. A week prior to departure, I called all of my friends to say good-by, including James. When I said good-by to him, there was a moment of silence on the other end. He finally said, "Jerry, I have an unusual request to make and I urge you to give it serious consideration. I would love to join you on your tour and act as your valet."

I was stunned. "You must be joking! Why would you want to do that?" He replied, "I have always wanted to be on the inside, to learn what it is like in show business and how an entertainer conducts his daily life on the road. You will not pay me anything. I will pay my own way and (in giggling excitement) I will be your man, James!"

I said, "Believe me. It is not glamorous. The life that you live is glamorous. Take my word for it, you will tire of it quickly." After hearing the request, my first thoughts went a little astray. I knew that he was not homosexual because of my knowledge of his many female conquests. He continued to insist. I let him know that I would give it some thought and inform him of my decision in the morning. In retrospect, I felt that it might be fun. I would certainly have the advantage of his sophisticated knowledge of European cities, and since performing in Europe was relatively new to me, without question, I needed all the help I could get.

I agreed, with the stipulation that if, for any reason either of us felt uncomfortable, we would be honest about it and act accordingly. He quickly agreed.

This was the beginning of a remarkable but comparatively brief friendship. Having received my approval, he lost no time in preparations. He visited every elegant men's shop in London, looking for the proper attire befitting a "gentleman's gentleman". When he showed me his purchases, I was amazed at the detail. He took his duties seriously but it seemed so incongruous for him to be doing it.

When James began his duties he answered phone calls and acted as servant/butler. Whenever I gave a cocktail party, he laid out my clothing for the evening and made all of my business and social appointments. He played his role to the hilt and was enjoying every moment. I must admit that I thoroughly enjoyed the attention.

My first engagement in France was Le Cirque Medrano, in Paris. My London agent had booked it. James and I were shocked and dismayed to find that I was working in an actual circus.

It was a smaller version of Madison Square Garden with one large sawdust ring in the center plus the elaborate high wire and trapeze equipment hanging from the ceiling. It had a seating capacity of two thousand and I was told that the week had been sold out!

I appeared at 10:00 A.M. for rehearsal and was greeted warmly by Mr. Medrano, the owner. I asked about the orchestra and he pointed to a huge platform mounted near the top. Musicians had already begun to set up and I was shocked to see that it was an all brass band! I told Mr. Medrano that none of this was going to work. My music accompaniment was written for a regular orchestra. He was, to say the least, upset by this news.

Medrano proceeded to explain that he had spent a great deal of money promoting this show. It seems that I was the first musical performer to ever appear there. In addition, Borah Minnevitch and the Harmonica Rascals were also opening at the Alhambra Theater at the same time, and there was a press war as to who could generate the most publicity. Medrano had an excellent, creative flair and he seemed to be doing a far better job. He obviously had a lot riding on my appearance.

He said, "What can we do about the music?"

I said, "The fact that I'm opening tonight doesn't give us much time! I do have a suggestion but it will be a radical change to what you had planned."

He said, "Anything! Please, what do you have in mind?"

♪

Grapelli & Reinhardt

I replied, "There is a duo working at a jazz cafe called Le Jazz Hot. Their names are Stephan Grapelli and Django Reinhardt. If we can talk them into working with me, I promise you that it will be an exciting show. We will also have to rent a piano and get them to provide a pianist."

Medrano was quite familiar with the names of Grapelli and Reinhardt and saw great possibilities for additional press coverage. The two musicians had a fabulous reputation in Paris and getting them to work Le Cirque Medrano was going to be quite a challenge.

He said, "Come to my office and we'll get them on the phone."

It was still morning and I had doubts that anyone would be there. Miraculously, Django answered the phone. After a fairly brief discussion in French, Medrano turned to me with a huge grin and nodded, YES!

I couldn't believe that he had pulled it off. I said, "Don't forget to remind them of the pianist."

The negotiations were accomplished in less than five minutes! Medrano arranged for a 2:00 P.M. rehearsal. I asked him if he had a wooden platform that could be carried into the ring to accommodate the trio and me. He did have one available so now it was up to me to completely change the material in my show. James and I went through all of my music to choose an appropriate program. I was getting increasingly more excited about the prospects of playing practically an all jazz program.

> *...inviting five hundred orphan children for a private afternoon show...*

In his enthusiasm, Medrano came up with a brilliant promotional idea. How about inviting five hundred orphan children for a private afternoon show and I would attempt to teach them a popular French song called, *Valentina*. He was going to contact the M. Hohner harmonica representative in Paris and purchase five hundred tiny, one octave harmonicas, use the clowns in the show to distribute them to the kids and arrange for newsreel coverage to be shown in all of the movies! I agreed that it would be great.

The trio showed up at 1:30 P.M. and with much hand shaking and back slapping, we got down to rehearsing. After rehearsing two numbers, I decided to delete the rest of my regular music. We worked out an ad lib program instead. The opening night audience was remarkable, as if I had planted all two thousand of them as shills. They screamed their delights, one number after another. I was thrilled with the response. I then announced that I was going to play, Ravel's Bolero. There was an immediate hush in the crowd and I gave it my best shot. At the finish, everyone began to hiss me! I couldn't believe it. The audience response changed from love to hate! I jumped off the platform and ran to my dressing room. I told James to pack up everything. He was baffled but didn't say anything. Suddenly Medrano charged into the room "What are you doing? Get back to the stage."

I said, "Are you crazy? Did you hear them hissing me?"

"Hissing you? That wasn't hissing! They were yelling, Biss! That means "more" in French!" Two thousand people yelling, "Biss" sure sounds like hissing to me! He grabbed a harmonica, slapped it into my hand and pushed me back into the ring. I did three additional encores.

Several days later, Medrano scheduled the benefit performance for the orphans. When the clowns handed out the harmonicas, there was immediate pandemonium. The kids would not settle down. I couldn't speak French so all I could do was gesture with my hands for them to be quiet. While all of this was happening, the newsreel cameras were rolling. I tried my best to get the children's attention but was ignored. My temper was beginning to take over and I finally shouted,

"Will you shut up, you little bastards?!"

> *...they had a full-face close-up of me shouting the obscenity.*

Medrano got a copy of the newsreel and invited us to his apartment to view it. I had forgotten about the newsreels and had also forgotten what I had screamed at the kids. There it was, in beautiful black and white. The newspapers did not forget either. To make matters worse, they had a full-face close-up of me shouting the obscenity. I visualized it being shown as a news clip of "the Ugly American" in all of the movie houses. Well, here we go again! Another faux pas catastrophe right on the heels of my British Royalty disaster. Once again, I found myself on the side of the angels. No citizen feedback, no indignations, no nothing! I was living a charmed life. Medrano, on the other hand thought it was terribly funny and his "public relations" mind began spinning wildly. He knew that the viewing public would respond to it favorably. Vive La French public!

On my first free afternoon, I was anxious to stroll the streets of Paris just to drink in the sights and sounds of this historic city. My

God, I was in Paris! James knew a girl there, as he did in every city that I played, so he was off, "doing his thing".

A young man approached and said, "Excuse me. I hope that you don't think me rude but are you an American?" The gentleman was well dressed, had a charming personality and seemed to have an over-all likeable attitude.

"Yes, I am. How did you know?"

He laughed and replied, "I guess it's the way that you walk. I spotted it immediately." "Obviously, you are also an American. Do you live here?" I inquired.

"Yes, I do. I have lived here for over three years." We introduced ourselves and continued to walk together. He said, "Look, if you don't have anything better to do, I would like to show you around."

I jumped at the chance and we walked for over an hour. After a while, he said, "This city doesn't really come to life until dark. What are your plans for tonight?" I explained that I was working at Le Cirque Medrano and it would be pretty late by the time I was through.

He smiled and replied, "Don't worry about it. I'm on vacation this week. I'll pick you up at the stage door." I agreed and we left it at that.

I actually forgot about him until I left Le Cirque that evening and discovered him waiting for me. We took off and he began to explain why the city was so different at night. I didn't agree but remained silent about it. I was still enjoying the tour when he said, "There is one thing that you have not seen." We turned the corner into a dark alley. I became slightly confused but did not anticipate anything ominous. I heard a strange click and turned around to discover that he was standing in front of me with an open switchblade! He continued in his friendly manner. "I'm sorry to do this to you, my friend but please give me your wallet, watch and ring."

I began to shake with fright, not knowing what would happen. He continued to smile. "Please don't make me use force because I will, if necessary. Just hand them over and you can be on your way." I tried to control my trembling voice. I waited as long as possible and said,

"Take what's in my wallet and my watch but please, not the ring." I was wearing a diamond ring that was given to me by my grandmother.

"Either give me the ring or I will cut your finger off..."

He said, "Look, you are wasting my time. Either give me the ring or I will cut your finger off, and believe me, I will cut it off!"

I don't know how I gathered the courage but I quickly brought my knee up as hard as I could into his groin, causing him to drop in screaming agony. I ran like hell, hailed a cab and went to my hotel. I wanted to leave Paris as quickly as possible. It was a frightening experience and I knew that as long as I remained there, I would be looking over my shoulder.

I told Medrano of the incident and he suggested that I file a police report. Two days later, the police called to inform me that they had caught my "friend" and that I would have to come to the station to identify him. Medrano and James went with me. When I identified my assailant, I couldn't resist saying to the culprit, "I'm sorry I had to do this MY FRIEND. But you asked for it, you sonofabitch!"

The rest of the Le Cirque engagement continued to do very well. I received more press in one week than I received anywhere else in Europe. Medrano had me doing radio interviews, appearing in homes for the aged and he actually arranged for me to do a show in a Paris prison. The prisoners went wild over my show and proceeded to stomp their feet and yell out requests. It was just one of many enjoyable experiences that I had, thanks to the remarkable imagination of Medrano.

One of the many things that impressed me during our Paris stay was watching James' reaction to this kind of life. I would occasionally glance at him and watch his expression as the audience responded to my music. His interest increased as he observed the reaction from the prisoners. He told me later that he expected hostility from the prisoners but was pleasantly surprised.

My next engagement was on the French Riviera. I performed in a posh gambling casino, Le Casino de la Jetee, in Nice. It was built on a pier that stretched along the shores of the Mediterranean. It was a magnificent venue in which to perform. The casino hosted a full orchestra and an exquisite restaurant besides the slots, tables and paraphernalia associated with casinos plus a fabulous show room. Incredibly, I was only required to do one show per night. The booking was for two weeks giving James and me ample free time. We had entire days and parts of each evening to ourselves because my one show did not start until 8:30 P.M. The show-room was filled every night.

> *I suggested we take a motor trip to…Monte Carlo.*

James knew many interesting people on the Riviera and he contacted all of them. The show-room was filled every night. James told me that he knew a great looking lady in Nice but hastened to assure me that there were more where she came from. We did "that" for a few days, until I was exhausted. I told him that I needed some rest. If I were to continue to perform my best in the evening, our daytime sojourns had to slow down a bit. I suggested we take a motor trip to a place that I had dreamed about for a long time, Monte Carlo.

James quickly responded, "That's a marvelous idea! It's only a couple of hour's drive from here and the scenery is spectacular."

We arranged to drive there the following morning. He insisted on driving because the narrow, winding roads were quite treacherous and he had driven it before.

"Spectacular," was an understatement. The steep cliffs of the Riviera with its hairpin turns were a thrill all by themselves. To have the glorious, turquoise Mediterranean sparkling in the background like so many thousand diamonds, caused me to gasp in disbelief.

We reached the Italian border and discovered the gate up and the guardhouse empty. That seemed a bit strange but we dismissed it from our minds. We drove across the border and continued on our way. It never occurred to me to bring my passport and I confessed my oversight to James. He was so accustomed to running off to foreign ports that he carried his passport with him at all times. He apologized for not reminding me, but I waved it off as something unimportant.

When we arrived in Monte Carlo, it was everything that I had expected except smaller than I had imagined. All of the action revolved around a cobblestone square. The famous Casino was, of course, the focal point. It was surrounded by quaint cafes and flower shops. The Lookout Point gave a breathtaking view of the entire Riviera.

Our first stop was the Casino. Gambling casinos in Europe were strange to me so I remained an observer. James played baccarat and walked away with a bundle. He was recognized by many of the dealers and was, of course, treated royally.

We decided to have lunch at one of the cafes. In the middle of lunch, James excused himself and was gone for about fifteen minutes. When he returned, he had a smile on his face. He said that he knew a countess who owned a villa in Monte Carlo. He called her, and she was so pleased to hear from him that she invited us for cocktails.

We drove into the hills above Monte Carlo and just as we came out of a hairpin turn, there appeared before us an exquisite Spanish-style villa. The Countess was standing outside as we drove up. Such a vision of beauty! James introduced me to Countess Felicia McDonald!

He explained that she was married to an Irish banker! She was exquisite with an eggshell white skin, dark blazing eyes and a figure that was beyond description! I guessed her age to be thirty, at the most thirty-five. James told me later that she was fifty-two! She and James spoke of many things that were foreign to me. She played the perfect charming hostess and inquired about me and my profession. She was quite taken when I informed her that I earned a living playing the harmonica.

I quickly glanced at my watch and knew that it was time for us to be heading back.

When we left Monte Carlo, I decided to drive and once again, we were graced with the heavenly view of the rocky coast. We finally reached the Italian border, but this time the gate was down and guarded by two soldiers. I stopped and the guard leaned over and said, "Your passports, Signors." I meekly admitted that I had left mine in Nice, but added that we had crossed the same border that morning and we were not stopped. The soldier smiled and walked into a small building. Soon, an officer followed the soldier out and I was asked to step out of the car. We both got out and one of the guards moved my car over to the side. I was escorted into the building and placed in a small jail! The officer questioned me as I constantly glanced at my watch. I told him who I was, and where I was appearing, etc. The officer smiled and said, "I'm sorry to dispute you, Senor, but I saw the show at the casino and you are not Jerry Adler." I was about to show him my driver's license but suddenly realized that it had my legal name on it, Hilliard Gerald Adler. The "Adler" was not enough. I then remembered that I had a harmonica in the glove compartment of the car. A guard was sent to fetch it and I proceeded to play some of the songs that I played in my show. This entire scene was turning into a Hollywood "B" musical!

I played and played as the three Italian idiots sat there enjoying the music. Not satisfied with that, they started asking for requests! It was now 9:00 P.M. and my show was scheduled for 8:30! The officer suddenly opened the jail door and said, "You are free to go."

We did not stop to argue. James and I ran to the car and were about to leave when the officer leaned down and said, "I knew that it was you all the time. I just wanted my men to hear you play."

I was dumfounded. "You what?"

He said, "I am sorry, Senor, I hope that we have not inconvenienced you."

"Inconvenienced me, you probably got me fired!"

"A suggestion, Senor. Always carry your passport." He saluted and waved us on.

I angrily started the car and took off like a rocket. I broke every speed law in France. We finally arrived at the casino at 11:15. I found a note pinned to my dressing room door. It read, "Come to my office."

Well, this was finally it. Three strikes and I'm out. I knocked on the manager's door and heard, "Entre." I entered and he was at his desk looking at some papers. He did not bother to look up but handed me an envelope with one week's pay.

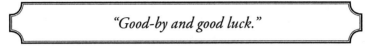

"Good-by and good luck."

I said, "May I please explain what happened? It was not entirely my fault."

"You missed your show in my casino. Good-by and good luck."

The following morning I reached my agent in London by phone, explained what had happened and he was forced to cancel three other French cities which represented the completion of my bookings.

That was the end of my French tour. James was disappointed that it had come to an abrupt end. After an emotional farewell dinner, I assured him that he had been a great companion and I looked forward to seeing him again on my return to London. We embraced warmly and he reluctantly went back to Bombay.

Two days later, I was back in London. Sad to say, I never saw James again. When World War II broke out, James enlisted in the RAF as a fighter pilot. He was one of the first to be shot down.

My parents returned to the U.S, and I went with them to Baltimore. It didn't make much difference to me because my goals were clear. Baltimore as a home base was of no importance. My base could be anywhere. However, being home in Baltimore meant everything to my mother. She was finally back with her sisters and in her own home. None of us fully appreciated how important that was.

We returned home because Larry had hired a professional manager in England and he was right to do so. If the truth be told, my father did not know anything about being a manager and was incapable of negotiating deals. Larry did not object early in his career because of his loyalty to Dad. However, when it became apparent that my Dad was a hindrance to Larry's advancement, he was forced to make a change. To my knowledge, my father had always been an unhappy, frustrated man who hated his old job as a plumber, especially after having had a taste of the good life as Larry's manager. Dad was determined that he would never be drawn back into the plumbing profession again.

When World War II broke out, Dad silently began to make drastic changes that would soon involve Mother and me. We never discussed his problems nor was there any open discussion about anything. God forbid, no opinions from us. We did not have a clue about what he had planned to do.

...we were moving to California to start a new life.

One day, he returned home with a used pickup truck. He announced to Mother that we were moving to California to start a new life. Determined not to slip back into the demoralizing kind of work that he despised, no one could blame him for the move. But at least he owed us the courtesy of a discussion! He just began loading the truck and announced that he was driving to California that very day and that he would send for us. He did not have the vaguest idea of what he would do when he got there.

He had taken a considerable amount of money from my bank account as well as money from Larry's which in his mind, he believed he had earned. After lunch, he left Baltimore, and left Mother and me sitting at the table in a state of shock! How could he justify such a move without listening to the family he was leaving behind?

I looked at my mother and realized, for the first time, what a terrible wrong had been committed against her. She began to sob uncontrollably.

I put my arms around her and whispered that everything would be OK. I did not have the slightest idea of what I was talking about.

Once again, she was about to be uprooted and moved to unfamiliar territory far from the security of her family and friends. I knew how miserable Mother's life had been in London, filled with fear and isolation. Once again, the change of lifestyle would so overwhelm her that this time, "panic" turned to depression. None of us were familiar with the signs or consequences of a nervous breakdown. She quickly started to mentally deteriorate and never came out of her acute depression. Mother was a dear, loving and sensitive flower who inwardly cried with each change. The joys and challenges that the rest of us welcomed devastated Mother. She had no resistance left.

When my father arrived in Los Angeles, he set about to purchase a retail business. Dad did not know a thing about running a retail store but that did not seem to bother him. He located a housewares and gift shop and was convinced that this would be it. He purchased the business immediately, without waiting to find out if it met with our approval. He called and told us to take the earliest train to Los Angeles. We promptly left but were still in shock about the move. I could see what it was doing to my mother but I was helpless to do anything to boost her spirits.

Dad met us at the train station and was so exuberant about the store that he failed to see the obvious deterioration in Mother.

Mother's illness placed a great strain on all of us. Dad and I were like confused children, attempting, without success, to "make Mother well". We did not have any moral or physical support from family or relief from the day-to-day strain. Our family and friends lived three thousand miles away. Out of desperation, we explored the area of psychiatry and finally called the Los Angeles Medical Association for advice. A doctor's name was recommended. Unfortunately, in those days, mental illness was dealt with in one way only - electric shock treatment! That drastic approach was still in its infancy and psychiatrists knew very little about it except to experiment on human beings and then wait to see the results. Within a period of six months,

Mother received one-hundred-and-nine shock therapy treatments which did nothing more than scramble her brains to a point of no return. I cannot blame my father for approving of such treatment because there did not seem to be an alternative. He did not know any better, nor did the psychiatrists who performed these hideous treatments.

When the shock therapy began, we were at the mercy of a part of medical science that was foreign to us. At best, shock treatment was a brief, temporary relief to Mother's acute anxiety. This treatment was to continue for the remaining thirty-five years of her life. These years were spent in and out of mental institutions.

From Stage to Film

My career was about to make a slight readjustment from performing in shows, theaters and nightclubs, to also performing in motion pictures, providing background music, plus TV and radio, variety, and talk shows. I began receiving studio recording calls to play background music for many films. I was usually the soloist with a huge studio orchestra and I thoroughly enjoyed it. Perhaps calling my contribution as "soloist" is a misnomer. Background film music is music that is written to enhance the mood of a scene with the composer striving to keep his music unobtrusive but effective. It was my first exposure to the technical side of motion pictures and it proved to be an exciting experience. Each film had its own series of technical problems and they all required knowledge of musical application as dictated by particular scenes.

I gained tremendous experience in most of the major studios and also had the opportunity to meet stars on a one-on-one basis. Many times, I was required to dub in my harmonica for a star whose role required him or her to play the harmonica and look as if they were actually playing it. This necessitated many private instruction lessons to show the actors the finer points of holding the instrument and the proper movements.

By its flamboyant nature, the entertainment industry is open to public admiration and scrutiny, plus unfounded rumors, trumped-up scandals and tales of the most irreverent kind were often fabricated by publicists working for the studios. In the years when I was actively engaged in entertainment, I had the opportunity as well as the pleasure of working with many famous actors. I found them to be, for the most part, hard-working, dedicated people who took their craft seriously and displayed their human side in a more appropriate manner than the spin artists from the studios portrayed them.

The public seems to get a vicarious thrill at the thought of well-known personalities squirming in annoying discomfort. This is not to say that the film industry did not have its share of sleaze. However, having spent the last sixty-six years in many phases of show business, I consider myself to be a fairly good judge of what is true and what is fiction. The next sections profile famous individuals with whom I worked, played with and sometimes loved in the 35 years I was engaged in the film industry. They are true insofar as I remember them.

Mary Astor and Dane Clark

One day I received a call from a gentleman from CBS Radio. He told me that Mary Astor, the film actress, was just starting a radio series featuring various actors and performers in a contest format. Actors would do scenes with Miss Astor and performers, such as singers and musicians, would do one song. At the end of the show the winner was decided by the level of audience applause, and those with the highest ratings would be asked to return for the next week. I agreed to do it and was pleased to win first place. I won for three straight weeks. On the fourth week, I was competing with a singer and an actor who's name was Bernie Zanville. I recognized immediately that Bernie was going to be very strong competition. I didn't mind losing to such a talent but was amazed when I won for the fourth time. Zanville was furious and made it quite clear that I didn't deserve it. Zanville went on to bigger and better things and changed his name to Dane Clark.

Charles Laughton

I struck up a wonderful friendship with Charles Laughton. Charles had invited me to lunch at the famous Trocadero Restaurant in London. I had never dined at a top-rated restaurant in London and had mixed emotions about it. I could not pass up the opportunity to dine with Charles, so I bit the bullet and accepted. After we had been seated, the maitre d' brought our menus. Charles asked if I would care for a drink and I quietly declined. I was pretty damned nervous in such surroundings and Charles sensed it.

> *I could not pass up the opportunity to dine with Charles...*

"For God sake, Jerry, relax! You're supposed to be enjoying it!"

I mumbled my apology and began looking over the menu. Everything was in French. Now what do I do? I leaned over and whispered that I could not read French. He said, "Don't worry about it. I will translate it for you." He named the specialties of the house in English and I couldn't understand what he was saying!

In desperation, I said, "Do they have any soup?"

"SOUP?" said Laughton in his best Captain Bligh delivery.

"Yes, soup. What's wrong with that?"

"Nothing, I suppose. Let's see, they have bouillon."

"What's a bouillon?"

"It's a clear beef broth."

"That's fine. I'll have bouillon."

I must explain that I have had a habit since early childhood that I have been teased and criticized for many times. I enjoy ketchup in soup. It doesn't matter what kind of soup. It can be chicken soup, vegetable soup or any other kind of soup. It made no difference.

The waiter brought the bouillon and I blithely asked, "Do you have any ketchup?" Unfortunately, I asked about ketchup just as Charles took his first bite of escargot.

Charles began to laugh and choke at the same time!

"Ketchup, sir?" said the waiter in a state of shock.

"Yes. I would like some ketchup." The waiter was making me hostile. He left our table and disappeared into the kitchen. I happened to glance up later to see our waiter talking to another man wearing a very tall, white hat. The waiter finally returned to our table, excused himself to Charles, ignoring me completely and removed my bouillon without a word. The restaurant refused to serve me! It never occurred to me that I was asking for something that is never used in such restaurants. All the while, Charles was laughing and choking on his Goddamned snails! I was mortified. I never got to eat anything except a roll and butter. However, justice was mine, for it was now time for Laughton to squirm, and squirm he did! I had learned that he dreaded being asked for an autograph, especially in a public venue like a restaurant. The Troc was famous for its excellent food and celebrity clientele. Many tourists, mostly American, would dine there with the expectation of a close-up look at a famous star. Charles spotted the dreaded interlopers before I did. He began to tremble and quickly broke into a sweat.

"What's wrong?" I asked.

"Oh, God. Look toward the entrance." He began to mop his brow nervously with his napkin.

I did not see anything unusual. He leaned over and whispered, "Fucking American tourists!"

The maitre d' was about to show them to a table, but the wife spotted Charles. I could see that she was insisting that they be shown to their table by way of Charles. As they got closer I heard a strange, guttural noise and was shocked to hear it coming from Charles' throat. Just as the couple reached our table, Charles leaped to his feet, threw himself halfway across the table and screamed in the lady's face,

"Oh, look! There's Charles Laughton!" The lady turned ashen and her husband quickly took her arm and moved her forward. I thoroughly enjoyed Charles' discomfort.

Vivian Leigh

In 1937, I had signed a contract to work on a film in England, titled St. Martin's Lane. It starred Charles Laughton, Vivian Leigh, Rex Harrison and Tyrone Guthrie. Laughton and Guthrie were cast as street buskers, or as we say in America, street entertainers. Guthrie was supposed to play the harmonica. I was hired to record his music as well as instruct him on the finer points on how to hold the instrument.

Vivian Leigh was, in my opinion, the most exquisite woman alive! Working on the set in her presence filled my days with great excitement. I found it very difficult not to stare and my desire for her was overwhelming. She was always warm and friendly to me and obviously realized that I had a mad crush on her. She invited me to lunch in the studio commissary on two occasions. Sitting opposite her was more than I could stand. Gazing into that exquisite face caused me great discomfort as well as made me extremely horny. I made a promise to myself. This was the lady that I was going to marry despite the fact that she and Lawrence Olivier were engaged! I was also convinced that the twelve bottles of champagne that I had stashed away in Baltimore, would impress the hell out of her. The strange behavior of an idiot teenager!

Working with Guthrie was a pleasure. He was eager to learn as much as possible about the harmonica and was determined that he was going to look like he was actually playing. His desire for perfection required hours of practice alone which allowed me more time on the set to be close to Vivian. I sneaked glances at her at every opportunity and hoped that it was not obvious, especially to her.

Imagine, sitting in the back seat with Vivian.

We had been working late one evening due to shooting delays and my usual ride back to London had already left. London was over an hour's drive and I did not have any idea who would give me a lift. Vivian heard about my dilemma and volunteered to give me a ride in her chauffer-driven limo!

I began trembling with excitement. Imagine, sitting in the back seat with Vivian. Just the two of us! If only the guys in Baltimore could see me now!

There were smoked glass windows between the driver and us, providing complete privacy. We were ten minutes into the ride when I felt her hand on my knee! Things progressed rapidly. Suffice it to say, it was my first and greatest sexual experience in the back seat of a limousine, or anywhere else for that matter!

♬

Edward G. Robinson

Edward G. was a true gentleman in every sense of the word. (He liked being called Edward rather than Ed or Eddie). He was a quiet, soft spoken, conservative gentleman not at all like the gangster parts that he portrayed so well. He was also a serious art collector and had built a collection that was the envy of collectors throughout the U.S.

He was equipped with a dry wit, a remarkable ability to speak on most subject such as politics, sports, education – you name it! He was an avid reader but was a loner. He seldom attended Hollywood parties.

One of the things that bothered him was the public misconception of his motion picture persona. With ten years of retirement behind him, he continued to receive an extraordinary amount of fan mail. The vast majority had to do with questions about his knowledge of notorious gangsters and thugs. He had a good-natured attitude about such mail and felt complimented that his portrayals were considered so real that the public assumed that he was a legitimate hood.

Edward G. Robinson became involved in political causes. As with so many actors of his day, he found himself embroiled in the McCarthy hearings. He was forced to testify and ordered to name names. He was not prepared for the vicious attacks as well as the unfounded accusations that he was a Communist dupe. His denials were shouted down by the members of the House Committee on Un-American Activities which left Edward a beaten man. He suffered a nervous breakdown as a direct result of the unfounded accusations, destroying a brilliant career, and along with it, a charming and very gentle human being.

♫

James Cagney

Jim was a pussycat. A tightly packed bundle of dynamite and a great gentlemen of the film industry. His screen image as "tough guy" was as far removed from the real Cagney as was that of his close friend, Edward G. Robinson, whose life revolved around art and art collectors. Cagney was married to his craft and like Edward G., was also an art collector. In addition, he was a better than average painter. He also had the good sense to know when to relax and have fun. Cagney's relaxation was bowling! He organized a team at Warner Brothers which he called, "The Mob". He loved the sport and played whenever possible. I will never know why I was chosen to join his team. I was not a regular employee at Warner Brothers and his team consisted of the "mob" who worked on many films with him. Alan Hale Sr., Frank McHugh, Alan Jenkins, John Garfield, and me. We bowled nearly every Saturday night at the Sunset Bowling Alley, a converted motion picture studio in Hollywood. He was quite aware of the thrill that the fans got from watching us bowl. The alley owners had to establish strict rules for the observers. They were allowed twenty minutes and then had to leave to allow others waiting in line outside. To compound the problem, we had several celebrity viewers as well. Bette Davis, Paul Henried, Sidney Greenstreet, Peter Lorre and Sylvia Sidney.

♫

Gene Kelly

One of my all-time favorites in the film industry was Gene Kelly. The public in general have mistakenly tossed the word "genius" around, about certain individuals in their chosen field. So much so that it has lost its meaning. Gene was an authentic genius in his choreographed dance routines. His vivid imagination was astounding and his well of original ideas remained full throughout his career.

> *...he was even brutal in his desire for perfection.*

What he created in the world of dance will never be duplicated. Gene was a tough taskmaster and pity the poor partners who did not meet his standards. A perfect example was Debbie Reynolds. Debbie was nineteen when she was cast in her first starring role opposite Gene in the classic *Singin' in the Rain.* Unfortunately her knowledge of tap dancing was her limited ability to do the simple "time step". He drove her mercilessly for weeks at a time until her feet were bleeding! He insisted that she learn every choreographic move of his creation until he was satisfied. Some would say that he was even brutal in his desire for perfection.

On a personal level he was warm, charming and witty. But when working before the camera, it had to be his way or no way at all.

I had known Gene for a number of years in New York before he became a Hollywood star. We shared a close relationship including the period when he signed a 12-year contract with MGM. I was privileged to be invited by him to watch the shooting of his classic *Singin' in the Rain* number which took three full days to shoot. Being exposed to the continuous shower of water on the first day caused his costume to shrink and he became ill from this constant exposure. On the second day he was running a fever of 102 but he insisted on completing the scene. That unforgettable number became what the motion picture industry still considers to be the most spectacular individual dance performance in films.

Gene and I remained close friends for over fifteen years. When he became a star at MGM, I was working on various films at the same studio. I always arranged to find the time to drop by on his shooting stage to see him. Whenever he spotted me he would stop what he was doing to introduce me to one and all as his "longtime friend". He always managed to make me feel very important. I will always be grateful for his friendship.

His tenure at MGM was not always a happy one. He had a bitter relationship with the head of the studio, Louis B. Mayer. They had many arguments and serious disagreements about artistic differences and their feud was common knowledge in the industry. Gene tried desperately to break his contract without success.

After his final year at MGM, Gene tried many projects that were not commercial successes. One in particular was his desire to make a full length film titled, "Invitation to the Dance". A daring idea which was shot without dialogue or story line. The film was simply dancing. It was spectacular in concept and artistic presentation but it failed miserably at the box office. He poured much of his own wealth into it and I feel that it eventually destroyed him. Gene Kelly died in February 1996 at the age of 84.

♪

Bette Davis

Contrary to popular belief, Bette Davis was unpretentious, always considerate to her fellow actors and stage crew, and was, as once stated by one of the crew, "One of the guys". She was capable of being feisty when driving home a valid point. These outbursts had mostly to do with how a particular scene should be played. With it all she was a consummate professional but always kept things humming on the shooting stage.

My first day on the set was a shocker. I immediately recognized the throaty voice of La Belle Davis before I ever saw her. She was talking and laughing with many of the working crew, sharing a bawdy joke. Her laughter could be heard above everyone else. I had a preconceived idea that Bette would display a grandiose manner, being ostentatious with flamboyant behavior. I was wrong on all counts.

Her human side quickly became more revealing...

When George Cukor, the director introduced me to her, she greeted me warmly and quickly made me feel welcome. Her human side quickly became more revealing, making her easy to talk to.

By the time we became close friends, she was influential in arranging for me to perform at several fund-raising dinners in which she was involved. She also opened many doors for me to meet many of the most famous stars in the industry.

A couple of years later, I enlisted in the Army Air Corps and was ordered to report to an entertainment unit at Santa Ana, California. It was basically a propaganda unit that provided radio shows for the U.S. as well as our troops stationed all over the world. The most influential stars in Hollywood were contacted to participate in these shows. We also performed a one-hour show on Wednesdays and Fridays featuring our magnificent 45 piece orchestra made up mostly of studio musicians. It was on those nights that I was called upon to perform as soloist. One afternoon I was overjoyed to hear the Bette Davis was to be the featured star on our Saturday night show. When she saw me she rushed over to greet me.

Bette had become involved with the Hollywood Canteen. It was tightly run, and no outsiders were admitted. She had asked me if it was possible to invite our entire orchestra to the Canteen to perform with me as soloist. I checked with my commanding officer and he quickly approved. It turned out to be quite a memorable evening.

When I was sent overseas to the South Pacific, Bette promised to write, but only if I promised to answer. She also became my "Hollywood Mother". She knitted sweaters and socks for me despite the fact that I was on the Equator, the hottest place on earth! Her "Care" packages became the topic of conversation with my fellow GIs. Her letters were hysterically funny and I regret that I never saved them. I still miss her and her loud, gaudy laughter.

Jean Harlow

I suppose, the magic word for this lady should be "fascinating." Jean Harlow was the first and most "fascinating" film star I had met in my early years in the industry. She was, at that time, the biggest star on MGM's star roster despite her tender age of seventeen.

Her demeanor belied her age. She was the quintessential "flapper" of that era, and she played it to the hilt. Most of us on the MGM lot were dumbfounded by her ability "take over" in any given situation. A good example was her behavior in the commissary at lunch time. I cannot say that she was demanding nor rude but she had a "fascinating" way of getting her way without being obvious.

She knew that she was the darling of the studio but we were never aware that she tried to push her weight around. The studio executives treated her like a piece of sensitive crystal and I sensed that she loved every moment of it.

I believe that they were shooting "Grand Hotel" at the time. The fine actress, Marie Dressler was also starring in the film and I was told that Dressler was annoyed at the way the top executives fawned over Jean. The two ladies seemed to get along well on the set but it was also obvious that Miss Dressler did not approve of the special treatment being given to Miss Harlow.

> *...Jean reminded me of Lucille Ball.*

In retrospect, Jean reminded me of Lucille Ball. She was a bit cocky and considerably loud in her desire to get attention. I never got to know her well but she insisted that I address her as Jean instead of Miss Harlow. I never had the opportunity to work on any of her films but our paths crossed on numerous occasions on the MGM lot.

She was a fun-loving young lady that reveled in the constant attention that was showered on her. However, I found her to be a kind and generous person who was not prone to putting on airs. One of her favorite fellow actors was Carol Lombard. They were close friends and so much alike and yet, so different.

Jean's career was shockingly brief and sad. She died at a very early age.

♫

Sammy Davis Jr.

The year was 1938. I first met Sammy when he was working with his father and uncle. The act was The Will Maston Trio, featuring Sammy Davis, Jr. We were appearing at the Capitol Theater in New York City. Headlining the bill was the king of comedy, Danny Kaye. That was the whole show except for the line of gorgeous chorus girls.

...he became a physical wreck prior to going on stage...

My first impression of Sammy was of his amazing energy. He was a marvelous dancer and singer but when I observed him and his partners warm up before their stage entrance, Sammy was geared to explode! He would bounce on his toes, twitch and grimace and, in general, look like a clock that had been too tightly wound. I later learned that he became a physical wreck prior to going on stage and literally threw up everything in his stomach prior to making his entrance. Once on stage, he was the consummate professional and was the focal point of the act. I had never seen anything like that in my life!

We became close friends and spent much time together. In those days we performed five shows per day with a first-run motion picture between each show. To keep ourselves amused we created our own "challenge contest." Meaning that I would play a fast jazz riff on the harmonica and Sammy would try to duplicate the riff with his taps. We honed it to such a fine point that we used to break each other up by me creating a musical pattern that made it more difficult for Sam to recreate in dance. The game was performed backstage while the film was in progress. We spent countless hours doing this to the delight of on-lookers such as Danny Kaye, stage hands, chorus girls and musicians from the orchestra pit.

Word soon spread to other vaudeville houses in close proximity to ours that Sammy and Jerry were "doing their thing." Eventually nine or ten acts would drop by and enjoy the fun.

Sammy was never able to conquer his physical problem of acute nervousness. I can only assume that he did not have an ounce of flesh on his bones. He once asked me how I was able to calmly walk on stage and do my act without a trace of anxiety. I couldn't give him a logical answer because I have never had the experience of feeling nervous before a performance. Excited, yes, but never nervous.

I knew from the first time that I had seen him perform that he was destined for stardom. My only fear was that his color would stand in the way. Remember this was 1938. However, his rise to fame was quite rapid. Unfortunately, by the time he became a star, the army drafted him and he was about to experience the living hell of what it was like to be a black serviceman. His inevitable confrontation with the "red neck" element created major problems for him. He was beaten unmercifully several times and was once actually tarred and feathered for simply being black!

Sam was eventually honorably discharged and was quickly back in show business. By coincidence, I was also in the service and we were discharged within two weeks of each other. He had broken away from the Will Maston Trio. His father and uncle realized that they were holding him back so finally, Sammy was on his own. We worked on the same bill several times and reestablished our favorite game.

In the course of his incredible career, he managed to lose an eye in an auto accident while in Las Vegas. He studied for and eventually converted to Judaism, became a key figure in Sinatra's Rat Pack, and was a personal friend of John F. Kennedy.

Sammy Davis, Jr. was a perfect example of a human being living his life in perpetual motion. He was a class act as a dancer, singer, impressionist and actor. Who could ask for anything more?

Lucille Ball

Lucy was a free-wheeling icon. At the age of eighteen she had a fierce desire to be a Hollywood star. She certainly had the looks. She was an attractive red head with an hour-glass figure that turned many heads as she deliberately walked in many areas on the lot where she would be noticed. Lucy cursed a blue streak, loved telling bawdy jokes and always enjoyed the attention she created in a crowd.

> *She cursed, laughed out loud and in general was "one of the guys".*

One of her first accomplishments in Hollywood was having been chosen by Samuel Goldwyn as a "Goldwyn Girl" in a Danny Kaye film. Being a Goldwyn Girl meant parading down a staircase with other young, beautiful women wearing exquisite but glitzy costumes. She was particularly proud of the fact that she never wore underwear! She went so far as to ask young men on the set to "touch her behind" to prove that she was not wearing panties! She was simply a totally outgoing individual that did not believe in the typical restrictions imposed on young, attractive girls. She cursed, laughed out loud and in general, was "one of the guys"!

Her major desire was to be a comedienne in films. Instead, she was given serious and sometimes dumb parts to play. She relaxed when told to "let her hair down" and be herself. And "be herself" she did until she was noticed by a casting director at MGM who observed her clowning around on a rehearsal stage.

Lucy and I remained good friends and got along very well. She recognized in me the perfect straight man to her silly and sometimes bawdy humor. Desi came into her life at a much later time in her career. They were the perfect team despite the fact that they had long, drawn-out fights that were sometimes physical. Lots of personal items were involved and their dressing room was usually littered with broken perfume bottles, chairs, etc. There were many confrontations between them, and everyone was advised to stay clear until the arguments subsided.

Lucy and Desi soon became the most powerful and influential team in television. They bought their own studio (formerly RKO) and produced many hit comedy series besides the classic "I Love Lucy" show.

Lucy never changed. She did mellow a bit but still slapped me on the back when she felt that something funny had occurred between us. We worked together in several USO shows to entertain the troops during WW II, but eventually lost touch.

♫

The Marx Brothers

I first met the Marx Brothers, when I was 21, at the Friar's Club in Beverly Hills, an elegant country club patronized by the cream of Hollywood's actors, writers, producers and directors.

I had been invited there to have lunch with George Burns. The meeting with the Marx Brothers was not anticipated. This occurred on a Sunday afternoon and it was pretty crowded. The club was filled with the elite of the motion picture industry and I, of course, was enthralled.

George said, "Have you ever met any of the Marx Brothers?" I excitedly replied, "No, I haven't!"

He nodded to the left and said, "Well, there they are, all four of them. Ya wanna meet them?" I could not believe that he was being so casual about it! "Come on," he said. "Let's go join them."

We walked over and the greetings between George and the Marx Brothers were animated and set me off into gales of laughter. Admittedly, I was so stunned by the immediacy of it that I had difficulty controlling myself. George introduced me to them individually and I tried desperately to be as calm and casual as possible. I had pictured in my mind what they might be like in person. Other than Groucho, they were not what I had expected. Chico did not look like Chico nor did Harpo look anything like his professional persona. Without the blond wig and salaciously wicked look, he simply was not Harpo! I was shocked to realize that Harpo had a voice! I handled the introduction to Chico much better but I nearly "lost it" when Groucho said, "How do you do, young fella." The voice was unmistakable. However, without the cigar, the painted eyebrows and mustache, something seemed to be lost in the translation. I was not that familiar with Zeppo, the straight man of the family.

> *...Chico was the financial genius of the group and Harp...the historian...*

We were invited to join them and extra chairs were brought to the table. This allowed me the time to compose myself, and I finally felt relaxed. I protectively kept a low profile and let them do the talking. Fortunately, George Burns was in rare form and he had all of us practically falling off our chairs. I was told later by George, that Chico was the financial genius of the group and Harpo was very much the historian and book reader. Groucho could not have been anything but Groucho. He related stories that caused us to hold our stomachs with laughter! For example:

They were under contract to MGM and were about to shoot the film, "A Night at the Opera." They had set up a meeting with Irving Thalberg, the young executive producer. When they arrived at his office, they were kept waiting for over one hour. Not accustomed to that kind of rudeness, Groucho went to the commissary and purchased a bag of marshmallows and returned to the waiting room. There was a huge fireplace in the room and Groucho lit it and then told his brothers that they should all remove their clothing and sit around the fire roasting marshmallows. Needless to say, when Thalberg's secretary came in to tell them that Mr. Thalberg would see them, they ignored her and continued roasting and eating their marshmallows in the nude. She let out a scream and rushed back into Thalberg's office. At this point in the story Groucho took a long pause, removed a cigar from his inside jacket pocket, lit it and said, "Thalberg never kept us waiting again!"

♫

Jackie Gleason

> *...the greatest harmonica player in all the world...!"*

During my early years in show business, I had the opportunity to work with many famous stage entertainers. One of my favorites was Jackie Gleason whom I considered to be a brilliant performer. He had the magic to charm his audience at will. My friendship with Jackie lasted for twenty years. We worked in vaudeville together and we always got along. Jackie was a heavy drinker but it never seemed to get in the way of his performances. I once watched in amazement when he walked off stage and the stage manager had to catch him as he fell over, dead drunk! Many years later, he starred in his own radio show on CBS from Hollywood. I was engaged as a steady on the show. When I arrived for rehearsal, I could see that the years had not been kind to Jackie because of his drinking problem. Most of the time, he was impossible to deal with and he would burst into a flaming rage whenever he was challenged about pieces of comedy material, etc. I elected to stay out of his way for a while. At show time, I was standing in the wings to make my entrance after being introduced by Jackie. He began. "And now, ladies and gentleman, the greatest harmonica player in all the world, my good friend, Claget Gloondeen!"

Claget Gloondeen?

I was really flustered but I walked out and did my number. After the show, I asked Jackie why he had introduced me that way.

He said, "What way?"

"You introduced me as Claget Gloondeen!" He laughed, "Ah, that's nothing, pal. Don't worry about it. It will be right next week."

I was puzzled and very angry but I was not in a position to make waves. The following Saturday, I reminded him to please use my correct name.

He looked at me in astonishment. "What's that for? I always introduce you properly!" I had a strange feeling that I was about to catch it again.

Jackie introduced me. "Ladies and gentlemen, here is a young man who plays the harmonica like you have never heard before. A true artist! Let's bring him on with a big hand! Here he is, Troman Finebalt!"

I was furious! After performing my number, I walked to the control room and began registering my complaint to the producer.

He said. "Please, Jerry. We'll straighten this out after the show."

When the show ended, the producer called a meeting of the entire cast, but Jackie, who hated production meetings, walked out, so we had it without the star of the show!

The producer was fair but blunt. "Look Jerry, I don't know what to say. I can only mention it to him and hope that he remembers."

I was on for sixteen weeks and my real name was mentioned twice by the regular announcer at the beginning and end of each show. Jackie's off-the-wall sense of humor – well, he thought that by introducing me differently each time would add spice to the show. Some spice. Despite my tremendous frustration, we remained friends.

When the radio show finally came to an end, Jackie went back to New York and soon became a household word in television. I had not seen him for eight years. After many seasons in New York, he finally moved the entire show to Miami where his popularity soared to new heights.

I received a call from my agent in New York asking if I wanted to work some condo dates in Miami. The offer was lucrative so I accepted. Knowing that Jackie lived there, I thought that it would be nice if we got together. I did not have his phone number so I called Ed Sullivan in New York and he gave it to me. I called Jackie and told him that I was coming to Miami and he shouted, "Clagett Gloondeen! HOW SWEET IT IS!" We talked briefly and then he said, "Look, I want you to be my guest while you are in Florida. I'll provide you with a car, you'll stay with me and we'll have a ball!" I accepted his generous invitation.

I had made previous reservations at the Holiday Inn but forgot to cancel. I am, and always will be, terribly forgetful. I arrived in Miami, took a cab to the Holiday Inn and was there for ten days when it suddenly hit me that I was supposed to be Jackie's guest! I felt horrible but knew that I had better call him. When Jackie answered, he climbed all over me, screaming that I was an ungrateful sonofabitch and that I was getting even with him because of the radio show! He had sent his limo to the airport to pick me up and of course, I never showed. He screamed, "I never want to see you again!" He slammed the phone down and, sadly, that was the end of our friendship.

♫

Gary Cooper

Gary Cooper was not the "strong, silent aw shucks" type of man most people envisioned, although he played that character in just about every film he made. He was decent, easy to get along with, not a bit temperamental and generally a very cooperative actor on the set. I worked on a number of westerns with him. His performance in "High Noon" convinced me that he was a far better actor than he had ever projected in previous films. Although I knew him fairly well, we never became close friends.

When Gary was working on a picture he never seemed to have the time to relax. He was all business and expected nothing less from cast and crew. Fortunately for me, he was a fan of the harmonica and would ask me to play. He seemed to get along with his female co-stars and rumor had it that when the studio was shooting "For Whom the Bell Tolls" he and Ingrid Bergman had an unforgettable scene which showed them sleeping in one sleeping bag. The story spread rapidly that he actually "made love" to Bergman in the sleeping bag. However, it was never confirmed.

Gary Cooper was also caught up in the McCarthy witch hunt for "supposed communists". Together with other stars like Robert Taylor, Adolph Menjou, Humphrey Bogart, and John Wayne he believed, for reasons of his own, to side with the House Committee On Un-American Activities. During that era of hysteria "Red baiting" was the order of the day, to reveal names of fellow actors. Cooper conceded, along with the others. This act of revealing names, proven or not, true or false, was responsible for destroying many reputations, careers and lives such as Zero Mostel, John Garfield, Lee J. Cobb, and Danny Kaye, to name a few. These other artists stood their ground and refused to capitulate to the "Committee" and their unfounded and unproven accusations. Of the whole group who ratted on their fellow actors and writers, Humphrey Bogart was the only one who truly "caved in" with apparently no regrets. The others, like Gary Cooper, were pressured and in retrospect, Cooper was shattered that he almost succumbed. It took an enormous amount of courage for him to follow the leads of Mostel, Garfield, Cobb and Kaye. He refused to answer their questions. However, he was considered "money in the bank" insofar as box office draw was concerned, so the studio sheltered him from the pressures and threats by the likes of J. Parnell Thomas and McCarthy's vicious committee. Mr. Thomas was indicted and convicted of wrong-doing unrelated to his Hollywood witch hunt, one of the crowning ironies during this time of hysteria.

Gary's obvious good looks, his manly persona clinched his popularity for years to come. His reputation lasted through all the remainder of his life. During the shooting of "High Noon," he was still hot at the box office.

♫

Larry Adler

My brother, Larry was the best harmonica virtuoso in the world and rapidly became a household name in the United States and Great Britain. Everything deservedly fell into place for him, and in a short time he was considered one of the highest paid entertainers in the United States. Several harmonica concertos were written for him by Ralph Vaughn-Williams, Sir William Walton, and by other famous composers.

Larry loved the limelight and the special treatment he received from many of the best known figures of the day. While living in England, after his divorce, he fell in love with a young and beautiful Lady Selina Hastings, Lady in Waiting to Queen Elizabeth. She in turn introduced him to Prince Phillip. Larry and Phillip quickly became close tennis buddies and Phillip arranged for Larry to receive a lifetime seat at center court for the Wimbledon matches - for free!

Larry was also an excellent writer and wormed his way into writing a restaurant column for a magazine distributed to all of the leading London hotels. This enabled him to be invited to dine at the finest restaurants, again for free!

> *The Committee asked him to state whether or not he was a Communist.*

Many years earlier, Larry settled down in marriage with a beautiful English model, Eileen Walsor. He enjoyed England and what it had to offer. He too put his own career and future on the line during the McCarthy era. Many good Americans were branded as communists or communist sympathizers. There was a witch hunt from coast-to-coast that became one of the darkest hours in our country's history. Our democracy was being challenged by a group of politicians who established the House on Un-American Activities Committee. They called before them hundreds of Americans including Larry. The Committee asked him to state whether or not he was a Communist. He refused to answer. From that moment on, he was considered a Communist or Communist sympathizer. He was refused employment (for to do so would endanger those who helped him); his wife left him and sued for divorce. Was he a Communist? Absolutely not! From his point of view, it was none of anyone's business! Larry moved back to London to live where he was well-known and respected

♫

Alan Gordon

One of my closest friends in Hollywood, was a wonderful gentleman named Alan Gordon. He had a public relations firm on Sunset Boulevard opposite the famous Ciro's nightclub. There was a continuous flow of exciting stories in and out of his office. Some true, others created for the sake of publicity for his clients.

Alan was kind and considerate to all of his friends and he was one of the most respected individuals in the publicity business. It was 1940 and the excitement and glamour of Hollywood was like a never ending roller coaster ride. Everyone seemed to be living the high life and it felt like the contemporary version of the roaring twenties. Alan was soft spoken, even-tempered and a true gentleman in every respect. His friends were, at times, a total contrast to his lifestyle. He knew the famous as well as the infamous, and was comfortable with both.

My first contact with him came in an unusual manner. When I worked on the Gleason show, I received a fair amount of fan mail. One particular young lady wrote to me every day. She would request certain songs and ask that they be dedicated to her. For some unaccountable reason, I was touched by her sweetness and sincerity and decided to call to thank her personally for being such a devoted fan. The only way that she knew my name was that the announcer at the beginning and end of the show announced it correctly. I was shocked to discover that this charming and lovable young lady was mentally retarded. I had first spoken to her mother and was then informed of the girl's condition. Her name was Ruth Gordon and her mother had informed me that I was the most important person in her life. I was deeply touched and asked if I could come to their home to meet Ruth. Her mother, excited at the prospect, asked me to dinner. I accepted and when I arrived, I was bowled over by the adulation. I then noticed Alan in the room, and was initially alarmed at his presence. But then I was told for the first time, that Alan was Ruth's brother!

I deliberately focused my attention on Ruth (she insisted on being called, Ruthie) and she was overjoyed. I asked her if she would like to see one of the broadcasts and she went wild. Alan promised to take her so I arranged for their tickets. I asked Ruthie if she would like to meet Jackie Gleason and she replied, "No, just you."

The following day, I received a call from Alan. He asked me if I had time to drop by his office. He greeted me warmly and invited me to sit down. He said, "Jerry, I can't begin to thank you for being so kind and understanding to my sister. It is the first time that anyone other than immediate family has shown her any attention. I mentioned the fan letters and he smiled and said, "Yes, I know about them. They were written by my mother but dictated by Ruthie."

Alan's public relations firm was located on Sunset Boulevard opposite Ciro's nightclub. His office was the hub for many exciting stories about Hollywood stars and starlets. Some were true while others were created for the sake of publicity for his clients. One such example got my name into the Hollywood gossip column. Alan has his staff plant a "hot" item with Louella Parsons, "Jerry Adler, popular harmonica artist is… playing *Here Comes the Bride* in the ear of Hollywood beauty, Stella Black". There was no such person as Stella Black!

Alan and I became the best of friends and he did much to get me press exposure. By a strange stroke of luck, I was able to repay the favors. I was driving in Beverly Hills and was about to pass the home of Orson Wells and Rita Hayworth. I noticed an animated argument going on in front of their home. I was close enough to hear everything. Rita was screaming at Orson that he would be hearing from her lawyer and Orson was bellowing at her to get the hell out of the house!

89

Rita Hayworth and Orson Wells

I was less than a mile from Alan's office so I rushed over and told him what I had just witnessed. He had his staff contact the top gossip columnists in town such as Hedda Hopper, Louella Parsons and Jimmy Fiddler. It became the Hollywood scoop of the year. RITA HAYWORTH FILES FOR DIVORCE. Alan received many compliments for his news releases. That may sound frivolous to some, but in Hollywood, it can make or break the credibility of a news source.

Alan Gordon was a unique and gifted individual. Not only was he the CEO of a major public relations firm but he also was an entrepreneur on many other projects. An example of his diverse interest was in junk yards, and not just any junk yards. He wanted ones that were related to World War II articles with the vast majority of items associated with film cameras, and outdoor shooting equipment such as camera booms. He found one in the San Fernando Valley that included, of all things, a complete army air corps fighter plane. His major interest in the plane was its gun cameras; cameras that took combat photography.

His fascination with these cameras eventually became the basis for a new project that converted these cameras into hand-held movie cameras. These cameras were eventually sold to the public and this "side interest" eventually became his major source of income. He also rented and sold the equipment to the motion picture industry.

♫

Ben "Bugsy" Siegel

One day, I stopped at Alan's office unannounced and noticed that he had company. I was about to leave but he spotted me and asked me to come in. "Jerry, I would like to introduce you to a friend of mine. This is Ben Siegel." We shook hands and Alan invited me to sit down. I did not have any idea who Ben Siegel was. He could have been Alan's tailor for all I knew. We had a pleasant conversation and Siegel mentioned that he had heard me on the Gleason show and complimented me on my musicianship. Ben was a strikingly handsome man and a very friendly, nice guy. We became friends later but at the time, I did not know about him and his reputation as one of the most dangerous gangsters in Hollywood. I was talking to Ben "Bugsy" Siegel! I only knew that he was always pleasant and pretty free with his money.

Ben and I had arranged to meet at a local shopping mall for lunch. After we left the restaurant, we passed Sy Devore's, an exclusive men's shop. He asked me to join him inside. All of the salesmen gathered around him as if he was a visiting potentate.

Ben ordered a couple of suits and then turned to me and said, "What do you like?" At first I did not know what he meant. Again, "So what do you like?" I replied, "What do I like about what?" "How about a nice new suit and maybe a sport's jacket and slacks?"

I said that I really didn't think that I needed anything.

"C'mon, it's on me! I want to buy you something nice."

...he was also a gangster and a killer.

I began to panic because I did not know how to deal with a situation like this. Here was a nice, generous man but he was also a gangster and a killer! How does one say no to such a person? On the pretext of saying that I had to go to the john, I found a pay phone in the men's room and called Alan and explained my problem.

He began to laugh and said, "What's so terrible? He wants to buy you some clothes!"

I said, "But I don't need any and if I did, I don't have to have someone buy it for me."

Alan replied, "Fine, so tell him that." "But I don't want to offend him." "Don't worry. You won't."

I returned to the store and told Ben that I appreciated it very much but I didn't need anything at the moment. Ben was very casual about it and said to Sy Devore, "If the kid needs anything, just put it on my bill."

We both walked out and it was never mentioned again.

♫

Virginia Hill

Ben asked me to do him a favor. His girl friend, the notorious Virginia Hill, who had been heavily involved with the Mob for years, was anxious to see the show at Earl Carroll's nightclub. He said that he wasn't interested in seeing the show and asked me to take Virginia. I felt a bit queasy about it but I didn't wish to offend him. Before I had a chance to respond, he shoved three one hundred dollar bills in my lapel pocket. I started to object but he held up his hand. "Please, you'll be doing me a favor." He asked me to pick her up at his home in Beverly Hills.

I arrived there quite nervous. She looked beautiful in a flashy way, and spoke with a deep Southern accent. She sensed my discomfort and seemed to enjoy it. She gave me a flirtatious wink, kissed Ben, took my arm and off we went.

I sat as close to my door as possible and kept looking from side to side nervously watching the rear view mirror to see if we were being followed! Needless to say, I did not relax for the entire evening. When I finally took her home, I ran to my car and made it home in record time.

I drove to Alan's office and related the entire evening as he roared with laughter. I said, "Alan, it isn't funny! Now, what do I do with the remaining one hundred and fifty that Ben gave me?" Alan said, "Do what you want. It was worth three hundred to Ben for you to take Virginia off his hands for the evening." I said, "Nope. I want to give the balance back to him." Alan again laughed. "How do you plan to do that?"

I said, "I'm going to give it to you to give to him." With that, I plunked the money on his desk and took off before Alan could stop me.

Ben eventually gained a new reputation as a hotel and casino owner by building the Flamingo Hotel in Las Vegas. It was the first super hotel on the Las Vegas Strip. It had been built with Mob money and there were many delays in construction. With underworld pressure barking at his heels, he was finally gunned down sitting in his living room. He was shot from his front lawn through a window. The assassin or assassins were never captured. Virginia Hill was eventually investigated by the Senate Crime Commission but never charged with any crime.

♫

Judy Garland

Judy Garland was a sweet, warm-hearted young lady with a monumental talent. Yes it's true, she did have a dreadfully destructive mother who made Judy's life a living hell on and off the set. Her mother's pet target was Louis B. Mayer, the head of MGM.

I was working on the film, "Babes on Broadway," starring Mickey Rooney and Judy. I had a minor role in addition to playing the harmonica. Judy's mother was responsible for many costly delays in shooting schedules. The director finally had had enough and asked that Mr. Mayer be called to the set. When Mayer heard about the many difficulties, he ordered Judy's mother off the set and issued an order to not allow her on the studio lot again. Judy was upset to the point of throwing up! It is small wonder that she turned to booze and drugs. Not that her mother was solely responsible. The constant pressures being put on Judy were beyond physical endurance. It seemed that she was bounced from one film to another without any kind of break, until she reached the point of collapse. Despite the volcanic episodes that Judy experienced at home, she never failed to give a "grade A" performance before the cameras. All of us who knew her well watched in silent horror as her physical and mental deterioration became a full-blown reality. How very sad to watch a brilliant career collapse before one's eyes.

I vividly recall a day when I was working on the MGM lot but not with Judy. I had heard that she was shooting "Meet Me In St. Louis" and I had always enjoyed watching her perform. I walked over to her set and she was sitting in her director chair crying hysterically. Several people were hovering around to calm her down. Someone had placed a wet towel on her forehead and her stand-in was gently massaging her neck. I looked around and noticed deep concern in the eyes of those in charge. It was now time to set up the next shot and when the director called for "places", Judy stood up and quietly walked into the set and took her place while the make-up artist freshened up her make-up.

When shooting a musical, a playback speaker is used which is actually the pre-recorded orchestra and vocal of the performer. This required that Judy lip-synch her pre-recorded vocal which is an art in itself. They were shooting *The Trolley Song* and she was supposed to be in a gay, carefree mood as she sang. I watched in stunned silence. She was brilliant and never showed a trace of strain. When the director yelled, "cut", Judy screamed and collapsed where she stood!

I dated Judy on a fairly steady basis and for a brief time, it looked as if it was going to turn into something permanent. Judy was 17 when we first started to date, and I was about 20. In less than a month, we were serious. We hesitated to broach the subject of marriage because deep down inside, we sensed it could never happen. She was already a superstar at 17 and had a great career in front of her. So we skirted the issue of marriage several times and once actually talked about running off to Las Vegas for a quickie marriage. However, she was wise enough to realize that she should check with her boss, Louis B. Mayer for his approval. As I anticipated, Mr. Mayer went ballistic on the phone to the point that even I could hear him screaming. "Judy, if you do this, your career is finished! I can guarantee that you will never work in any studio again!" I was sad but relieved at the same time. When she hung up the phone, she began to cry. I knew immediately that this was strictly out of my league. I was certain that she was destined to do incredible things with her talent.

♬

Mickey Rooney

I first met Mickey Rooney when I signed on for a couple of Andy Hardy films. He was the hottest property that MGM ever had. He made more money for that studio than Gable and Tracy combined. But like many child superstars, he was an arrogant, pushy kid with the knowledge that he had enough clout and chutzpah to get away with nearly anything. Mickey Rooney was a multi-talented performer as a dramatic actor, singer, dancer, and comedian. At times, he was generally an easy person to work with and in most cases lots of fun. But to many of the actors and crew at MGM, they saw him differently than the studio heads who pampered him and super-sized his already monumental ego.

With one exception, his amazing talent was never challenged. It was during the filming of "Boys Town" starring Mickey and Spencer Tracy. On a visit to the set, I chatted with Tracy. They had shot several scenes earlier and apparently Mickey had done something to irritate Spence. He commented, "This kid is a repulsive pain in the ass!" I knew at that moment he intended to straighten Mickey out. They were setting up the scene where Mickey is arguing with Father Flanagan (Tracy) about Mickey leaving Boys Town. They were ready for rehearsal. Spence quietly suggested to the director that they go for a take instead of rehearsal. They were all set and Mickey was ready. Tracy was supposed to slap Mickey, but instead, with clenched fist, caught Mickey on the point of the chin, sending Mickey sprawled on his back. The look on Mickey's face was priceless. He got up and charged at Spence. The entire company froze. Tracy grabbed him by the shoulders and whispered, "Sorry I whacked you with my fist kid but don't ever mess with me again." They eventually became close friends.

Mickey loved practical jokes. In later years he starred in a film with David Jansen, about the New York gangster/gambler titled "The Arnold Rothstein Story". I was one of eight men who sat at a table taking bets on the telephone. It was a small part but the scene actually opened up with a close-up of me saying into the telephone, "Honey, I told you to NEVER call me on this phone!" That was it. We rehearsed the scene and then Mickey walked up to me and said, "Jerry, for God sake, that's no way to read that line!" He proceeded to show me how it should be done. At the time I thought his version was totally unbelievable. But being the relatively new kid on the block, I took his advice. When they began shooting the scene I emoted my one line like Jackie Gleason screaming at his wife, Alice! The director yelled, "CUT"! He looked at me and shouted, "What the hell was THAT all about?" Mickey was sitting on the floor grinning at me and laughing like an idiot!

♫

Johnny Carson

I first met Johnny when he had a syndicated ½-hour radio show on KNX in Hollywood. He was as delightfully funny as he was later on TV. I was a musical guest on the show several times. It was obvious to me, at least, that he would become a household name on the infant entertainment media - television. He was a natural. He quickly developed a huge following, and it didn't take too long before NBC snatched him up to become the hottest late-night talk show host in the nation. I appeared on two of his "The Tonight Show" segments, once in New York and once in Hollywood.

Unlike most celebrities who thrived on attention, Johnny was a very private person and actually shunned the attention when he appeared in public. This attitude seemed to translate into "snobbishness" by those who spotted him in a restaurant or elsewhere. Nothing could be further from the truth. He was a gregarious, fun-loving, pleasant and an extremely bright person, but only in the confines of his "work area" which was, in his case, the TV studio.

> *I have never seen anyone consume such quantities of food as Johnny Carson.*

He considered it ill-mannered when someone would approach his table in a restaurant to ask for an autograph. He politely explained to the stranger that he was trying to enjoy his dinner and if they wished to wait outside he would be happy to accommodate the autograph. I have dined with Carson several times. Once we went directly across the street from NBC in Burbank which housed a well-respected steak house restaurant. Management always anticipated his arrival and they actually set aside a private dining area where he would not be disturbed. I have never seen anyone consume such quantities of food as Johnny. This included salad, soup, steak, french fries and topped off with an ice cream dessert to die for. I asked him how he managed to stay so trim. He said, "I suppose it's my good fortune to have the kind of genes that burn it off naturally. I also play a lot of tennis so I have never had a weight problem."

Johnny's incredible sense of humor and his devastating wit has carried him to astronomical heights. He is truly a very funny man. Anyone who remained the undisputed king of comedy on the "Tonight Show" for over 30 years, certainly cannot be ignored. His is a record that will never be broken. I am saddened by the likes of Jay Leno who assumed control of the show when Johnny Carson retired. It is tragic that we will never again hear the clarion call of "HEEEEEER'S JOHNNY"!

♫

Ava Gardner

Ava Gardner and I met in the strangest way. I had received a call for a soundtrack recording date at MGM. In a recording session, the music department adds background music for a particular scene. The music is composed especially for that scene and usually involves a full orchestra.

Ava was on the recording stage and my harmonica track was an obbligato to her singing. However, the studio felt that she could not sing well enough for the part and they hired a young lady, Marne Nixon to dub in the singing. During filming, Ava simply mouthed the vocal.

Ava, dressed in a skin-tight jump suit leaving little to the imagination, was there to listen to the vocal recording and familiarize herself with the music. Ava was a gorgeous girl She was voluptuous, sensuous, and appeared to have a preoccupation with showing off her body. If that were not enough, she had a low, throaty speaking voice that was terribly sexy. She was not well known at the time so, being the young, healthy male, I asked her out on a date. I was dumbstruck when she accepted.

We dated for five or six weeks before the MGM brass cracked down on who she should or should not be seen with in public. MGM had great plans for her. They wanted her to date the leading eligible young contract actors on the lot. It was obvious that we were strongly attracted to each other physically, but I never considered that it would become serious. MGM's timing was perfect. After five weeks, the glamour began to wear thin but we remained good friends. It was shortly after that that she became involved with Mickey Rooney, and eventually married him. As most of us know, that was a preordained disaster, followed by her torrid romance with Sinatra, and again, an unsuccessful marriage.

Ava was a very unhappy young lady who was never strongly drawn to motion pictures. She received dreadful advice from the studio, and was bitterly disappointed in the one film, "Showboat", in which she wanted to actually sing. She had a very nice singing voice and made a test recording of *Can't Help Lovin' That Man of Mine*. Her recording was wonderful but MGM in their remarkable "wisdom," had Lena Horne record the vocal. Hooray for Hollywood!

Louis Armstrong

I was performing at the Monteleon Hotel in New Orleans. At the conclusion of my show, a waiter handed me a note that read, "Please join me at the back table on the right hand side." It was signed, Louie. I had no idea who "Louie" was and I nearly disregarded the note as I walked to my dressing room. Then it hit me. Nah, that couldn't possibly be my old pal, Satchmo! I had not seen him in nearly five years when we worked on the same bill at a theater in Philadelphia. I quickly changed into my street clothes and walked to the back of the club.

As I approached the table, a man stood up with outstretched arms and a grin that glistened from ear to ear. Yes, it was my old and dear friend Louis Armstrong! He told me that he now called New Orleans his home. He had taken the time to see my show and wanted to catch up on the last few years. We talked, laughed and happily cried through much of the evening, one story leading to another, until closing.

> *Louie suggested that we take a stroll down Basin Street...*

Louie suggested that we take a stroll down Basin Street and mentioned to keep my harmonica close by. As we walked, many passersby recognized him, waved "hello" and he of course returned the greeting. I felt very proud to be with my friend, whom I refer to as "musical royalty" walking down Basin Street together. It just doesn't get any better than that. Dixieland music was "swinging" out from one of many non-descript store fronts. We walked in. Five white-haired black men were playing their hearts out to a crowded audience that seemed to be floating two feet off the floor. When the musicians spotted "the King" they shrieked with joy. "HEY, POPS! HOW'S IT GOIN' MAN?" etc. Within seconds, Louie was on the bandstand, asking for a trumpet. He let fly with a trumpet riff that sent the place in near hysteria. He played two or three numbers and then gave me a fabulous introduction and asked me to join them. I forget most of the songs that I played with them, but one. It was *Body and Soul.* Louie began by singing the first chorus while I played an obbligato. He then picked up the trumpet and we played a duet for the concluding chorus. The place was in a frenzy. We didn't leave until 3:00 a.m. My God, how I wished I had had a tape recorder! I cannot recall that I ever played better. When I finally returned to the hotel, got into bed and eventually fell asleep, I know that I had a smile on my face.

♫

Fred Astaire

I had known Fred Astaire since 1935 when he was teamed with his sister, Adele. They were headliners as far back as that. It was a forgone conclusion by anyone in the business who recognized exceptional talent, that Fred Astaire would soon be a star on Broadway. Nobody thought seriously about Broadway stars becoming motion picture stars. But Astaire was someone quite special in his creative ability, his remarkable interpretation of the dance and last but not least, his natural charm as a potential leading man in Hollywood light musicals.

I considered Fred a good friend in the heady days of New York, but we became much closer friends when he made his spectacular entrance in Hollywood by teaming with Ginger Rogers. The amazing irony of that professional coupling was the fact that they did not particularly like each other! That feeling lasted throughout their respective careers. At the conclusion of each film, one or the other promised that that film would be the last. However, their popularity soared to astronomical heights with each new film. They were both wise enough to finally realize that it was foolhardy to turn their backs on such a remarkable following.

I worked on three films with Fred. As long as I knew him, he was a pleasant, generous and fun-loving friend. He respected outstanding talent and constantly encouraged them to pursue and hone their talents to become something special. One day, he called me and told me that he had just discovered a sensational black singer and was anxious to back him on a record album. He specifically wanted me to back him with harmonica obligatos besides the impressive 80 piece orchestra that he had hired. Fred invested a large sum of money for the recording. The singer was quite good but I personally felt that he did not have that special "umph" to make him a singing star. I regret that the album never got off the ground and I learned later that Fred had poured over $50,000 in the production of this album.

Fred continued to flourish in films and soon struck out on his own to break in other partners such as Cyd Charisse, Eleanor Powell, Rita Hayworth and even Joan Crawford in the hopes of finding another Ginger Rogers. His was a fabulous career and one of his lifelong friends, Gene Kelly stated that the world would never see another Fred Astaire.

♫

William Randolph Hearst

I was 22 years old and was comparatively new to show business although I did have a few years of experience under my belt. I do not recall the exact date. However, my best recollection tells me that it was in June 1940.

I had received a telegram from Marion Davies asking me to please call her as quickly as possible, and she had included her telephone number in Santa Monica. I did not know the lady that well at the time. I recall I had met her when she arrived with a large party at Ciro's where I was performing. I called her and she said that Mr. Hearst was giving a large dinner party at San Simeon Castle in two weeks and wished to retain my services for a show along with Frank Sinatra, and Ray Bolger. She asked me if I would be interested and if so, to give her the name of my agent and his phone number. Needless to say, I was quite excited at the prospects of performing at San Simeon. My agent called me and he was also thrilled. He said, "I'm getting you two thousand dollars for a twenty minute show. You will be flown to San Simeon in Mr. Hearst's private plane and will stay overnight at the castle! Wow!

Sinatra, Bolger and I met at Burbank Airport and we were flown immediately to San Simeon. We landed at Mr. Hearst's private airport and then taken on the short ride by limo to the castle. We were each assigned a private bedroom where we had our own private maid! I was asked if I wished to go for a swim in the indoor pool. Apparently, Sinatra and Bolger were not interested so I had the entire pool to myself. There was a life guard/attendant on duty so I made the most of my luxurious surroundings. The pool was glorious with all of the beautiful tiles imported from Rome. There were a number of fantastic statues surrounding the outside walls of the pool and felt that I was having a heavenly dream. The attendant asked if I would be interested in refreshments which I politely declined.

When I concluded my swim, the attendant was there with a huge towel. I was then escorted to my room where all of my belongings had been neatly laid out. I showered in what appeared to be a Grecian bathroom that was breath-taking in size and decor.

The three of us had a 3:00 pm rehearsal with a fourteen-piece orchestra and it came off flawlessly. The show was scheduled for 8:00. There were nearly one hundred guests who dined in the main dining room which looked as if it had been carved from King Arthur's Court. The dining room table was in the center and every guest was seated. Although we were not formally introduced to the guests, I was able to pick out such notables as Marion Davies, Louella Parsons, Mary Pickford, Fay Wray, John Boles, Douglas Fairbanks Jr, Jeanette McDonald, Gregory Ratoff, Robert Taylor, etc. The women were exquisitely dressed in floor-length gowns and it looked like more of a beauty contest rather than a high-class social evening. As for the men, it appeared that they were attempting to out-dress the women. Douglas Fairbanks Jr. wore a gaudy multi-colored sash that looked very much out of place. I briefly met Mr. Hearst and thanked him for his cordiality, and that was that.

The show started on time and later we then had the opportunity to mingle with the guests. I was obviously the youngest person present and there was much fuss made over my talent. I ate it up! Who wouldn't? At 2:00 p.m. we were taken to the airport and flown back to Burbank. It was a day that I shall never forget. And I got paid for it!

Elizabeth Taylor

MGM brought this young, ravishing beauty to America from England at the tender age of 15. They were casting for the film, "Black Beauty" starring Mickey Rooney and, a yet to be cast, leading lady.

I was working on the set of "Babes On Broadway" starring Judy Garland and Rooney when I first saw this exquisite child - deep searching orchid eyes of unbelievable beauty with the face of an angel. My eyes were riveted on this vision and I could not help myself. I just kept on staring. I turned to glance around the set and discovered that every person present was doing the same thing, simply staring in disbelief. Louis B Mayer, head of the studio introduced his new "find" to everyone on stage, explained who she was and stated that they were preparing a screen test with her for the leading role in "Black Beauty". With a very feminine curtsy, she acknowledged everyone and they left. The shooting stage was buzzing like a disturbed bee hive.

> *...she was heavenly to work with and Spencer Tracy heartily agreed that she was too good to be true.*

I did not see Elizabeth again for two years which was, coincidentally, the final shooting schedule for "Black Beauty". By that time the studio frantically scheduled her for additional films, the first being, "Father of the Bride" starring Spencer Tracy, Don Taylor (no relation) and Elizabeth Taylor. Don was a close personal friend and he invited me on the set to observe some of the shooting. I was shocked to see how this child had suddenly blossomed into such a remarkably beautiful young lady of such exquisite proportions. Don said that she was heavenly to work with and Spencer Tracy heartily agreed that she was too good to be true.

I was finally introduced to her by Don. My first impulse was to sweep her up into my arms and never let go. The rest is history. We all know about her various escapades with Richard Burton, Nick Hilton, etc. She eventually became the most valuable female star in the history of motion pictures.

We saw each other at Hollywood parties, but I regret that I never got to know her as well as I would have liked. But I'm sure that I am one of thousands who felt exactly as I did.

♫

Marlene Dietrich
USO Tour

I never worked with Marlene Dietrich in films. However, I was fortunate enough to be part of a mammoth USO Show just prior to my enlistment in the Air Corps. The program consisted of Kay Kyser and his orchestra, Marlene, Lucille Ball, Desi Arnez, Linda Darnell and me. It was a two month tour of Army, Air Corps, Marine, and Navy camps throughout the U.S. It was a grueling tour and we performed at least five shows per week.

Marlene was remarkable. When she was introduced, a ground-swell of cheers arose from a G.I. audience of 30,000 or more at each show. She was warm and down-to-earth; sang popular songs, told jokes, talked to servicemen about their families, and got them to think about something other than the war - even if it was just for a few hours. It was electrifying to see a woman old enough to be the mother or grandmother of most of those in the audience, exude such sex appeal.

When we traveled by bus, she insisted that she be treated and accepted like everyone else in our group. She became involved in poker games and, at times, chatted about some of her colorful experiences from the past. We never tired of this fascinating lady and always encouraged her to tell more about her exciting career.

She did make one important point in expressing her political beliefs. She despised Hitler, and was saddened that her countrymen would accept that maniacal brute as their leader. Unknown to most U.S. citizens, Marlene Dietrich was on Germany's "Most Wanted" list. Dead or alive.

During some of the long bus rides from one camp to another, she would slap me on the knee and insist that I drag out the harmonica and accompany her on one or two songs. One day she asked if I would consider doing the same for the troops. It became an immediate hit and she decided to expand on this by singing close to me as she ran her fingers through my hair. The troops ate it up so we kept the act in for the balance of the tour.

We added one additional offering to our appreciative audience. Lucille Ball suggested Marlene recite "Lincoln's Gettysburg Address," while I softly played The Battle Hymn of the Republic. It turned out to be one of the highlights of our show.

Marlene was charming and generous and was always a pleasure to have around. At the conclusion of the tour she presented an engraved gold cigarette lighter to each of us. She was a beautiful, classy lady.

♫

Jack Benny

Jack was one of the dearest, most loved persons in show business. I cannot think of anyone who disliked Jack or had an unkind word to say about this comedic genius.

I toured with Jack in a USO show throughout the U.S, entertaining troops in the Army, Air Corps, Navy, Marines and Coast Guard. He was remarkably easy-going, warm and generous. Many have asked, "What was it about Jack Benny that made him so funny? His comedy was quite unique and unlike most other comedians, he never resorted to physical humor. He could get bigger laughs with a simple "look" into the audience than anyone I've ever known.

One evening Jack was interviewed on television by Dick Cavett. Cavett said, "Jack, I understand that you carry a considerable amount of life insurance." Jack looked at him in disbelief. "DO I CARRY A LOT OF LIFE INSURANCE! Let me give you an idea of the kind of life insurance I carry. . . . . WHEN I GO...THEY GO!"

I'm sure that most of you are familiar with a classic line from one of his old radio programs. They were doing a skit in which Jack is supposed to be held up at gunpoint on the street. The thug was played by the multi-talented Mel Blanc, the voice of Bugs Bunny, amongst many of his creative voices. In his best snarling voice, he said to Jack, "OK, buddy. . . your money or your life!" This was followed by a long silence. Mel again says, "I told ya, buddy, YOUR MONEY OR YOUR LIFE!" Again silence by a shorter pause when Jack finally blurts out, "I'M THINKING. . . .I'M THINKING!" This was pure Jack Benny genius performed with impeccable timing.

The following is a true story that his best friend George Burns liked to relate. He and Jack were like brothers and George almost made a career out of breaking Jack up with laughter. Burns was riding down the famous Beverly Hills, Rodeo Drive, in his chauffeur-driven limo when he spotted Jack on the other side of the street. He told his driver to stop, rolled the window down and called out, "Hey, Jack, come over here." Benny obediently started to cross the street. When he was within arm's length of the car, George ordered his driver to drive on. He turned to look back and saw Jack sitting on the sidewalk in hysterical laughter.

Jack Benny was truly one of a kind. It is sad to realize that comedy today has taken several giant steps backwards. There isn't anyone to replace this comedy icon.

♫

Henry Fonda

Henry Fonda was a private person, very much a conservative and a believer in God and country. He had a dry, witty sense of humor. He rarely told jokes but the few that he did tell, he quietly giggled at the punch line. His good friends were Jimmy Stewart, Spencer Tracy, Katherine Hepburn, Lee J. Cobb and Karl Malden.

I made four westerns with Henry and each character that he played was a prized performance. He intensely prepared for each role and performed with astounding focus. In his unforgettable portrayal as "Mr. Roberts" Jack Lemmon once commented, "My God, to have that kind of inner drive and passion and play it in such a low-key performance is breath-taking."

Henry was a serious individual and possessed an equally serious love of music. On some of our sets, he asked me to play his favorite songs. He was a very decent man and never failed to speak out against injustices of any kind, especially bigotry.

> *Henry went about his business without a lot of fanfare of notoriety.*

Despite his obvious love of his children, Jane and Peter, they had a history of friction. Both shared their father's sense of right and wrong and spoke out against injustices, but they had a different style than their dad. It appeared on the surface that Jane was everything that Henry was not. Jane was outspoken, constantly looking for a political fight and was vocal in embracing unpopular causes. Peter was more sensitive and reserved, but also supported the underdog. Henry went about his business without a lot of fanfare or notoriety. That's just the way he was.

As a serious actor, Henry had few equals. He literally poured himself into every role. He never received the kind of recognition that he so richly deserved. He never won an Oscar until his final project, "On Golden Pond" where he played the role of a retired, grumpy old curmudgeon - that was classic Fonda.

♫

Eddie Cantor

Eddie Cantor had always impressed me as being a loner. However, he was an original and, because of his unique talents, became a big star.

As much as I admired him as a performer, I can't say that I liked him personally. I had worked a couple of times with him in vaudeville but now I was working on one of his TV variety shows. On this particular show, he used six children to sing a song with him. The children's parts were complicated and difficult to memorize. At the first rehearsal, one of the little boys missed his cue and Cantor jumped all over him, shouting in the kid's face! The California State appointed guardian had to step in. California law requires that minor children must be supervised on the set and looked after during working hours. They rehearsed it again but this time, the child was so terrified that he burst into tears when it was time for his cue. Cantor stormed around the set shouting, "Somebody, get this kid out of here. He's fired!" The entire cast and crew were stunned that Cantor could be so cruel and insensitive. From that point on, we all did our jobs in a tense atmosphere. The press clobbered Cantor for a dreadful show.

♫

Betty Grable and Gwen Verdon

Betty Grable was a hard-working star. She began her career as a singer and dancer. Hollywood latched on to her as a "blonde bombshell" and 20th Century-Fox was just the studio to do it. Her first year as a "contract" player was pretty dull but then it happened - she rapidly climbed to stardom. With little experience in the industry, she was cast in light, fluffy comedies and did not seem to make much headway until she coaxed Daryl F. Zanuck into giving her a shot at a musical.

Her All-American beauty and exquisite figure were perfect for the type of films that she craved to do. Zanuck provided her with a remarkable dancing coach in Gwen Verdon. Gwen was a first rate choreographer and Betty an eager student. Gwen eventually went on to become a star in her own right, on Broadway in the hit musical, "Damn Yankees".

Betty had limitless energy and she could rehearse for hours without ever tiring. She knew her limitations as both a dancer and later as a singer, and was very comfortable in the kinds of musicals that made her famous. Working with fine dancers such as Dan Daily and Donald O'Connor seemed to be the magic formula for money-making musicals for 20th Century-Fox and Betty could not have been happier.

The studio hired me to work on several of her musicals. She was a joy to work with and what a "risk-taker"! Whenever a script called for her to assume a particular character that was totally unfamiliar to her, she simply plunged ahead and worked on it until the director was satisfied. She was adored by the entire stage crew as well as her fellow actors.

Her love affair with Harry James was the talk of Hollywood. It is unfortunate that she picked him to fall in love with. Harry was a brilliant musician but was also an acute alcoholic who, when drunk (which was most of the time) had an ugly temper which created some very difficult moments on the set. All of us who knew her well were shocked and disappointed when we heard that they would marry. Blind to his drinking problem, Betty Grable was in for serious troubles. Their marriage did not last and the torture of screaming battles on the set took its toll. Betty never recovered from her divorce and her thousands of fans quickly became disenchanted with the unfavorable publicity. They stayed away from her films and without an audience, the star quickly faded.

♪

Richard Boone

"Shit. The damned horse just peed all over our lunch!"

Richard Boone had always been one of my favorites. He was a remarkably underrated actor. I always felt that he was constantly laughing inside despite the fact that he took his profession very seriously. He was fun to be with and had the capacity to put everyone on the set at ease. A dedicated actor, he was always looking for new ways of doing things to make his popular TV show, "Have Gun Will Travel" more interesting. For example, instead of pre-recording the harmonica on a sound stage and playing it back on the set, he wanted to record it live while they were shooting the scene outdoors. We were filming "Have Gun Will Travel" in the San Gabriel Mountains, in a lovely, secluded area. It was to be a gentle, romantic scene between Boone and his lady love. The scene began with her spreading a blanket on the grass under a tree where Boone's horse was tied. In the story, she had prepared a lovely picnic lunch. The romantic scene with the snow-capped mountains in the background was perfect. We had to wait for the soundman to give us a cue to start shooting as soon as he knew that planes were not in the area, which could ruin a take. Boone's leading lady was seated on the blanket as Boone strolled into the picture and quietly sat opposite her. Everything was going great when suddenly, Boone yelled, "Shit. The damned horse just peed all over our lunch!" The entire company was in hysterics including Richard and the girl. He called to the cameraman. "I hope that you got that on film. I want to save that one for myself!"

They finally gave up trying to shoot the scene outdoors because each time they tried; somebody would crack up laughing and ruin the take. They rewrote the scene to be shot on a sound stage in the studio.

Boone was what we affectionately refer to as an actor's actor. Whenever he was shooting, other actors would appear on the set to watch the master at work. I was hired for several "Have Gun" segments and I never heard him flub a line nor did he ever become upset with actors who happened to be having trouble learning theirs.

Richard gambled with his career when he was at his popular peak. He suddenly packed it in and moved to Hawaii, built his own sound stage and lived the good life by renting his facilities to motion picture and TV productions. The entire Hawaii Five-O series was shot on his sound stage. He did not seem to miss the life of an actor.

♬

Spencer Tracy

Spence can best be described as a pearl in a sea of pebbles. I have never known an actor so proficient at everything and every part of acting in films. Watching him perform was like watching a good magician do magic. Spence's magic was the fact that he never looked or sounded like he was delivering lines. He had a remarkable gift and was perfect in every take. He knew his lines without thinking about them and had the additional ability to draw out the best in other actors. I spoke to people like Katherine Hepburn and Clark Gable about this natural gift and they both basically said the same thing. "He was a true inspiration to all who were fortunate enough to work with him." Mickey Rooney, not exactly a novice actor said, "I would give anything to be able to act as well as Spence." Mickey had a gigantic ego and for him to make such a statement must have meant that even he was humbled by the artistry of Spencer Tracy.

I have watched old Spencer Tracy movies on TV that were made in the 20s. I was stunned at the freshness of his performances. I worked on several films with him and will always remember how he made a point of making me feel important on the set. He loved the harmonica and always asked me to play his favorite tunes. Yes, he was a heavy drinker which may have been a contributing factor to his death, but it never affected his performances.

♬

Katherine Hepburn

Katherine was one of the first female super-stars I had met when I lived in Hollywood. I was working on a film at MGM, "Babes On Broadway," with Judy Garland and Mickey Rooney. When we took a luncheon break, Judy said, "Jerry, a few of us are skipping lunch to watch Katherine Hepburn work on Stage 4. Would you like to join us?" I was not about to pass up an opportunity like that. I believe the title of the film they were shooting was "Pat & Mike" starring Hepburn and Tracy.

Watching them together seemed to stir a remarkable surge of excitement that permeated everyone fortunate to be in the presence of pure genius at work. One of the things most fascinating was watching them perform, as well as observing the director. It was obvious to most of us that Hepburn and Spencer Tracy were taking huge liberties by deviating from the printed script. The dialogue was so electrifying that the director allowed them to continue undisturbed.

Katherine gave as good as she got and working opposite Tracy was a challenge that she adored. One of the things that I vividly recall was, at the conclusion of the scene when the director finally said, "Cut," Tracy looked around at nobody in particular and said, "I'm hungry. Let's go eat."

I finally got to meet this remarkable lady many weeks later. She made my skin tingle with excitement when she spoke to me. She was as down to earth as any star I have encountered. The constant thrill of being in her presence was beyond belief. We eventually became close friends.

One day I admitted to her how I had felt when I first saw her in person. She exploded into gales of laughter and in her exquisite vocabulary sprinkled with a liberal dash of profanity; she light-heartedly scolded me for thinking of her as anything or anyone special.

She was extremely strong-willed but as gentle as anyone I had ever met. Her love of Spencer Tracy was unconstrained and she watched over him like a mother hen with her chicks. She knew that he was a heavy drinker but never seemed to lecture him on the subject.

Kate was born and raised in New England and I would venture to say that had New England been a monarchy, Katherine Hepburn would have been it's Queen Katherine the Great!

♫

Jack Lemmon

Jack Lemmon could have been brilliant in practically any phase of show business. He was a gifted actor, an excellent writer and a fine pianist. Regrettably, he was also an alcoholic and an active member of AA. The only reason I knew about his addiction was that he quietly blurted it out on the set of a film that he was visiting. I happened to be working on the film and during a shooting break to change a set; Jack spotted an upright piano that was part of the set. He seemed to be drawn to it like bees to honey. He sat down and began to play. I was astonished at his musicianship and his superb inbred taste in chord structure.

George Cukor, the director called me over and suggested that I join Lemmon in song. Jack happened to be playing one of my all-time favorites, Rainy Day, so I whipped out my harmonica and quietly approached Jack and began to play along. He looked up with a wide, pleasant, startled grin and nodded approvingly. We finished the song and the entire crew burst into applause. Jack stood up, reached out his hand and said, "Hi, I'm Jack Lemmon. You play an exquisite harmonica!" I replied, "Thank you. I'm Jerry Adler and you play a brilliant piano." We laughed and he sat down and we ad-libbed a few more tunes until the new set was ready. As for the alcohol problem, he was informally interviewed by a reporter who happened to be on the set. I overheard most of it, and when asked about his addiction and how it began, he sadly dropped his head and replied, "I don't know."

I never got to meet him again but continued to watch for any new Jack Lemmon releases. I have always been a great fan along with millions of people throughout the world. One particular performance was one that he made for TV. It was a remarkable adaptation from a book titled, "Tuesday's With Morrie". His heart-wrenching, tender performance was sheer brilliance. Thank God, we have these films and videos to be released over and over again.

My major regret was that we never had the opportunity to meet and play again. I know that I was truly inspired on that memorable day.

♫

James Stewart

I was signed to work on a film titled "Pot O' Gold" starring James Stewart, Paulette Goddard, Charles Winnenger and Horace Heidt and his Orchestra. In the many years that I have worked in films, this was, in everyone's opinion, the worst film ever made. It was the brilliant idea of James Roosevelt, son of President Roosevelt, who decided to start a motion picture company called, naturally, Roosevelt Productions. How he suckered Stewart into doing it remains a mystery. Stewart was so unhappy with the film that he would show up on the set in the morning, fairly inebriated. He simply could not face another day of shooting this fiasco without first fortifying himself with booze.

Jimmy's role was that of a kind -hearted music store owner and, by chance, played the harmonica. Again, I was called in to do the dubbing as well as work directly with Jim for authenticity. He and I became good friends and he confided in me that he could not stand Paulette Goddard, and choked every time Horace Heidt read his lines. What saved him from going off the deep end was the fun that Charlie Winninger and I provided between takes.

> *...he was still determined to do his best to make the character believable.*

Despite his acute disgust with the film, he was still determined to do his best to make the character believable. He and I had many private meetings at the studio and he insisted that Roosevelt Productions pay me for my visits to his home. I taught him the finer points of how the harmonica should be held plus many other subtle inflections. He was an excellent student who really worked hard at it. He soon had it down to such perfection that he actually captured my facial expressions when he was supposed to be playing. I rarely met an actor who was so totally dedicated. He sat for hours just watching me play.

One day, George Marshall, the Director came to me and said, "We're running right on schedule and I would like to have a little fun with Jim to ease the tension. Do you have any suggestions?" I told him that the harmonica that Jim was using was rigged so that he could not play it if he tried. I had placed a strip of masking tape inside of the mouthpiece, blocking out all of the reeds. I suggested that I remove the tape without his knowledge. I knew of Jim's amazing reflexes and he would blow right into it, even knowing that he could not make it respond. Marshall said that it was a great idea and told me to set it up. I told Jim that I needed to clean his harmonica and he simply handed it over to me. I quickly removed the tape in private and replaced the mouthpiece and handed it back.

Marshall said, "OK, Jim, we're going for a take on this one." Everyone took their positions. Marshall yelled, "Roll em!" The scene was slated. As he blew into the harmonica, Jim played the first five notes, correctly! He stopped, stared at the harmonica and said, "Well I'll be a sonofabitch!" Everyone was laughing and Jimmy went crazy. He called me over and said, "You know what you have done, don't you? You have just made yourself my harmonica teacher!" Marshall had actually shot the scene and gave the clip to Jim to take home. All of the tension on the set dissolved.

Jim became excited about learning to play the harmonica. He insisted that it be a straight business deal in which I would come to his home on certain evenings and teach him as much as possible. After a few months, he became pretty good. When Jim went into service as a Private at Camp Roberts, California, I drove the long trip every Sunday to continue to teach him. When he finally became a General, he wrote to me and said that the harmonica was his favorite form of relaxation which he played while flying bombing missions over Germany.

♪

Louis B Mayer
American Federation of Musicians

What I am about to relate should not be construed as anything more than it really is. When faced with the unexpected, we do not always act wisely or as 20/20 hindsight would like us to. It was a very disturbing situation, and one in which I remember vividly. I was in the middle of recording background music at MGM for a film. We rehearsed the music twice and then were ready to go for a take. Background music is not the same as simply playing a popular song. The music is originally written to compliment a scene. The scene is displayed on a large screen to the conductor. The music cutter adds a black, vertical line that moves slowly across the screen. The conductor cues the orchestra as the line begins to move and fades the orchestra as it disappears off the screen. All timed to the split second. After rehearsing a couple of times, we were ready for a take.

> *Background music is not the same as simply playing a popular song.*

During the recording, Louis B. Mayer and a guest were seated on the sound stage enjoying the session. The recording engineer began the playback mixed with the film. They sat quietly and listened. At the conclusion, Mr. Mayer called me over and said, "Jerry, I would like you to meet James C. Petrillo, the head of the American Federation of Musicians." I reached out to shake his hand but he declined. I found out later that he had a fetish about touching people and never shook hands. He also washed his hands at least twelve times a day. "Young man, you play the harmonica very well!" he said.

I thanked him and was about to leave but he stopped me and declared, "You play so well that I think that you should be a member of the Musician's Union." I was making much more money than musician's scale so I said, "Thank you, sir, but I am perfectly happy the way things are."

"No, you're wrong, young man", he firmly stated. The harmonica should be established as a legitimate instrument, especially when it is played so beautifully. You deserve to be a member of the Union."

I quickly retorted, "Really, sir, I'm not interested in becoming a member, perhaps at a later date."

"No, I insist," he went on as he turned toward Mayer for support. "Louis, does your music department have a blank membership form?"

"Yes, I believe we do."

"Then, I insist!" A form was brought to the stage and I was highjacked into the Union! I am the first harmonica player to belong to the American Federation of Musicians.

♫

Sid Kuller

I like to refer to this story as "Once Upon a Hollywood". I knew a wonderfully gifted and colorful screenwriter named Sid Kuller. He was a legend to so many of the greats in this city that thrives on legends. The Saturday night parties at his home were considered to be "the bash" to attend if one was lucky enough to receive an invitation.

Kuller lived in the Hollywood Hills. His criteria for a deserved invitation was either musical talent or star beauty. The biggest stars in Hollywood used every ploy possible to gain an entrance. He lived in a very nice home but it was modest by Hollywood standards and he had to limit the number of guests to avoid overcrowding. One of the big reasons for its popularity was the entertainment - the stars would provide impromptu performances. Mickey Rooney actually kept a set of drums in Sid's garage. It was not unusual to share the evening with the likes of Mel Torme, Duke Ellington, Vic Damone, Judy Garland, Art Tatum and Mitzi Gaynor, who represented some of the "steadies". I had a standing invitation which I considered quite a compliment.

The audience this particular evening was a veritable "who's who" in the entertainment business: Lana Turner, Basil Rathbone, Van Johnson, Robert Stack, Hedy LaMarr, Linda Darnell, etc. It began with a simple buffet and then segued into what Sid lovingly referred to as "the shtick". Each person with any performing talent got up and did a few numbers and occasionally, a "surprise" guest would appear. One night, Art Tatum arrived with the legendary Bill "Bojangles" Robinson. The large throw rug was pushed aside and Bill and Art mesmerized the entire party with their fascinating taps and piano. On another evening, the "surprise" guest was Oscar Levant who proceeded to make it an entire evening of Gershwin, with Judy and Mel doing an ad-lib duet to some of Gershwin's great songs. The parties gained such notoriety that LIFE Magazine covered one of them with a five page spread called "LIFE Goes to a Hollywood Party". Those were the great old days. Parties like that no longer exist. When Sid Kuller died, the parties died with him and nobody has had the imagination or the know-how to make it happen again.

Hollywood has become a shadow of its former self and I consider that a real tragedy. It could have been one of the great classic glamour cities in the U.S. Instead, Hollywood parties have gained the dubious distinction of being the most drug infested gathering places in the film colony. Prostitution had become rampant and taking a walk down the once famous Hollywood Boulevard at night has now become a risky endeavor that puts one's life in very real danger.

World War II Years

Eddie Peabody

When Japan attacked Pearl Harbor, I told my parents that I wanted to enlist. They pleaded with me not to make a hasty decision. I tried to explain that my medical history would exclude me from combat. It never occurred to me to investigate the possibilities of the Special Service branch of the military. However, I tried to enlist but was rejected for, of all things, flat feet and classified 4F. I attempted to argue my way in but was told to go home. All of my family and friends were thrilled about my good fortune. However I had other ideas. I had read about an old friend from the days of vaudeville, Eddie Peabody, the great banjo player. He had received a commission in the Navy and was running a Navy Special Service unit in San Diego. I managed to get him on the phone and he urged me to drive down as quickly as possible. He felt that there was a definite need for my services in his unit. I drove to San Diego with high hopes. Eddie arranged for an immediate physical and they told me the same thing, flat feet. I tried to reason with them that flat feet would not prevent me from playing the harmonica. Trying to make a logical point with the military was like playing Hava Nagila for the German Army. Eddie felt terrible about it and I felt worse.

I learned about a Special Army Air Corps unit stationed in Santa Ana, California. This time I was going there prepared with my own private ammunition. I was taking a few of my orchestrations with me just in case. They were quartered in the old American Legion Hall and broadcast every Wednesday and Saturday throughout the U.S. plus Armed Forces Radio all over the world! They had a fabulous forty-five piece orchestra made up of the best studio musicians to come out of Hollywood. There were also a number of seasoned actors who participated in the weekly dramas that were broadcast every Saturday.

> *I am probably the only person who auditioned to get into the service.*

Saturdays were very special because of the availability of important stars willing to participate. There were a variety of famous people who drove from Hollywood and Beverly Hills to do the weekly show: Gary Cooper, Marlene Dietrich, Pat O'Brian, Rita Hayworth, Betty Grable, Jack Oakie, Edward G. Robinson, James Cagney, Humphrey Bogart and the list goes on. What a setup for me, but how could I get them to accept me? The Major in charge, was Eddie Dunstedter, a friend from vaudeville days. He had been the organist at the Orpheum in Minneapolis. I explained my problem to him and he asked if I had any music with me. I showed him what I had and he said, "Hand out the Begin the Beguine parts and let's try it." After we ran through it, he said, "I'll make a call and see what I can do." I was thrilled at the possibilities. He returned a short time later and said, "Report to Ft. McArthur and locate Captain Bernard Stowitz in Personnel. He has been briefed about your physical and 4F status. You will remain there for basic training and then you will be transferred to us." I am probably the only person who ever auditioned to get into the service.

I did not have any idea that it would be such a cushy job. No drilling, no calisthenics and no barracks! We were paid an extra allowance to board in private homes in Santa Ana. Some of the musicians who had their wives with them rented an apartment or small home. We did not have roll call and were only required to be present for special duties, rehearsals and shows. The clincher was that we were only forty miles from Los Angeles so we spent a lot of time at home.

I had been in the Service for six months when I earned my corporal stripes. I found complete contentment. Here I was, in the Service with my professional peers and enjoying every moment. It was a dream come true.

♫

Peter Hayes, Walter Long, Joe Bushkin, Frank Loesser

We had so much talent in our unit that, on occasion, a group of us were sent out to entertain other Air Corps bases. We had Peter Lind Hayes, a brilliant, imaginative comedian; Walter Long, an excellent tap dancer; Joe Bushkin, a top drawer jazz pianist; Frank Loesser, the genius who wrote and produced "Guys and Dolls." and Mario Cacozza, a magnificent singer who eventually changed his last name to Lanza; Mario's voice was untrained but still excellent. However, his potential was limitless but his ego would not allow him to realize that potential. He refused to listen to anyone's advice. His eating habits were not to be believed. He was only five feet seven inches, but he exercised every day causing his massive body to turn to solid rock. He weighed three hundred and twenty pounds and nobody could figure out how he was allowed into the Service. He also had a vicious temper that was hard to imagine and more incredible to witness.

♫

Mario Lanza

Many of our tours ended up in some desolate areas which made Mario very unhappy. He had been transferred to Santa Ana from an Air Base in Marfa, Texas, the hell hole of military America. He hated mess hall food and the only thing he ate there was breakfast. He always managed to find off-base restaurants for lunch and dinner.

My first experience in watching him devour food was in a mess hall in Phoenix. There was a huge sign over the door that read, "Take all you want but eat all you take". Mario proceeded to fill his tray with scrambled eggs. He loaded the whole tray with eggs and used another tray for hash brown potatoes, ham, bread and coffee. The mess officer was there and stared at Mario's trays in disbelief. I could read his mind. "That character had better eat every crumb on those trays." Mario went back for seconds! He despised Army food but loved eggs. He spent every penny that he made in the Service on restaurant food. We often went into town for dinner where he ordered four steaks with mashed potatoes and then topped it off with half a pie. We were the best of friends and spent much time together. I implored him to cut down on his intake but it fell on deaf ears. As we all know, Mario was a very handsome man and I was the first to tell him what a tremendous potential he had for films.

Our mode of transportation to the various camps was by Army "recon" (reconnaissance) car. We traveled across the desert during the day which was a big mistake. The temperature reached one hundred and twenty-five degrees and no air conditioning. We used two cars, one for the performers and the other for the quartet plus instruments. When we left Phoenix, we were assigned a new driver, a surly, six-foot-four redneck who had taken an immediate dislike to all of us. Unfortunately, we did not have any choice, so we took what we could get.

We were crossing the Arizona desert with all of the windows open, remained as still as possible and did little or no talking. We had decided that this was the way to conserve energy. As we drove in the choking heat, we heard the driver mumbling something about "Goddamned Jews". We had one Jew in the car, me. The remark came from out of nowhere. Peter was sitting next to me and urged me to ignore it. I was not about to pick a fight with a Neanderthal redneck! Anyway, it was too damned hot. I happened to glance at Mario and he was purple with rage. I reached over to calm him down and he pulled away. Apparently, he had had enough, and screamed at the top of his lungs," STOP THE CAR YOU FUCKING ASSHOLE!"

The driver said ,"What did you say?"

"YOU HEARD ME! STOP THE FUCKING CAR!"

He stopped the car and said, "Now what?"

"GET OUT!!"

"Wadda ya mean?"

"ARE YOU DEAF AS WELL AS DUMB? GET THE HELL OUT OF THE CAR!"

> *He had grabbed the driver's head and was bouncing it on the hard asphalt.*

The driver immediately got out and turned toward the door with his fists clenched. Before we could stop Mario, he shot out of his seat to the front, took a flying leap on top of the driver knocking him to the ground. We all jumped out and tried to pull Mario off. He had grabbed the driver's head and was bouncing it on the hard asphalt.. Mario was like a raging tiger! By this time, the driver's head was bleeding as Mario yelled, "Don't you EVER say anything about the Jew bastards again or I'LL KILL YOU!!!"

We finally stopped the bleeding on "Redneck's" head and he was able to take over the rest of the driving assignment to our next destination. At that point we were able to replace him with a human being!

I questioned Mario as to why he referred to Jews as "Jew bastards". In his incredible ignorance, he had assumed all along that it was perfectly natural to say it since he had heard everyone in his neighborhood use the same expression. Mario's formal education seemed to have come to a grinding halt just prior to entering high school. He was blessed with a magnificent voice and remarkably handsome features but little else. I finally explained that the expression was ugly and that it would be wise for him not to use it again. I thanked him for coming to my defense.

We had been gone for three weeks and were more than grateful to be back in Santa Ana. After our desert tour, I was determined to avoid the traveling show assignments whenever possible.

♬

Irving (Swifty) Lazar

One day, two Captains arrived at Santa Ana from Washington. One happened to be an old friend, Irving (Swifty) Lazar, the most respected literary agent in the country. He had received a commission when war was declared. He greeted me warmly and introduced me to his partner, Captain James Landis. Swifty said, "Do you have any idea why we're here?"

I said, "No, sir, I don't."

"Hey, you can drop the Sir, Jerry."

"Thank you, Swifty. So tell me, what's going on?"

> *Moss Hart has written a wonderful dramatic show and we are recruiting talent...*

"We are here to look for talent for a new Broadway show on behalf of Army Emergency Relief," he explained. "Moss Hart has written a wonderful dramatic show and we are recruiting talent from the Air Corps installations throughout the country." I excitedly replied, "Hey, that sounds great. I hope that you find what you're looking for."

"We have. You are one of them. Believe me, Moss will have a great spot for you."

I suddenly became panicky. "But I don't want to go to New York!"

He replied casually, "I'm sorry about that, because you are going. We're also taking Peter Lind Hayes, Walter Long, Joe Bushkin and Mario Cacozza."

I went directly to Col. Dunstedter's office and told him. I was sure that my old friend would come to my defense.

He said, "Yes, I know."

I shouted, "What do you mean, you know?"

Dunstedter looked at me sternly. "I would suggest that you remember where you are. You will address me as Sir and conduct yourself properly."

"But Sir, you can't do this to me!"

"I'm not doing anything to you, Jerry. Those two officers have top priority from Washington. There isn't anything that I can do."

"But Sir, you promised that I could stay here."

Dunstedter was losing patience, and his self control was remarkable.

"Look, my hands are tied. Their orders came from General Arnold. Just do the best that you can."

I apologized for my outburst, saluted smartly and did an about face and walked out. We had one more week there before receiving our two-week furlough prior to going to New York.

♫

Melville Ruick

The final week became a memorable event. One of our officers was Maj. Melville Ruick, a former announcer with CBS who produced most of our shows. He was so enthralled with his own image that he was a constant pain in the ass.

♫

Joe Venuti

One Saturday night, instead of a dramatic show, we featured the great jazz violinist, Joe Venuti with his orchestra and vocalist. Ruick was on a constant ego trip to impress our guests with his "knowledge" of radio broadcasting. He did strange things in the control room. He would ask the performers to move an inch one way or the other from the microphone, as if that slight movement made any difference!

On this particular day, he pushed Venuti too far. Little did Ruick know that he was picking on the wrong man. Joe Venuti was an off-the-wall legend, especially in New York where he would do wild and crazy gags just for his own amusement. For example, one day he called for a recording session in New York. He hired twelve bass players. He told each man to meet him on the corner of 47th and Broadway to be picked up by bus. He hid himself with his camera across the street and took a picture of twelve bass players huddled in the cold, holding their basses. It was a funny sight and all he wanted was the picture. There wasn't any recording session. However, he paid every man for the session anyway.

Maj. Ruick drove Venuti crazy. Joe knew that he was dealing with an egomaniac and had concocted the perfect anecdote. When the musicians took a break after rehearsal, he called his group together and said, "Look, this guy is a real fruit cake. Here's what I want you to do. When we go back in for the dress rehearsal, I want silence from everyone. Pantomime as if you are playing but do not make a sound. I'll take care of the rest."

> *He then went berserk and smashed at the controls with his fist…*

When they went back into the studio, Ruick, in the booth, pressed his intercom button and said, "OK people, let's see if we can run it straight through." He cued them with his finger, Joe gave the downbeat and everything was silent. Ruick looked puzzled and said, "I can't hear a thing, Joe!" Joe pantomimed answering him. Ruick said, "I still can't hear anything!" He began twisting dials and was becoming angrier by the second. Ruick said, "Can we try it once again, please?" Joe nodded and gave the downbeat. Still dead silence. At that point, Ruick lost control and began pounding on the console which is the heart of the system. Still nothing. He then went berserk and smashed at the controls with his fist, breaking all of the glass covered meters plus several sound dials. He had destroyed the system! An emergency call was placed to NBC to explain the problem and the network had to replace the program with a different show. Venuti never told Ruick what he had done. The band simply packed up and left!

I spent two short but lovely weeks at home on furlough and made the rounds of visiting my friends as well as organized a couple of parties before taking off for New York. Our orders were to fly by commercial airliner and go directly to the 44th St. Theater and report to our commanding officer, Colonel Dunham. Lazar had performed a miraculous feat by getting the best stage hands, electricians, scenery designers, musicians and actors who were either in service or were about to be drafted. Everyone working in that show was a professional. The only civilians were Moss Hart, his stage manager, Jerry Whyte, plus a number of female walk-ons who were either wives of some of the actors or regular outside civilians from Actors Equity.

Col. Dunham told us to find seats in the theater and wait to be called. Four days later we were still sitting, not knowing what we were to do. We didn't even know that the title of the show was, "Winged Victory."

We had many fine actors and some of them were quite well known. Edmund O'Brian, Lee J. Cobb, Karl Mauldin, John Forsythe, Red Buttons, Barry Nelson and others. Mario had already been assigned to the two hundred man chorus conducted by Lt. Leonard DuParr. Sgt. David Rose was our orchestra conductor and arranger. Our orchestra consisted of fifty studio musicians.

♫

Winged Victory

Auditions were finally scheduled and that took an additional two weeks. It was finally decided who would play the male leads: Mark Daniels, Don Taylor, Barry Nelson, Edmond O'Brian and Lon McAllister. One liners were given to Lee J. Cobb, Red Buttons, Peter Lind Hayes, John Forsythe, and Kevin McCarthy. The female leads were Elizabeth Fraser, Olive Deering and Phyllis Avery, all seasoned Broadway actors.

The logistics in organizing a production like "Winged Victory" were mind-boggling. We had four hundred and fifty Air Corps personnel plus fifteen civilian women. The Air Corps had to requisition several hotels close to the theater. We were bunked four to a room so Army bunk beds had to be brought in and the regular furniture moved out. We were given the opportunity to choose our own bunk mates so mine became Ray McDonald, my old friend from the Ed Sullivan days; Tommy Farrell, a funny comic, Mario and me - the four Musketeers.

The theme for "Winged Victory" reflected the trials of a group of youngsters, from various walks of life, eager to join the Air Corps to become pilots. Their first meeting was at an Air Corps Cadet Depot. The central theme was based on the training that they experienced before they would ever see a plane. Everyone expects to become a pilot, but at the end of the training period their scores determined which of them washed out and eventually became bombardiers, tail gunners, etc. The remainder who passed received their wings in a dramatic graduation scene, and became Second Lieutenants. The night before graduation, the cadets have a huge bonfire party on the beach where they all get pretty drunk. Ray and I were featured in an impromptu dance and harmonica number. That was it for my contribution. Ray got stuck with stand-in duty as an officer for the graduation scene.

Each actor shared a dressing room with five others, making life in the a bit crowded. I figured out a way to have a dressing room to myself. I approached Moss with an idea. How about having our own PX in the backstage area? He thought that it was a great idea and had it officially cleared with Col. Dunham. This also called for a promotion for me to Sergeant. A jeep was requisitioned and I drove to Mitchell Field Air Base on Long Island for my supplies once a week. I had my own dressing room plus my PX inventory and I had my own jeep! The items that I sold were impossible to buy in the drugstores such as Kleenex, facial cream, perfume, etc. When word got out, I became the darling of all the girls in the show. One of them was Helen Eastman who did a walk-on. She was a very attractive young lady and I fell in love! Well, I thought I did at the time. I dated her and we took many long walks up and down Fifth Avenue. One day we stopped at an exclusive ladies hat shop with one hat displayed in the window. It was a pink pillbox and Helen said, "Isn't that attractive?" The following day, I went back to the shop. I forget what it cost but it was well beyond my means, but I bought it anyway. After I gave it to her, I found out that she had been dating many of the guys in the company! I was crushed! Didn't she know that I was madly in love with her?

"Winged Victory" was the first Broadway show to utilize two revolving stages. The audiences were astonished at the instantaneous scene changes and each scene received a standing ovation! The sold-out house was filled with audiences pumped with patriotic fervor. The show remained a sellout for over a year.

After the Broadway show, arrangements were made for a national tour. When we closed in New York, Col. Dunham decided that the full company of men would assemble in front of the 44th St. Theater and march down Fifth Avenue to Grand Central Station, singing the Air Corps song. The police had diverted traffic and hordes of people lined the sidewalks waving small flags while others wept openly, shouting, "Give 'em hell, fellas!" Of course we were all embarrassed by this blatant charade. Little did the public realize that we were on our way to Philadelphia for a two week run. That was the beginning of the U.S. tour.

Taking the show on the road was not an easy task, considering the kind of scenery involved, plus the ongoing problem of keeping order within the ranks. We traveled by special train which consisted of a series of converted box cars plus four freight cars for our scenery, and two dining cars. We stopped every morning for calisthenics. Each time that we stopped, the Red Cross appeared magically from out of nowhere with doughnuts and hot coffee for the "fighting G.I's". After calisthenics, we would have an impromptu softball game until the train was ready to leave. The Red Cross ladies must have been baffled by a bunch of beautiful girls standing around cheering our softball game. Where did the girls come from?

Our stage manager, Jerry Whyte was about to be drafted so Moss Hart arranged for him to enlist. He was a key figure in the production and they couldn't afford to lose him. He was sent to an induction center and returned to us four days later with six stripes and a diamond in the center on his arm! A TOP SERGEANT! Many of us were furious! Most had been in service for over a year and some had not made Pfc. However, in retrospect, we realized that his rank was necessary for him to maintain control over the men.

The Philadelphia Theater had five floors of dressing rooms! On the wall of each floor was a speaker with an intercom switch tied in directly to the stage manager's desk in case of emergency. My dressing room was on the fifth floor next to the speaker. Sgt. Whyte had the volume turned all the way up. When he announced to the cast to get ready for the first scene, it nearly shook my teeth loose. I rushed over to the speaker, pressed the intercom switch and said, "Sgt, can you please turn the volume down?" Whyte came on the horn immediately. "Who in the Goddamned hell said that?"

"It's me, Sgt. Adler."

He yelled, "You sonofabitch. Get your ass down here immediately!"

Everyone backstage was listening to our conversation on the speakers.

When I reached the stage, he said, "Don't ever touch that button again! Do I make myself clear?"

The show was in progress and it seemed impossible that the audience could not hear Whyte's outburst. I replied stiffly, "Yes, Sergeant. You have made yourself clear."

I turned and left in a rage.

He continued to yell, "Listen, you little bastard, you get your ass back up there and don't come down until you're called!"

I nodded but was furious for the rest of the show. Many of the cast tried to calm me down and said things like, "He always does that. Don't let it bother you."

I did not sleep that night. I had been embarrassed by him and the entire cast had heard it.

The following morning, I visited the Colonel's office, walked in and saluted. The Colonel returned the salute and said, "What can I do for you, Sergeant?"

I explained in detail what had happened. The Colonel looked at me absently and said, "I'll have a word with him."

"I'm sorry, sir, but that will not do. I demand an apology from Sgt. Whyte, after the show tonight in front of the entire cast."

The Colonel looked at me as if I had lost my mind. I continued. "I have been in the service long enough to know about certain Army regulations, Sir."

The Colonel, realizing that I had legal rights in the Army, said "What else do you want, Sergeant?"

"I respectfully request, Sir, that you call Sgt. Whyte to your office now and explain my demands."

"Demands? What do you mean, demands!"

"Sir, I consider this a serious breach of my rights. If Sgt. Whyte is not willing to accept my demands, he leaves me no choice but to file formal charges against him in a court martial."

He looked at me startled. "Those are very serious charges, Sergeant."

"I know that, Sir."

He shrugged his shoulders. "OK, you are certainly within your rights to do so."

He called Whyte and asked him to come to the office immediately. When Whyte opened the door, it swung toward me, hiding me from his view. Whyte was impatient, which seemed to annoy the Colonel. He didn't help matters by saying, "I'm very busy in the theater , Colonel. What is it?"

The Colonel was becoming angry. "Sergeant, I am giving you the benefit of the doubt because you have only been in uniform a very short time. First of all, when you enter my office, you come to attention and salute. When you address me or any officer, you say, "Sir". Is that clear?"

I could see Whyte's neck get quite red but he said, "I apologize, sir. It won't happen again.. Now can you please tell me what this is all about, Sir?"

"Sgt. Whyte, I have a formal complaint filed against you by Sgt. Adler."

That sonofabitch used the intercom during the show and . . ."

The Colonel was flushed. "Hold it right there, Sergeant! Sgt. Adler, (nodding toward me) intends to press court martial charges against you."

Whyte wheeled around in a rage. The Colonel continued. "Before you make matters worse, I suggest that you calm down and do some listening."

The Colonel (bless him) read Army regulations to Whyte spelling out the consequences if found guilty. Whyte turned ashen.

Whyte looked at me, eyes blazing. "OK, Adler. What do you want?"

I told him what I wanted and he yelled, "You want WHAT?"

I replied, "Sergeant, I have never been more serious in my life."

It was a tough thing for Whyte to do but then, he didn't have much choice. The irony is that we eventually became good friends. The one important thing that I was looking for besides his apology, was that he never verbally abuse anyone again.

That evening, in front of the cast after the final curtain came down, Whyte did apologize.

♫

President Harry S. Truman

General Hap Arnold, Commander in Chief of the Army Air Corps once told me that he was going to speak to President Truman's secretary about having me perform at the White House. I had done several shows for Gen. Arnold and we became good friends. It sounded glorious but I didn't place too much stock in it. It wasn't that he didn't mean it. I assumed that he had more important things to think about. Like winning a war!

One morning, while still in "Winged Victory" in New York, Col. Dunham summoned me to his office. He smiled and handed me a slip of paper with a phone number.

"Sir, do you know who it is?"

"I certainly do. It's President Truman's private secretary! You may use my phone if you wish."

I began to tremble with excitement. I placed the call and was put through immediately. A charming voice said, "Sergeant, General Arnold tells me that you are quite an artist on the harmonica."

I didn't know what to say.

I heard a soft laugh. "I'm sorry, I did not mean to put you on the spot. I want to know if you are available to fly to Washington next Saturday to perform for the President."

> "...she wants me to fly there next Saturday to play for the President!"

I asked her to please hold for a moment. "Sir, she wants me to fly there next Saturday to play for the President!"

"Well, for God sake, tell her that you will be there."

"What about the show?"

The Colonel replied, "Don't worry about it. I'm sure that Zeke Manners can fill in for you on the accordion." Zeke was an excellent musician and I knew that he could handle it. I told the secretary that I would be honored!

She said that official orders would be cut and I was to report to Mitchell Field. A military passenger plane would be there to fly me from New York to Washington. She gave me the departure schedule and said that a staff car would be waiting for me in Washington when we landed. I thanked her and hung up. I didn't sleep for four nights. I was so keyed up with excitement that I was not a bit tired. I knew that the lack of sleep would catch up with me but hoped that it wouldn't happen while I was in the White House!

I was aboard an Air Corps passenger transport with ten high ranking officers. When we landed, I spotted a staff car with the driver holding a large card with my name. I introduced myself and he handed me an identification badge that I had to pin to my uniform. He told me to keep it on at all times until the performance.

We arrived at the White House and I felt like I was riding on a magic carpet. The guards waved us through the security gates and we drove to the corner of the building. I was then escorted by two Marines to a beautiful lounge and was asked to wait. Shortly, the President's secretary walked in and warmly shook hands with me. She explained what would be happening for the rest of the day. The rehearsal with the orchestra was set for 3:00 P.M. However, prior to that, we would be served lunch in the V.I.P. dining room. After lunch, those who were interested would be taken on a tour of the White House. The show was scheduled for 8:00 P.M. in the East Room. The other entertainers were Jack Haley, Marge and Gower Champion and Phil Regan, the singer.

Truman was my political hero and I was tingling with excitement. Rounding out the audience were members of Congress and the Senate including their wives. Of course, Bess Truman was there as well as their daughter Margaret.

We were told to keep our performances to fifteen minutes each, so I chose my strongest material. Suddenly I heard a drum roll and a male voice shouted, "Ladies and gentlemen, the President of the United States!" My skin started to tingle as I peeped through the curtain and watched the President and his family walk forward to their seats, as the Orchestra struck up *Hail to the Chief.*

My performance was received with tremendous enthusiasm and the President was the first to start a standing ovation. I took my final bow and started to leave when the President called out. "Young man! Do you know the Missouri Waltz?"

I was taken by surprise and nervously replied, "Yes, Mr. President, certainly do."

"Would you like to do it with me?"

The audience went wild as the President came on stage and took his seat at the piano.

He said, "Perhaps I'd better warn you. I only play on the black keys."

"That's OK, Mr. President. I'm not prejudiced."

The President and the audience laughed, thank God!

We played it together and the audience stood up and cheered. He smiled and shook hands with me while the White House photographers took our picture. Not content to walk off while I was still ahead, I said, "Forgive me, Mr. President. I do not mean any disrespect but you make a far better President than you do a pianist." The room rocked with laughter and the President laughed just as loudly.

It was a moment in my life that I will always treasure.

♫

An agreement had been reached with 20th Century-Fox to make the film, "Winged Victory". Daryl F. Zanuck was the producer and the director was George Cukor. The cast remained the same with the exception of the women. Zanuck insisted that we use some of his stock players such as Jeanne Craine and Judy Holiday. The only one who was obviously miscast was Judy, a brilliant comedienne. They gave her the part of the wife of Edmund O'Brian, a dull and lifeless role that caused her great frustration and personal humiliation.

Arrangements were made with Army Engineers to construct wood-sided tents on the beach at Santa Monica. This was our "base camp". Our job was to wait for a studio call and when we were not at the studio, we played a lot of volleyball to kill time.

When the film was completed, we pulled up stakes and were on our way again to continue our tour. The next stop was San Francisco. Tommy, Ray and I became the Three Musketeers. Mario was happy eating his way into oblivion.

Tommy was our comedy relief. He was one of the nicest, happy-go-lucky individuals in the company and was a genuinely funny man. The three of us were always picking up girls in malt shops, etc. until Ray dropped out because of his heavy romance with Elizabeth Fraser. Ray and Liz eventually married. Tommy was the son of the famous film comedienne, Glenda Farrell. He was her only child and she constantly called to plead with me to "take care of my baby".

One day, Tommy and I met two very cute girls in a drugstore. We told them that we were in the show and they became excited. We asked them to meet us in the lobby of the hotel. We had strict orders that we were not to bring women to our room. However, we did not take the order seriously.

After the show, Tommy and I rushed to the hotel, showered, shaved and dressed for our dates. When Tommy got out of the shower, his body was covered with ugly, red welts. I called the house doctor and his diagnosis was that Tommy had hives. His suggestion was to find a drugstore and buy a large bottle of Calamine lotion. I rushed out and bought the largest bottle that I could find and then ran back to the hotel. Tommy was going mad with a terrible itch. I covered his body from neck to toes with the pink stuff. The girls called from the lobby. Tom said, "Ask them to come up". When they saw Tom, they shrieked with laughter and one of them said that he looked like a hairy popsicle. The dates were obviously off and we hoped to make it another night. Right after they left, the phone rang and it was Glenda, Tommy's mom. I did not wish to worry her but she inadvertently solved my problem. She said, "How's my baby?" I replied, "In the pink." That seemed to satisfy her and I turned the phone over to Tommy.

Occasionally we would change room partners. One or two of the company would have a fight or misunderstanding so this became a fairly common way to deal with the situation. One day, Red Buttons asked us if he could switch to our room and Mario agreed to make the exchange.

Red Buttons

We were appearing in Chicago and had arranged a secret knock on the door of our hotel room. If the response was answered by a loud cough, we were to disappear for a while. I had gone to the room and knocked. I heard the loud cough and turned to leave. The door opened and Red stuck his head out gesturing me to come back. He stage whispered, "Jerry, you gotta help me out. I've got a broad in here that refuses to quit! I just can't handle it anymore! She's taking a shower now so please, come in and take my place in bed."

I looked at him like he was nuts. "What am I supposed to do?"

"Just come in and take over. She is such a nympho that she won't know the difference."

"I can't go in there without letting her know!"

"Sure you can! Believe me, she'll never know the difference. Even if she does, she won't care!"

I thought about it and finally said, "What the hell. OK, why not?"

Red was already dressed so I quickly rushed in, removed my clothes and immediately got under the covers. She was showering and my vivid imagination was working overtime. I was really ready. The longer I waited, the hornier I got. I finally became impatient and went to the bathroom. The shower was on but NOBODY WAS THERE! I opened the door to our room and saw Red, Tommy and Ray on the hallway floor laughing their heads off. Naturally my "buddies" could not keep it to themselves and the story spread throughout the company. I was bombarded by "cute" remarks by everyone including the women. I was never a devious person but I was determined that I would get even but none of my ideas materialized.

We continued across the country, appearing in every major city until our final performance in Norfolk, Virginia. Moss Hart had arranged a huge farewell banquet and everyone was wondering what would happen once "Winged Victory" was history. Ninety percent of the men were discharged on the spot. The other ten percent were to be sent overseas as entertainment units for the fighting troops. The Air Corps also arranged for Mickey Rooney to be transferred to us to work in one of the units. Our unit consisted of Peter Lind Hayes, plus a fellow named Gant Gaither who would act as spokesman for our unit. Walter Long a dancer, Danny Scholl and John Tyers, singers, and Joe Bushkin, pianist and conductor, and me. We received a two week furlough and our orders were to report to the San Pedro Naval docks in California. Our unit was scheduled for a tour of the Pacific while the rest of the men went on to Europe. We were upset that everyone else was going home for good, but ours was not to reason why. I decided to spend my furlough at home in Los Angeles.

When our unit met in San Pedro, we were told that we would be going by troop ship but the destination was secret. While waiting for further news, we planned a mini revue that had a simple story line. Within one week, we boarded our troop ship. During the crossing, we rehearsed the show and used the soldiers and sailors aboard as guinea pigs to test our material. They went crazy over the show and yelled for us to do it again! We were convinced that we had a tightly knit unit.

♫

Winged Pigeons

We arrived in Hawaii grateful to be in one piece. Our unit manager, Gant Gaither, was bright and knowledgeable about getting things done quickly and cutting through red tape whenever necessary. He also had a marvelous, dry sense of humor. We had to come up with a name for our unit. After much discussion, we settled on "Winged Pigeons" - a spin-off of "Winged Victory".

We docked in Honolulu and ordered to Hickam Field. A truck transported us and when we arrived, we were assigned to a Special Service Officer. Gant went to the Headquarters building and met with our Officer, Capt. Horace Grim! The name sounded like trouble. We eventually had a meeting with him and he turned out to be very pleasant. He suggested that we schedule a show on the base so that he could evaluate it. Ten days later, we put on an outdoor show for ten thousand airmen and sailors. The area was jumping. They screamed for more. We had passed with flying colors.

Another meeting was scheduled with the Captain the following day and he was obviously excited. He said, "You boys are really terrific. Each of you are strong enough to head your own unit. Of course there will be promotions for all of you. What do you think?"

> *…we put on an outdoor show to ten thousand airmen and sailors.*

Gant was now put to the test. He said to Captain Grim, "Sir, I really don't think it's a good idea. This unit has prepared themselves over many months of honing and refining the show. To break us up would be a total disaster." It did not take him long to convince Grim that it was a foolhardy idea. We remained together, thanks to Gant. Our orders were to go to the forward areas by troop ship. We were baffled. We were in the Air Corps! Why a troop ship? It was obvious that Grim had failed to requisition a plane. We all went outside in front of our barracks to discuss possible alternatives. Our orders were to report to the dock by truck at 8:00 A.M. the next morning. We sat there pitching dumb ideas between us trying to figure out how to avoid the troop ship. As we were talking, Peter looked up and saw a familiar face walking past. "Hey, isn't that General Scanlon's driver?" I had performed a number of shows for Scanlon in Washington while in "Winged Victory". I said, "Yes, it is!" I called to him and he walked over, recognizing all of us. I asked, "What are you doing here?"

He replied, "General Scanlon is now commanding general of Hickam Field."

Peter leaped to his feet. "Wow! There's our answer! Where is the General now?"

"He's off the base and will not be back until tomorrow morning."

Peter said, "Jerry first thing in the morning, go over to his office and explain everything. I'm sure that he will come through for us."

"Wait a minute. Why, me? That's Gant's job. Besides, we're to report to the ship at 8:00 A.M. tomorrow."

Peter said, "It's got to be you. You know him and we don't."

"That's fine but what do I do about the troop ship?"

"Don't worry. We'll hold the ship for you."

I don't know whether I was simply dumb or terribly naive. I tried to picture them holding up a troop ship for me!

At 7:00 A.M, our guys boarded a truck and were delivered to the ship. I walked to Headquarters and it hit me that after 8:00 A.M, I would be officially A.W.O.L! When I reached the office, it was locked so I sat on the floor and hoped that he would show up soon. I looked at my watch. It was 7:45. Five minutes later, I heard footsteps and I jumped to attention. Two officers and a Sergeant were heading my way. One was General Scanlon! The Major unlocked the door and they walked in. My God, the General didn't recognize me!

I regained my composure and walked in. I approached the Major's desk, saluted and said, "Sir, it is urgent that I speak to the General immediately!"

"State your business, Sergeant."

"Sir, it is very personal but really urgent. Just tell him that Sergeant Adler is here. I'm sure he will understand. Surprisingly, the Major did not challenge me. He entered Scanlon's office and I heard, "YOU MEAN MY FAVORITE HARMONICA PLAYER IS HERE? SEND HIM IN!"

The Major seemed dazed but gestured me to enter.

I walked in, saluted and then reached over to shake his hand.

"How the hell are you, Adler?"

I quickly interrupted. "I'm fine sir. Sir, time is running short." I quickly explained the problem.

"Troop ship my ass!"

He quickly picked up a phone and was immediately connected to the troop ship dock.

"This is General Scanlon at Hickam Field. Do you have an entertainment group on your manifest called The Winged Pigeons? You do? Great! Put those men on a truck and return them to the air base."

The General told me that I should join my unit when they arrived in front of Headquarters and he would have orders cut for a C-47 transport to take us to our destination. I pumped his hand gratefully and thanked him for the quick action. I saluted, did an about face and ran out of his office.

I had committed the unforgivable. I had gone over the head of my superior officer. The truck arrived in less than an hour and they all had broad smiles on their faces. I told them to keep their mouths shut until after we boarded the plane. It didn't take long for Capt. Grim to hear about it. I knew what was on his mind as I watched him coming toward us from Headquarters building. He was very deliberate in his heavy strides. We were in a high truck and the tailgate was above eye level. The Captain was so angry that he stared at the tailgate without looking up.

"OK, I want to know who went over my head." We all remained silent.

"That's fine. You are all going to remain on the truck until I have been notified that the plane is ready for departure. Nobody is to leave this truck." Suddenly a staff car flying General flags on the fenders and heading our way came to a stop. Capt. Grim snapped to attention and saluted. The General acknowledged the salute, stuck his head out and said, "Everything OK, Adler?" I nodded weakly and saluted. The General yelled, "Good luck boys. Maybe I will be running into you later." When the car pulled away, the Captain said, "Adler, I want to see you at the rear of the plane as soon as we board." He turned and left us sitting in the truck. When he disappeared, everyone began slapping me on the back. I angrily shoved them away and told them to leave me the hell alone. I had an "appointment" with the Captain and was not in any mood for further conning from my "buddies". I had been suckered into breaking every military rule in the book and had to defend myself. I silently planned my strategy to avoid being busted down to private. The thought of losing my hard-earned stripes because of my stupidity did nothing to calm my anger. I was at the Captain's mercy and he knew it. I had to work on a counter attack.

We finally boarded the plane and I walked back to where the Captain was sitting. He had calmed down considerably. He spoke to me in hushed tones despite the loud noise of the engines revving up. I knew that he was pleased that someone was able to find a plane but he still had to save face. He said, "You realize that I'm going to have to bust you to private."

I was not going to submit so easily. "Look, Captain. I urge you to not make a big deal of this. I'm sure that you did your best to get us a plane. Simply put, it's who you know that counts. I stuck my neck way out to get this plane so why don't we sit back and enjoy it?"

He stared at me for a while and then smiled. "To hell with it. Go forward and buckle up."

Who you know is really what it's all about.

> *...we were on our way to Guam to do our first official show.*

When things settled down, our Captain informed us that we were on our way to Guam to do our first official show. We were excited about finally going to work. He also told us that we would be on our own because he had to return to Hickam Field. We were pleased that we did not have an officer breathing down our necks.

After landing, we were taken to our quarters. Gant went with the Captain to iron out the details. When they returned, the Captain shook hands with all of us, wished us luck and he was gone.

The next morning, we reviewed our format and on the same evening, presented our show. They shouted their approvals until hoarse -- all of that talent without the trappings of young, desirable girls. I have always had strong opinions about stars like Bob Hope bringing young starlets overseas whose main contribution was to display their bodies for sexual arousal. I am light years away from being a prude but I consider that kind of exposure to GIs serving overseas a frustrating and dangerous experience. Compare that to a Jack Benny show and you will better understand my reasoning. Jack's show consisted of Ingrid Bergman, my brother, Larry and Martha Tilton, the vocalist with the Benny Goodman band. All of them wore uniforms or fatigues. No sexual displays and no double meaning or suggestive jokes. The Jack Benny shows were a great success!

Before going overseas, I had arranged to have my harmonicas packed in special wrappings called silicagel. The same material used to ship airplane engines and critical parts. They were then placed in an airtight wood box. I carried several extra harmonicas with me in my duffel bag and planned to open the box only when it became necessary. The harmonicas that I had been using were rapidly going sour so I knew that it was time to go to the box. I became physically ill to find all of my harmonicas black with rust! I panicked. Remember, when in doubt, panic. I went to the Special Service Officer and explained my dilemma.

He said, "That shouldn't be a problem. We will have a message sent to your parents and they will buy new ones and ship them over." "Sir, I wish that it was that easy. Harmonicas are made in Germany and there isn't a single harmonica in any music store," I said.

"Sergeant, I don't know what else I can do!"

I thanked him and walked out thinking all kinds of horrible thoughts. I was in a desperate situation and needed to find a solution, quickly! I suddenly got a bright idea. It was pretty far-fetched and a hell of a long shot but I had to try. I returned to the office. I said, "Sir, would you give me an authorization to send a message to General Arnold?" He stared at me in disbelief. "Sergeant, have you lost your senses?"

"Please, Sir. I will assume full responsibility."

He laughed. "Sure you will! What's that supposed to mean?"

"It means what I said, Sir. I know the General personally. I performed many shows for him in Washington. If anyone can find harmonicas, he can."

He actually gave me a written order to send the message!

I sat down and worked on it for over an hour before I was satisfied that it was worded correctly. It was sent immediately and now came the waiting period. I did not have any idea of what General Arnold planned to do, if anything. I simply hoped that he would appreciate my problem. An answer was received the following morning!

"Harmonicas will be shipped as quickly as possible. Signed, General Arnold." I saved that message and it is part of my prized scrapbook.

Needless to say, I gained new respect from everyone in Special Service. I thanked the Special Service Officer for sticking his neck out on my behalf.

From Guam, we went to Saipan and performed many shows for the Air Corps as well as the other branches of service. We remained there for a month. While in Saipan, we received word from Intelligence that a large group of Japanese were hiding in the hills adjacent to the steep cliffs. We also found out that they were mostly elderly men, women and small children who were hiding in the many caves that dotted the hills. It seems that they had a shortwave radio and were receiving propaganda reports from Tokyo, warning them that if they were captured by the Americans, they would be tortured and killed.

Intelligence had one soldier proficient in reading and writing Japanese. One of the officers suggested that the soldier use a bullhorn and explain in Japanese that they should all surrender and that they would be cared for properly. The soldier said that he was too nervous to use the bullhorn. The officer tried everything to get him to change his mind but he flatly refused. It was then suggested that he write everything out phonetically and they would find someone to read it. The Intelligence officer figured that one of us from the "Winged Pigeons" could do it with conviction. Peter Lind Hayes and I were chosen. We climbed to the top of the hill and simply read what was written. Peter took part of it and I took the other. Our pleas (in Japanese) were ignored. We turned to walk down the hill when we heard screaming from the caves. We turned to watch in horror as hundreds of old men, women and children rushed from the caves and leaped off the cliffs! Over three hundred people lost their lives in this manner. We were helpless to do anything. It was the most hideous sight that I can ever remember and the picture still remains burned into my brain.

♫

One day, a soldier arrived at Headquarters looking for me. A runner had been sent to track me down. As I raced back to Headquarters and confronted the soldier, he told me that a Captain Sinclair was waiting for me on the tarmac next to the airstrip. I thanked him and ran as fast as I could and looked up and down for the Captain. I finally spotted an officer standing in front of a C-47 looking for someone. I saluted and said, "Sir, are you looking for Sergeant Adler?"

He smiled and said, "Yes, are you Sgt. Adler?"

I smiled broadly and shook my head in the affirmative.

He returned my smile and said, "Please follow me."

We entered the plane and my heart sank because it was completely empty!

The Captain turned and said, "Is this what you're looking for?" He handed me a box from under the pilot's seat.

I took it from him and ripped the package apart. There it was! Twelve brand new harmonicas still factory wrapped!

The Captain said, "Sergeant, I don't know who you are but you obviously know the right people. I flew this plane all the way from England and I will be heading back pretty soon." I thought it best not to reveal the circumstances. I shook his hand and thanked him and he turned and headed for the Officer's Club.

It was two years before I found out how it happened that I received the harmonicas. Gen. Arnold was informed that there was a factory in the town of Trossingen in Germany that made harmonicas and accordions for the German Army. He ordered an O.S.S. team of infiltrators to go in and smuggle these harmonicas out. They successfully performed this hazardous duty without one casualty!

♫

Mickey Rooney & the Slate Brothers

To every GI, mail call was the highlight of the day. One day, I received a letter from Ray McDonald from somewhere in Germany. He related an incident that has become a classic. It had to do with Mickey Rooney and his ongoing determination to get out of the Army as quickly as possible. One of the guys in Rooney's outfit was Henry Slate, one half of a comedy team, The Slate Brothers. Henry had a wild imagination and he came up with a solution for Mickey.

He said, "How badly do you want to get out of the Army?"

Mickey replied, "I'll do anything. Just name it and I'll do it."

"OK, but you must follow my instructions to the letter. If you do, I can promise you a plane ride back to Hollywood."

Mickey became very excited and promised to do as he was told.

> *"Private! What in the hell is that on the toilet seats?"*

"First, go to the PX and buy a jar of peanut butter. After you do that, walk around the camp smoking cigarettes and throw the butts on the ground. Sooner or later, a sergeant or an officer will come along and put you on latrine duty. Now, here's the important part. Scrub down the latrine so that it sparkles like diamonds. You then take the peanut butter and smear it on a couple of toilet seats. When the officer in charge comes in with his sergeant to inspect, he will compliment you on the excellent job until he spots the toilet seats. If I am any judge of human nature, he will roar, "Private! What in the hell is that on the toilet seats?"

You then walk over to the toilet, dip your finger in the peanut butter, taste it and say, "Shit, sir!"

Mickey roared with laughter but Henry insisted that it would work. Mickey was on his way home within one month.

♩

Tyrone Power
Peter Lind Hayes

While in Saipan, Peter Lind Hayes ran into Lt. Tyrone Power. He was a Marine fighter pilot and was there for a few days having his plane checked out. I had worked on several films with Ty at Fox He saw our show and became so enthused that he went to Marine Headquarters and requested a temporary transfer to the Army Air Corps to be assigned to us as our pilot! The Marines, after having seen our show, were very accommodating and even supplied us with a small transport plane. It had ten bucket seats and enough room for our props. Ty was in seventh heaven and so were we.

Our next stop was Iwo Jima. There was heavy fighting still going on but surprisingly, we were cleared to go. We took off two days later and arrived at 2:00 A.M. in a blinding rainstorm. When we landed, we were surrounded by armed Marines and they all had their rifles pointed at the plane. The officer in charge was furious. "Who in the hell are you and who authorized you to land here?"

Before any of us had a chance to say anything, Gant shouted, "Point those things somewhere else! One of them might go off!"

Gant handed the officer our authorization and orders. Gant continued. "Sir, it is pouring and we are getting soaked! Will you please direct me to your commanding officer?"

The Captain looked bewildered. "Sergeant, you've got to be kidding! It's O-two-hundred-hours! The General's asleep!"

Gant replied, "Then wake him up! We just can't stand around here in this deluge!"

The whole time that this was going on, we could hear rifle and cannon fire. Nothing fazed Gant. We were all awed by his insistence so we followed him out of curiosity to see what would happen. The rain was coming straight down and the air was suffocating - hot and humid. We reached the General's tent and the Captain quietly entered.

After a slight pause, we heard a sleepy but booming voice say, "The Winged WHAT?" He stepped outside in his shorts. The General was a small, muscular man with premature white hair. Even in his shorts, he looked like a man in charge. Gant saluted and spoke first. "Sir, we regret this terrible inconvenience but we have been ordered here to provide entertainment for your men." The General sleepily glanced at our orders, turned to the Captain. "Put these men up in tents and_____."

> "Sergeant, you salute the uniform, not a man in his underwear."

Gant said, "Excuse me, General. We cannot possibly sleep in tents! We have a considerable amount of valuable electronic equipment and it must remain with us at all times." The General shrugged and mumbled, "OK, Captain, put them up in the mess hall until morning." That seemed to satisfy Gant who again, saluted. The General looked annoyed. "Sergeant, you salute the uniform, not a man in his underwear."

Gant apologized and saluted. The General looked at him in disgust and returned to his tent. We walked back to the plane and, with the assistance of several Marines, unloaded and carried everything to the mess hall. Cots were brought in and we all slept well, considering the constant bombardment of gunfire and cannon that sounded too close for comfort. We awoke in the morning bathed in perspiration. The heat and humidity was unbearable. How could the fighting men, in full uniform, function under such conditions?

The rain had stopped and everything that we touched felt like rotting slime. Our heavy equipment kept sliding out of our hands and simple movement sapped our energy. The cots were quickly folded to make room for the Marines and us to eat breakfast. This was followed by all of us pitching in to set up our equipment on an outdoor stage. An announcement was made on loudspeakers about our show. It was scheduled for 2:00 P.M. and the Marines were excited about seeing it.

It was a small, outdoor theater setting in a natural bowl. There were no seats. Everyone sat on the ground which was nothing but thick mud. That didn't seem to bother them. Thousands of Marines suddenly came from every direction. The area was packed. There were Marines sitting in trees so far back that it was impossible for them to see the show. About thirty minutes before show time, I saw some men hauling in folding chairs that were placed in the front of the men sitting on the ground. They set up three rows of chairs for approximately fifty people. I asked one of the men who the chairs were for. He said that it was for the General, his staff plus a group of nurses from the field hospital. I spoke to Gant about it and we agreed that it was unfair and extremely inconsiderate. We informed the ranking noncom of our feelings and stated that we would not perform under these circumstances.

Word soon reached the General's aide and he quickly arrived in his jeep. He demanded to know what was going on. Gant never lost his cool. He spoke calmly and politely and told the Colonel that there would not be a show as long as those chairs were there. The Colonel nearly blew a fuse. "Sergeant, I do not want to hear anymore arguments or discussions. You are to put on your show as soon as the General arrives with his staff."

Gant replied, "I'm sorry, Colonel. The decision is mine to make and I have made it."

While Gant and the Colonel were going head to head, the General and his staff arrived in jeeps. Before the Colonel had a chance to say anything, Gant approached the General and briefly explained the problem. The General looked out at the sea of faces who were now yelling and whistling for the show to start.

"You're absolutely right, Sergeant. Colonel, please have those chairs placed to the side so that they do not block the men's view. "As soon as the men began removing the chairs, a wild cheer reverberated all over the place and the men sitting in trees were told to come forward and sit down in front. The General and his party watched from the side. We had made our indelible mark on Iwo Jima.

Our first opportunity to entertain the wounded in the field hospital came the following morning. We were not prepared for what lay in store for us. Teenagers, just kids with limbs blown off but there they were, nearly all of them smiling. As we entered the ward, Joe Bushkin had brought his accordion and he accompanied us as we put on an impromptu show. It broke my heart to see the innocence in the faces of the wounded. I played as many requests as possible and the others sang along and danced. All of the wounded were covered with mesh nets to ward off the thousands of insects trying to feed on their battered bodies. When it came time to leave, several of us had difficulty holding back tears.

> *...I volunteered...to play for a few guys in fox holes.*

Later that evening, I volunteered to go to the forward area and play for a few of the guys in fox holes. That was one of the advantages of playing the harmonica. I could go anywhere without any problem. I remained forward for two hours, running from one fox hole to another. It was exciting and very frightening at the same time.

We were on the island of Tinian, a mere twenty miles from Saipan. Those two islands plus Guam, accounted for all of the B-29 strikes against Japan. The famous Enola Gay, the B-29 that dropped the first atomic bomb, was part of our own bomber squadron in Tinian, yet nobody knew about the bomb including the crew of the Enola Gay! When they finally received their orders for the mission, they were not aware of what they were carrying until they opened their sealed orders when they were half way to Japan. We heard about the explosion on short wave radio from San Francisco, an eerie silence covered the entire island like a phantom blanket. Then photographs started coming in showing the amazing destruction of an entire city from one bomb! It was as if all of us had been ordered not to speak.

♫

Peter Lind Hayes and I had started a running gin rummy game when we were on Saipan and played at every spare moment. I enjoyed the game but he was a fanatic about it. He insisted on playing for pretty high stakes to "keep it interesting". That made me very uncomfortable despite the fact that I was winning. We were playing at the time and my heart wasn't in it. Peter had a logical attitude about it that was frightening to me. He said, "I realize what we have done, but we all know that it will shorten the war and save a hell of a lot of American lives. Now deal the cards." We were back to playing gin rummy as if our watches had stopped temporarily and then magically started again.

At one point, Peter owed me over one thousand dollars which I felt, was straining our relationship. One night, we were playing when we unexpectedly heard rifle fire and guys yelling. Several of the men ran out to see what was going on. They came back shouting, "THE WAR'S OVER! THE JAPANESE HAVE SURRENDERED!" I grabbed Peter by the shoulders and shouted, "PETE, THE WAR IS OVER AND WE'RE GOING HOME!" He gave me a chilling stare and said, "Deal!" I looked at him in disbelief.

"BUT PETER, IT'S OVER! DON'T YOU UNDERSTAND?" He just sat there waiting for me to deal. I said, "To hell with it. All bets are off and all debts are canceled. I'm going home!"

Peter said, "I'll tell you what we'll do. One more game, double or nothing." I reluctantly agreed and I beat him. He wrote me a check and I sent it home to be deposited.

♫

…my father had…a heart attack.

I was killing time doing some much needed practicing when I received a message to report to the Red Cross office. It never occurred to me that it might be something serious. The executive officer in charge handed me a message saying that my father had suffered a heart attack and I was to be shipped home immediately! In those days, a serviceman was automatically sent home if an illness in the immediate family created a hardship. They were unable to provide me with any details and I did my best to keep calm. My orders were cut and I was free to leave on the next available flight to San Francisco. The planes on Tinian were mostly B-29s and I was not too keen on flying in them due to their overall track record so I waited for a C-47. I gathered all of my equipment together including a Japanese sword and rifle that I had removed from a dead Japanese soldier, had a brief farewell with my buddies, and was off. I had nagging, emotional thoughts about my father and was feeling guilty about leaving my buddies behind. The thought of actually flying back to the U.S. seemed unreal..

I boarded the C-47 with a full load of soldiers. Our first stop was Guam for refueling and then on to Hickam for one more refueling. Two hours later, we were on our final lap. Next stop, San Francisco! The California coast line finally came into view amid cheers which rang out from all of us. We were coming in at night and as we made our final approach, a huge electric sign lit up on top of the main terminal. WELCOME HOME!

After we landed, I was on my own. I went directly to the PSA Airlines desk and showed them my emergency papers and was given a priority ticket to Burbank, which was just three miles from our home! I then called my mother who wept with tears of joy. I told her that I would be home in approximately three hours. From there, I ran to the airport restaurant and ordered a quart of milk and two huge slices of lemon meringue pie from the startled waitress. After gulping down my milk and pie, I grabbed my equipment and burped my way to the boarding gate. The wait seemed to take forever, but our flight was finally called. They told me that I could not carry all of my gear aboard the plane so they had someone check most of it through baggage including my sword and rifle. It was only an hour's flight from San Francisco to Burbank and it was the longest hour of my life. When we finally arrived, I gathered up my equipment and took the first available cab home.

Mother was standing outside waiting for me. We embraced and of course, we both burst into tears of joy. My first question was, "How's Dad?" Mother said that he was doing fine and was anxious to see me. I also noticed that she seemed in stable condition but I was reluctant to pursue the subject. I refocused on the reason for my early homecoming. We drove to the Good Samaritan Hospital and Mother was looking me over and quickly decided that I had lost too much weight. She would remedy that immediately. Dad looked pale but was in fairly good shape considering the heart attack.

Dad soon left the hospital to recuperate at home, as I took over the running of the store. Two weeks later, he felt well enough to come back to work. At the first opportunity, I drove to Ft. McArthur and was told that I had enough points for discharge. I was processed, issued a "ruptured duck," a discharge pin and was out!

♫

Jean Ludwig

> *After four years in the service, I felt strongly about getting married...*

While in the Service, I had kept a running correspondence with my first sweetheart in Baltimore. Her name was Jean Ludwig and we wrote to each other on a pretty steady basis. After nearly four years in the service, I felt strongly about getting married and raising a family. Jean was the obvious choice if still available. I called her and in the course of our conversation, asked if she had a new boy friend? She assured me that things were just the same. I said that I was preparing to drive to Baltimore to see her and she sounded very excited. As I drove across the country, I allowed myself to day-dream about the rosy future, picturing Jean as the mother of our children. It all seemed to fit perfectly.

I arrived in Baltimore and drove straight to Jean's home. It looked like the world had continued on it's inevitable future and had left Jean's street the same as it always was. I was brimming over with nostalgia as I walked up the steps to the front door. She had not changed a bit. If anything, she was more beautiful. When I entered, emotions flowed freely. After settling down, I spent about a half hour with her mother and sister but I was anxious to get her out of there so we could have some privacy. We went to dinner at a quiet, elegant restaurant. I don't remember where we dined but the environment was a perfect setting for me to pop the question. It didn't take long to realize that Jean had not given serious thought to marriage. We jabbered frantically throughout the meal and I tried to impress her with the fact that we had been childhood sweethearts and my feelings for her had never wavered. I told her that I loved her and she responded by saying that she felt the same way.

I said, "So what's the problem? Let's get married!"

Jean looked at me forlornly and said, "Are you planning to live in California?"

"Of course! That's my home! You'll love California!"

"I don't mind that Jerry, but if we get married and live there, I will be without my family!"

I said, "We will always have the opportunity to visit them. My career is in California. Where would you expect us to live?"

She looked at me tearfully. "I can't. I just can't leave my family."

I was shattered! I had not anticipated this turn of events.

I pleaded and implored, asking her to please reconsider but she was adamant.

Although it was heart-wrenching, I knew that I had to make a decision to break it off. The rest of the evening was a disaster. I took her home and told her that I still loved her. Emotionally and physically drained and confused, I started to question whether I was being stubborn, unreasonable, and unfair. The following morning, I was back in my car, driving back to California. The ride back was mental torture. I was ill prepared for such a setback but, deep down inside, I knew that I had made the right decision.

♪

When I returned to Hollywood, I was anxious to re-establish my studio contacts. Many of the soldiers were still overseas and musicians were hard to find. I spent the next few years working in most of the major studios, recording background music for films.

> *Television was rearing its ugly head. Vaudeville theaters*
> *and nightclubs rapidly became history.*

Being in the service for nearly four years created a Rip Van Winkle effect on the realities of show business. Television was rearing its ugly head. Vaudeville theaters and nightclubs rapidly became history. People remained at home watching the best entertainment on a picture tube. My heart sank at the prospect of digging for fool's gold in the world of disappearing show business. Sure, there were the isolated dates still available such as Las Vegas, Reno and Tahoe, but that was not enough to sustain a future.

Not long after I returned home, I received a phone call from Peter Lind Hayes. He was starting a new TV show in New York and invited me to appear on the show for one entire week! By coincidence, my brother was appearing at a club in New York called "The Village Gate" It was the first engagement that he had been offered since his traumatic move to England during the McCarthy horror days. This was a rare opportunity to spend time with Larry. At the end of each show I would rush down to the Village Gate to be with him. During dinner one evening Larry said, "You know Jerry, I'm really surprised at you." Startled, I asked him why. His replied, "You know how important this date is for me. Why didn't you suggest to Peter to contact me to appear on his show instead of you? You didn't need the engagement?" I was stunned. This was the first time that Larry and I had a major disagreement. I left the club in a daze and walked over four miles back to my hotel. I was stunned by what he had said. Needless to say, I did not sleep that night.

The next morning he called and asked me to join him for breakfast. I was reluctant to join him. However, I finally decided to meet with him. With much difficulty, he apologized. "Jerry, I have never been so ashamed of anything in my life. Saying what I said to you last night…can you forgive me?" We both realized how much we cared for and trusted each other even after all the years of not having much time to spend together. I assured him that although I was momentarily shattered, I did understand his reasons for saying what he said. I replied, "Of course I forgive you. Now please, let's put it to rest."

Peter received numerous phone calls about the show, and my engagement was extended 2 more weeks giving more time to spend with Larry. The last two weeks flew by and on my final evening in New York, Larry and I embraced and we were, once again, brothers.

♫

Edna Lichtenstein

I had been dating a girl named Edna Lichtenstein. She was two years my senior and it never occurred to me to think of her romantically. One day, she wrote to her cousin in Minneapolis, telling her some very nice things about me. She also mentioned that she was too old for me but felt that she (her cousin) and I would make an ideal couple. Her cousin, Sylvia Gandel was looking for a good reason to leave Minneapolis and was longing to live in sunny California. She quit her job and took a train to Los Angeles.

♫

Sylvia Gandel

Edna invited me to dinner where I first met Sylvia. She was charming, pretty, bright and had a wonderful sense of humor. We dated many times and I finally introduced Sylvia to my parents. When they met her, it was love at first sight. They were thrilled that I had met such a marvelous girl, and in a not too subtle way, urged me to propose marriage. I urged them to "stop pushing".

After the war, many items that were rationed and other household items were scarce. But Dad's store still carried some of the hard-to-find items. One day, Mother informed me, "Sylvia Gandel called and wants to buy a GE steam iron."

I replied, "So what's the big deal? Sell her one."

"Sylvia doesn't have a car and it's too far for her to travel to pick it up. I promised that I would have you deliver it to her."

Mother was a great lady but had one hell of a devious mind when it came to getting her son to marry the right girl. Without admitting it to my mother, I was just as anxious to see Sylvia again. I called her and told her that I would deliver the iron. I also asked her out for dinner. I knew that she enjoyed exotic, Cantonese food so I made a reservation at The Beachcomber, one of the nicest restaurants in Hollywood. The ambiance was perfect and the food delicious.

♫

Sylvia Adler

From then on, we dated steadily. Her values were similar to mine and we seemed to drift into a very comfortable relationship. Six months had passed and I knew in my heart that I had finally found the woman of my dreams. I proposed marriage to her in the unlikely atmosphere of her mother's kitchen! She accepted my proposal and we were married three months later. She never did pay for the iron.

At the risk of being burned at the stake for using such a horrible cliche, our marriage was "made in heaven". We were ideally suited to each other, and very much in love. Our first child, Michael was born on January 2, 1947. He was a beautiful baby who loused me out of a great tax write-off by being born two days too late. Our daughter,

Susan was born on February 19, 1948. She was born with more hair than Elvis.

Apartments were practically impossible to find. Mother and Dad invited us to live with them but that was looking for trouble. We finally found a very small apartment with a pull-down bed, and small kitchen but it worked. We were happy in our own little place and managed to enjoy our marriage to the fullest. When Michael was born, we were faced with a problem. Where would we put him? When we brought him home, we set up a crib in the kitchen next to the stove! I went searching for a larger place but nothing was available at any price. Fortunately, Michael was a remarkable child who seemed to be happy at every waking hour. We couldn't believe it! He slept through the night and I do not recall ever having to get up at night to change him. Ten months later, Susan was born! We no longer had the luxury of playing tick tack toe with our children and simply had to find a larger place. With extreme trepidation, I discussed the possibility with Sylvia to move in with my parents but only on a short-term basis. I promised that I would look for a home as soon as possible.

We gave up the apartment and moved in with Grandma and Grandpa Adler. I knew that I could not risk my parents becoming too accustomed to having the children around so I went on a serious house hunt.

Within two months, I found a home in North Hollywood, a part of the San Fernando Valley. I was able to use my GI Bill to purchase the house and we moved in. We bought used furniture temporarily and we were happy. We were also the only Jewish family on the block but that didn't seem to be a problem.

There were plenty of kids in the area, so when our children were old enough to play outside, they had many friends. We were the first family on our street to purchase a TV set. It was so small that we had to buy a Plexiglas bubble that was placed in front of the screen to enlarge the picture. The entire neighborhood would gather in our living room to watch it, but not at the same time!

We had been living in our new home one year when we noticed activity on the empty lot opposite our house. After much inquiry, I learned that a Catholic church was to be built. I was pleased about that for a number of reasons. It would dress up the neighborhood and would definitely increase property value. It took a year and a half to complete the construction. Early one Saturday morning I noticed the priest walking down the steps of the church. He stopped at the corner and looked in all four directions. I would guess that he was in his sixties, and could double for the Irish actor, Barry Fitzgerald. He then proceeded to walk towards our house. I guessed what his mission was on that sunny morning, and when he arrived at our front door he twitched his shoulders nervously and rang the doorbell.

I opened the door, smiled and said, "Good morning, Father. Would you care to come in?"

When he spoke, I was positive that it was Barry Fitzgerald! His body language was nearly identical to Fitzgerald, with that quaint way of looking at you over his glasses. An Irish brogue said, "Top o' the marnin' to ya!" He walked in and immediately introduced himself. "M'name's Father Bauer and "iym" the priest of that there church."

♫

Father Bauer

As he settled into a comfortable chair I asked, "Would you care for a drink, Father?"

I was thinking of a pleasant soft drink or perhaps a cup of coffee, considering the time of day.

The Father said, "Oh, that would be luvly. Do ye happen to have a wee bit of Scotch?"

Scotch! I went to the bar and poured him a healthy shot.

"Now, Father, what can we do for you?"

He replied, "Well, as ya know, we are a brand new church in the neighborhood and I wuz about to make the acquaintance of all me neighbors."

We were fascinated with this charming leprechaun. He looked the perfect part to appear on the face of a St. Patrick's Day card. We did not want him to leave before he stated the reason for his visit. So I tried to drag out the obvious. I attempted to make small talk but he too became anxious to get to the heart of his visit. I went right to the point by saying, "Correct me if I'm wrong, Father. Would I be assuming correctly that the purpose of your visit is to find out who is and who is not Catholic in the neighborhood?"

He looked genuinely startled. "Well! That's exactly right! Yer a very perceptive young man. Would ya mind tellin' me your religious denomination?"

I smiled and said, "I hope that this does not come as a disappointment, Father. We're Jewish."

Without missing a beat, he said "Jewish, are ye? Well, that's a hell of a start!"

Father Bauer and I became very close friends through the years. It broke our hearts to learn that he had died from a massive heart attack while delivering a sermon. I was honored when the assistant priest asked me to act as honorary pall bearer at his funeral. Father Bauer was a jolly man with a great sense of humor. We never discussed religion and when he died, I knew that I had lost a good friend.

I was always kept busy by the studios and had more work than I could handle. The pay was quite lucrative and I enjoyed it for a while but my heart still belonged to performing on stage to a live audience. I contacted my New York agent and told him that I was ready to go back to work.

♫

Glen Campbell & Bobbi Gentry

One day, an agent called and asked if I would be interested in going on a college tour with Glen Campbell and Bobbi Gentry. Here was an opportunity to play to a live audience again. I discussed it with Sylvia and asked if it would be OK with her, and wanted assurance that she could handle things alone while I was gone. She assured me that she would be fine.

On the day of departure, I embraced my family and told the kids to take good care of Mom. The tour was going to be in the deep South including such states as Georgia, Mississippi, North Carolina, Alabama, and Louisiana. We anticipated a grueling schedule. The musicians and I traveled by bus and Campbell and Gentry went by air. We had a ten piece band and the Musician's Union asked me if I would volunteer to act as Union representative. I reluctantly agreed as it appeared to be a technical rather than active assignment.

We left Los Angeles, drove during the day with the usual rest stops, and slept in crummy motels. When we finally reached the South, we arrived at the first college town early in the morning. We checked into a motel and tried to sleep for a couple of hours before rehearsal at 6:00 P.M. When we arrived to rehearse, we tested the sound system and set the lights. After the show, the bus was loaded with our equipment by the local stage hands.

The shows were received with great enthusiasm at every college. Campbell was a marvelous performer with great charisma, and of course, Bobbi Gentry was hot with her new recording of *Ode to Billy Joe* I had a fifteen minute solo spot and that was the show.

One night, while appearing at Mississippi State University, Campbell introduced me, "Ladies and gentlemen, it gives me great pleasure to introduce you to a terrific harmonica player and our favorite bar mitzvah boy, Jerry Adler!" The intro got a big laugh as well as applause and I did my act although I was furious inside. After the show, I confronted Glen and asked about the introduction.

He said, "Hell, I thought it was funny. It got a big laugh, didn't it?"

"It certainly did . . . at my expense."

"Don't get so damned touchy. That's one of the things wrong with you people."

"What do you mean by YOU PEOPLE?"

"Aw, c'mon, Jerry. It was just a joke and a damned good one at that."

"I fail to see the humor in it and suggest that you delete it in the future."

"Hey, nobody tells me what to do in my show."

"Are you saying that you refuse to take it out?"

"You're damned right."

"OK, I guess the next move is mine."

"That's right. Whatever-the-hell that's supposed to mean."

I called an emergency meeting of the band and explained the problem. I gave them an official order not to rehearse or play the next show. They were all in agreement. Glen was not aware of the meeting so when we arrived at the next date, the musicians showed up at rehearsal but refused to play. Campbell was puzzled.

"What the hell's going on around here?"

I said, "As the Union rep, I have ordered the band not to play unless you promise to delete your remark."

Glen was fuming. "Well, we'll just see about that." He went to the phone to call the Hollywood Union office but realized that we had a three hour time difference. The office would not be open for two hours.

He said, "Can I at least get you guys to play the rehearsal until the Union office opens?"

They all turned to me and I shook my head, "No."

He looked at me with pure hatred.

"You're fired!"

I said, "That's fine, but I'm taking the band with me and you're going to pay our air fare back to Los Angeles."

"You can all get in a hell of a lot of trouble with the Union."

I said, "Please don't make any rash decisions, let's wait until the Union office opens and we'll get this settled once and for all."

We all went to lunch and at 1:00 P.M. Glen placed a call to the president of the Union. They spoke for a while and then Glen turned to me and said, "He wants to talk to you."

I gave my version of the story and the Union President said, "You are absolutely right and I have told that to Glen."

I thanked him for backing me up and Glen reluctantly dropped the "joke".

While we were preparing to be on our way to the next concert, a student came to me and said, "A lot of us heard about your trouble this morning and I would like to shake your hand for standing up to Mr. Campbell. He went on to say, "I didn't think that it was funny at all." I was touched, "Thank you for sharing your sentiment and for taking the time to come back and see me."

The tour lasted for four more weeks and although I did not have additional problems with Campbell, I, as well as the rest of the musicians were extremely anxious to return home. Performing college concerts by bus is not exactly the cream of show business engagements. We finally arrived back in Los Angeles and it felt great to be home again.

♫

William Holden and Buddy Clark

Columbia Studios engaged me to dub in a harmonica solo for a kid named Billy Gray. The film was a real stinker called "Father Was A Bachelor", which starred William Holden and Virginia Grey. Billy was cast as a farm kid who was supposed to be a whiz on the harmonica. Holden's role was that of a carefree, singing hobo. That is the meat of the plot. Holden could not sing a note so the studio hired a fine vocalist, Buddy Clark. Buddy had the same vocal timbre in his voice that matched perfectly with the speaking voice of Holden.

We were on the recording stage, pre-recording the harmonica and Buddy's voice. These tracks would be played back on the shooting stage. Holden had a difficult time lip-synching because he had a tin ear and did not know anything about music! Buddy was backed up by a huge orchestra conducted by studio musical director, Morris Stoloff. They were recording a simple children's song called, *The Big Rock Candy Mountain*. Buddy was standing on the six foot platform so that the sound engineers could watch his every move.

♫

Marilyn Monroe

Freddie Karger, the music coordinator for Columbia, was just entering the sound stage with a young lady when the red warning light went on in conjunction with a loud bell. This was to let everyone in the vicinity of the stage know we were about to record, and opening the studio door was prohibited until the light was turned off. They made it just in time and the recording take was slated, meaning a verbal announcement was made on a mike from the sound booth. Example: "This is take one, Buddy Clark, fishing wharf scene, "Father Was A Bachelor". Roll for speed." The orchestra began the introduction and Buddy began to sing. While he was singing, Karger and his lady friend quietly moved forward. When they got close enough, Buddy found himself staring at the most exquisite blonde that he had ever seen. She was wearing a white, pleated skirt and a pale pink angora sweater. Buddy was singing the lyrics, "Oh, the buzzin' of the bees, in the chewing gum trees, 'neath a soda water fountain . . . Holy Jesus!" He was completely lost at the sight of Marilyn Monroe! She was unknown at the time but not for long. Buddy and the orchestra had to re-record it.

♫

Ira Gershwin

I received a call from my brother in London. He said that the BBC was preparing a TV Special on George Gershwin. George Gershwin was the elite of the music world. He and I had become good friends and we knew each other well. George Gershwin was born September 26, 1898 in Brooklyn , N.Y. He had two brothers, Ira (the elder) Arthur, and a sister, Frances (Frankie). His father, Morris Gershovitz, son of a mechanic and grandson of a rabbi, and his mother, Rose. Morris shortened the name to Gershvin, George changed it to Gershwin.

He said of his childhood years, "Music never interested me and I spent most of my time with the boys on the street, skating, and in general, making a nuisance of myself." However, he also recalled this vivid scene when he was a child of six. "I stood outside a penny arcade listening to an automatic piano leaping through (Anton) Rubinstein's Melody in F. . . . To this very day I can't hear this tune without picturing myself outside the arcade on 125th street, standing there barefoot and in overalls, drinking it all in avidly."

Knowing that I visited his brother Ira quite often in Beverly Hills, he thought that it would be a great idea for me to interview Ira at his home. The BBC would send a cameraman immediately.

Ira had been in poor health for a long time and I was reluctant to tax him with such a project. I called Ira's wife, Leonora and explained the show. She also had doubts about Ira having the stamina to do it. But she promised to ask and call me back. Ira insisted that we do the show. I called Larry and told him to send the cameraman as soon as possible. He arrived within forty eight hours and came directly to Ira's home. I explained to Ira that I would be interviewing him and had prepared a list of questions that I had formulated the night before and hoped, would be appropriate. We seated ourselves near one of two grand pianos in the living room and the interview proceeded without a hitch. We had finished in one take! The whole thing ran for ten minutes. I thanked Ira for his generous contribution and his obvious delight in doing it. He insisted that I remain for tea. We seated ourselves at a small table. He said, "I never did ask you. Do you play the piano?"

"Not really. However, I do enjoy searching for chords to match a particular melody." "Go over to that piano and tell me what you think of the touch."

> *"That's the piano that George used to compose the Rhapsody in Blue."*

Of course, it was beautiful. Ira casually said, "That's the piano that George used to compose the *Rhapsody In Blue.*"

I pulled my hands away as if I had been stung. How dare I touch the piano that George Gershwin used for composing!

Ira laughed and encouraged me to continue. "Please, Jerry. There's no reason for you to feel intimidated."

I continued to play and then Leonora came into the room and nodded to me that I should excuse myself. The strain was beginning to show on Ira's face. I thanked him again for his generosity and cooperation and promised to show him a copy of what we had done as soon as it became available to me.

Two weeks later, Larry said that the show was a tremendous success and the interview was a real highlight. He thanked me for taking the time and trouble to help out.

I said, "I would certainly appreciate a video copy of the show or at least the interview portion." He didn't anticipate any problem and promised to have it mailed to me. Later he called to say that the BBC told him that they never saved any film and the entire show was erased after it had been broadcast!

♫

Judy Garland. The Finale

I heard about Judy's farewell performance at Carnegie Hall scheduled for April 23, 1961. I don't remember most dates, a chronic affliction, but I remember this one. I told Sylvia that I wanted to fly to New York to see the concert. She knew about my past relationship with Judy and assured me that is was okay with her. My thoughts about Judy drifted to our time together and so many more memories went through my mind as I entered this magnificent concert hall. There was electricity in the air and the behavior of the audience was super emotional, almost frightening. And all this before they began the overture or raised the curtain! The talented Mort Lindsey was her arranger and conductor. I had known Mort when he was with Dot Records in Hollywood. When the overture began, I was seated far back in the theater. Even so, I sensed a surge of excitement beyond imagination at his orchestration of the overture.

The house lights began to dim and the kettle drum crashed through the thickened air of excitement. My skin buzzed as if I had put my fist into an open socket. The orchestra soared as the trumpets and trombones blasted the first five notes of *The Man That Got Away*. So help me, people around me were sobbing uncontrollably. *The Man That Got Away* was followed by *The Trolley Song* and then came *Over the Rainbow*. The response from the audience was seconds away from turning into a riot! And then came Judy's entrance. People jumped from their seats and rushed to the front to greet her, shake her hand, or simply get close to her.

This tiny, frail figure walked on stage and a huge roar arose from the audience. Dear Judy sang her heart out. I have never seen or heard her perform better. I readily confess that I joined with the audience in my own tears of joy. Her timing, her control, and savvy were there to enjoy. She sang twenty-six songs and left the audience screaming for more. This was the concert to end all concerts. The rest is history. There will never be another Judy Garland - Ever!!

> *...I received a call...asking if I would be interested in performing at...a few condominiums.*

While working on a film at Warner Brothers, I received a call from an agent in Florida asking if I would be interested in performing at the Beach Theater, an old vaudeville house in Miami Beach, plus a few condominiums. Condominiums are very big in Florida. During the winter season and portions of the summer, entertainers are invited to their clubhouses or auditoriums to perform. It's a major industry and they have booked names like Milton Berle, Tony Bennett, Steve and Edie Gorme and many more.

Howard Keel

I had heard much about the "condo entertainment industry" in Florida but was never exposed to it. After my stint with Warner Brothers ended, I left for Florida, and arrived at the theater. Howard Keel was giving his closing performance and I stayed to watch the show. I went backstage to say hello and try to get some pointers from him regarding the audience. His first question was, "Did you bring any cassette tapes?"

I was puzzled. I honestly did not know what he meant.

"Tapes! Cassettes to sell in the lobby!"

I had never heard of an entertainer pitching his own tapes.

He said, "Follow me." We walked to the front of the and there was a huge display loaded with nothing but Howard Keel tapes!

He said, "Jerry, my salary here represents a fraction of what I make on these tapes!"

I was fascinated and wanted to know more.

He said, "They sell for ten dollars. I give the house a dollar a piece to sell them and my average take in sales of tapes for one week runs approximately five thousand dollars." I was stunned. I did not know that promotions like this existed in the theater. I would keep this in mind on my next trip to Florida.

♫

Jan Murray, Anna Maria Albergetti

This was my first experience with an all Jewish audience since I worked the Catskills as a kid. I had forgotten how open and gregarious they could be. I shared the bill with Jan Murray, Anna Maria Albergetti and a belly dancer! Jews are big on belly dancers. They featured four stage shows a day with a movie in between. The first film started at 11:30 A.M. The was packed with fifteen hundred people All of us in the show eagerly awaited the opening. I was all fired up when the M.C. introduced me. He gave me a generous introduction and brought me on to warm applause. I opened with a medley from *Fiddler On The*

Roof. As I was about to go into my next number, I heard a voice yell, "Mr. Adler!"

"I instinctively turned to the wings but nobody was there. I started again but this time, the interruption was more forceful.

"Mr. Adler!"

I then realized that the voice was coming from the audience. I could not afford to ignore it. I responded, "Yes, what is it?"

He quickly asked, "So tell me, how's yer brudder?"

I was shocked but felt that I had to go along with this strange behavior.

I said, "He's fine, thank you. I appreciate your interest."

I continued with the show. At least I played the first three notes of the next number before I was interrupted again.

"I understand dot he's living by Englund."

There are fifteen hundred people in the theater and this man is talking to me as if he was in my living room! The audience began to heckle the man, sprinkled with a few boos. I visualized my show going down the drain.

I said, "Yes, he does live in England. Sir, are you satisfied?"

"So how come he lives dere for soch ah lung time?"

> *"For God sake, will you let the boychik play?"*

"He likes it there, I suppose, because ....Sir, I do appreciate your interest in my brother but this is not the time nor the place to discuss it. If you like, I will be happy to meet you in the lobby after the show."

As I said that, a voice from the other side of the theater, yelled, "For God sake, will you let the boychik play?" For those who do not know, boychik means young man.

For my next performances at the Beach, as suggested, I brought my cassette tapes. A very nice Jewish lady in charge of the candy counter was also responsible for selling my cassettes.

On the morning of my opening, I walked to the lobby to be sure that the tapes were prominently displayed and that she had plenty of stock. The theater was still closed. She looked at me forlornly. "I ain't sold nuttin' yet! Not ah single tape!"

I said, "The theater hasn't opened yet!" She looked concerned.

"But I ain't sold nutton!"

"Please, I appreciate your concern. When the theater opens and after we do our first show, I'm sure that you will be selling some tapes."

That seemed to pacify her. I started to leave through the front door of the theater but she stopped me. "So, vare you goin?"

I replied, "I'm going outside to look at the front of the theater."

"It's chilly outside. You'll put on ah sveater so you vunt ketch culd."

This is where the definition of "Jewish mother" originated. Here is a woman, in all innocence, expressing concern about the health of a total stranger!

On Saturday night, it was impossible to get near the theater. I had seen elderly people standing in line for most of the day to get tickets for the evening show. That evening, as I looked through the peep hole from backstage, I could hear and see the people in the front row. A lady turned to another lady. "I gotta go to de ladies room. Vud you mind, you'll vatch mine seat?" The lady nodded yes. As soon as the first lady left, a man ran down the aisle and sat in the seat. The lady said, "Hexcuse me, dis seat is taken." The man stared straight ahead and said, "No resoived seats." The woman said, "But de lady just vent to de toilet! She's coming right beck!" The man continued to look straight ahead. "Sorry, no resoived seats." The other lady finally returned. She yelled, "Hey, vot you doink in mine seat?"

The man was adamant. "No resoived seats."

The woman turned into a raging animal. "I'll give you vun sekund to get out from mine seat!"

Once again, he said, "No resoived seats."

The lady swung her heavy purse full force into the man's face, screaming, "I'll give you, no resoived seats, you gonnif! Get de hell out from mine seat!"

The man jumped up immediately, holding his face and ran to the back of the theater.

This was the first of my many performances at condominiums in Florida. They bring in at least two shows a month, mostly on the east coast with its predominantly Jewish population. The number of condos is staggering. One can work four months of condos twice a week without one repeat. They usually have two acts which are backed up by a trio, consisting of piano, bass and drums. It is, for obvious reasons, a seasonal activity and begins the last week in October until the end of March. After that, most residents leave for cooler climates.

Condos in Florida can provide the greatest wealth of comedy material by simply listening to the residents, who are, without question, the most receptive that I have ever experienced. However, they have strong opinions about talent and are very vocal in their approval or disapproval. Fortunately, I have been very successful and have never been subjected to anything less than an enthusiastic response.

I refer to this as "innocent" Jewish humor...

Here is still another example of natural, Jewish humor. I refer to this as "innocent" Jewish humor, meaning that the person involved is unaware that she/he had become the star of a typical, humorous anecdote. I was booked into two condos in one night. Thank, God, this is no longer practiced. It becomes a physical and mental nightmare. The condos can be thirty or forty miles apart, so time becomes critical. I would complete my first show while a car and driver waited to rush me off to the next condo. Definitely no time for small talk. As I rushed to the car, I heard a loud shout from the hallway,

"Vait, Mr. Odler Jost ah sekund I vant you should sign mine pitcher."

She was running as fast as her little legs could carry her. I was surprised to see her holding an 8 x 10 glossy photo of me!

I said, "Where did you get this?"

She matter-of-factly replied , "I took it off de billboard outside!".

171

It is important that you understand that she sincerely felt that she had done nothing wrong. It was done in all innocence as if to say, "Doesn't everybody?"

After one of my shows, a lady asked. "Mr. Adler, I nuticed you got a guld ring on yer fingeh. You married?"

"Yes, I am."

She looked at me with disdain. "Feh! You couldn't do me no good."

I jokingly said, "Just a minute. I'm sure that I could, but it would only be a one shot deal."

She gave me a haughty glare and said, "Are you talkin doity to me?"

I completed my tour of Florida and returned to my work at the studios.

♫

Nelson Riddle

There have been many moments in my career that have made me feel proud, but none more than the many recordings I made as guest soloist with musical giants such as Nelson Riddle, David Rose and Henry Mancini, to name a few. The music from the film, "The Alamo" contained a haunting melody titled, The Green Leaves of Summer. I received a call from Nelson Riddle asking if I would do the solo for a Capitol Records recording. Nelson's arrangements were exquisite and that session remains one of my all-time favorites. Another recording was from a film called "The Little Fugitive". The music was composed by a very talented gentleman who is also a dear friend and fellow harmonica player, Eddie Manson. The title of the song was the same as the film and the arrangement by David Rose was beautiful.

♫

George Burns and Harry Cohen

One day my wife, Sylvia and I received an engraved invitation to a birthday party. It was to pay tribute to Harry Cohen, President of

Columbia Pictures. Cohen was one of the most powerful and most feared in the industry. I doubt that he ever had one person whom he could call a friend. However, his power was such that one did not refuse this invitation. It still remains a mystery as to why we were invited. I had never met him although I did a considerable amount of recording at his studio. Although he attended many of my recording sessions, we were never formally introduced. The party was to be a black tie affair. I had not planned to go because one, I never had much respect for Cohen's reputation and two, I have always disliked parties with hundreds of people milling around kissing each other in "mid-air" as if they loved everybody! However, I knew how nuts Sylvia was about meeting celebrities. I also knew that she would go mad wondering what to wear. This was going to be a rare opportunity for her. Imagine being in the same room with the cream of the Hollywood elite. I decided to ask if she wanted to go and was not surprised to hear her say, "yes!"

Two days later, I received a call from George Burns asking if I had planned on attending the party. It wasn't necessary to ask, "What party?" I told George that we were going and he asked if I would be good enough to pick him up because he hated going there alone. Of course we were delighted.

We picked him up and on the way he said, "Wanna have some fun tonight?"

I said, "Sure. What's the point of going if we can't have fun?"

"I'll make a bet with you, Jer. Just to make it more fun."

"What kind of bet?"

"How about betting me a buck?"

Hell, I could be a swinger for one buck.

"Ok, George, what are we betting on?"

"You know that Jack (Benny) will be there."

"Yes, I assumed that he would."

"I'll bet you a dollar that I can break Jack up without saying anything funny or making a funny face."

"What in the hell are you talking about? What are you going to do?"

George was sitting in the back seat but I could feel his silly grin. "You'll see."

We arrived at the party and George left us quickly reminding us, "I'll be back later."

Sylvia and I joined Gene Kelly and Henry Koster, the director. We made the usual small talk and Sylvia was in heaven. About ten minutes later, George returned.

"OK, Jer? Are you ready?"

I nodded and he said, "OK, here we go."

We excused ourselves from Kelly and Koster and followed George through the crowd. We soon found Jack chatting with Mr. and Mrs. Gregory Peck. Jack greeted us and introduced Sylvia and me to the Pecks. I thought that Sylvia was going to have a coronary.

George stood there silently bending his forefinger. Jack happened to look at George and suddenly fell apart with gales of laughter. He laughed so hard that he physically dropped to the floor, pounding his fist on the carpet. We all stared at Jack blankly, unable to understand what caused him to fall down laughing.

I looked at Jack in astonishment. "Jack, why are you laughing?"

People around the room were staring at Jack in disbelief.

He was still laughing and tears were running down his face. Jack pointed at George and said, "Did you see what George just did?"

"Yes, I did. What was so funny about somebody bending his finger?"

Jack just sat on the floor and laughed, "NOTHING! But George did it!"

George looked at me. "Gimmie my buck."

♫

Dinah Shore

Dinah Shore, was one of the most delightful ladies in the entertainment business. For years I had admired this marvelous bundle of talent. Following her career closely, I rarely missed the opportunity to hear her sing on TV or radio. Dinah had the great gift of lyric interpretation, better than any female vocalist I had ever heard. She was a song-writer's dream come true.

Dinah and I had done a number of live shows together and were very good friends by the time her TV shows appeared. As a guest on the "Dinah Shore Show", I was given the full hostess treatment. She made it her business to become personally involved in each production, seeing that her guest's talents were featured properly.

Our first meeting on the set of her show was filled with warmth and graciousness. When I entered the stage, she broke off her conversation with one of the executive producers, turned towards me, and greeted me with outstretched arms! What an unexpected welcome! She said, "Oh Jerry, I'm so pleased to have you on the show." I was overwhelmed with her generous praises. From that point on, everything floated like fine silk.

Dinah and I had made several recordings together and I played backup to her singing on many of her Chevrolet-sponsored TV shows. We were also very good friends and anytime one of her sessions required the use of a harmonica, she insisted that it be me. One day I received a call from Dinah asking if I would like to work with her on her newest album. The title of the album was *Bouquet of Blues*. It was also the name of the song that she wanted me to do and I was prominently featured. Harry Zimmerman, the musical conductor had written a beautiful arrangement and we proceeded to rehearse. I felt a bit uncomfortable about the part that he had written for me but didn't say anything. We rehearsed it six times and each time, it seemed to lack something. Her producer bellowed over the intercom that something was not quite right musically. After several more rehearsals, she finally said, "Hold it, I know exactly what's wrong." She walked over to my music stand, picked up the music and tore it in half! She put her arm on my shoulder and said, "Jerry, just play what you feel." I did and we recorded the song in one take. Everyone loved it except her long-time conductor and music arranger, Harry Zimmerman.

Zimmerman seemed quite miffed that the part he wrote for me did not meet the producer's approval or Dinah's. But music is more than just a bunch of notes on a page - what we did, worked, and besides, it was Dinah's album! I performed again with Dinah at a huge fundraising affair in Palm Springs for her favorite charity, the Palm Springs Children's Hospital. She went on to organize and sponsor the Dinah Shore Golf Classic, raising additional millions for the Children's Hospital.

♫

Jackie Kennedy

Lieth Stevens, a very talented arranger and conductor called to tell me that he had written a score for a TV Special on the life of John F. Kennedy. The President had just been assassinated and CBS was rushing a documentary to be broadcast as quickly as possible. The show was called, "Young Man From Boston".

The harmonica was featured throughout the entire film. Shortly after its release, I received a lovely autographed photo of Jackie Kennedy in appreciation for my music. Her photo still adorns the wall of my office.

♫

Mario Lanza

I had been working as a free-lance musician for several years when I was told that I would be doing a small recording in, "The Great Caruso". That really excited me because I had not seen Mario since "Winged Victory". I appeared on the recording stage and he was on the usual high platform, rehearsing. All of the studio executives were there just to listen to the great Lanza voice. Mario was down to one hundred and sixty pounds and looked fabulous. MGM spared no expense by hiring a large section of the Los Angeles Philharmonic to augment the existing MGM orchestra. It was a glorious sound. Mario stopped during one rehearsal and proceeded to scream at Johnny Green, the conductor, plus the entire orchestra. Nobody seemed to make any effort to stop his tirade. I was embarrassed by his ugly behavior, star or no star. There were at least twenty women in the orchestra and the filthy language spewing from Mario was disgusting. Without thinking, I yelled, "Stop making an ass of yourself!" The stage became deadly silent and all eyes turned toward me. Mario jumped off the platform and came charging at me.

"Who in the hell do you think you are, talking to me like that. Get the hell off this stage right now!"

I looked at him and said, "Fine. I'm leaving. It's obvious that you don't remember an old friend. I'm Jerry Adler and I am ashamed of..."

Suddenly, tears came to his eyes and he threw his arms around me, sobbing. I tried to push him away but he refused to let go. "Oh, my God! Jerry, please forgive me for not recognizing you." He grabbed my hand and pulled me into the control room. He ordered everyone out and then sat me down and proceeded to sob his heart out, telling me that the studio was killing him, how terrible he felt, etc. We talked for over an hour while everyone in the studio was biding their time waiting for Mario to make up his mind. This display of temperament was costing the studio thousands of dollars a minute!

I finally said, "OK, you got it off your chest. Now get back out there and behave like a gentleman and apologize to everyone for your disgusting outburst." He was like a meek lamb. He embraced me again and promised that we would get together again and talk over old times. He did as he was told and did apologize for his behavior and they began rehearsing. I finally got to my small musical number and never saw Mario again.

♫

Kirk Douglas

I was to appear in a film and record the music for "The Juggler" starring Kirk Douglas. The big surprise came when the studio asked me if I would be interested in going to Israel on location. My answer was an immediate, "Yes!", and I was instructed to get my passport in order plus certain shots. They were leaving as quickly as possible but first, they had to choreograph the dance at the studio with professional dancers. As it was explained to me, I was to appear in a massive traditional Hora dance around a huge bonfire with two hundred dancers. The scene would open with a close-up of my hands holding the harmonica to my mouth. The camera would pull away as I played a slow version of a particular Hebrew melody with quickly increasing tempo, thereby starting the dancers into their traditional Hora.

I went home to pack my things and was told to await a phone call from the studio. I received a call the next day. I was told that all plans had been changed. The film would be shot in Israel but our scene would be shot on the back lot in Burbank!

♫

My studio calls were getting to be less frequent and my yearly income began to plunge dramatically. I had a family to support and the only thing that I was qualified to do was play the harmonica! I did not wish to worry Sylvia about my problem because she worked full time raising our two children, I might add that she was doing one hell of a good job. I decided to consult with my good friend, Alan Gordon. I have never taken advantage of our friendship but I needed to talk to someone with whom I could reveal many of my private thoughts. I also had tremendous respect for his insight and knew that confiding in him would not go any further.

We arranged to have lunch together and I poured out my problems. His first response startled me. "Jerry, you have one serious fault that I have been aware of for a long time. You have a habit of selling yourself short. You feel that your only talent is just in music. I disagree. Whether you know it or not, you have a wonderful writing talent. I have received enough letters from you to recognize that. Why don't you try to get into something that utilizes that imaginative head of yours?

"Like what?"

"How would you like it if I called an old friend, Earl Muntz and ask him to see you?"

♫

Earl Muntz

Earl Muntz had been a flamboyant used car dealer and had gained notoriety with a great ad campaign, using as his logo, a cartoon character of Napoleon, suggesting that he was out of his mind and was giving used cars away. Having milked the used car industry for all it was worth, he finally gave it up and started a car stereo company.

"What in the world would I do with Earl Muntz?"

"Earl has a successful car stereo business going and he needs people who can write copy regarding the constant flow of new stereo units, etc. I also understand that he is expanding into manufacturing 4 Track car stereo tapes. You would be ideal for reviewing the new tape releases."

I said, "Alan, I am extremely grateful for your confidence and your advice. However, I want to be up front with you. You know that my number one love, outside of my family, is performing. If things begin to open up, I want you to know that I will chuck any job if I know that I can get back into show business."

Alan said, "That's fair enough. However, you might find that you like what you are doing as a writer."

Alan called to set up an appointment. I went to see Muntz at his office, with much trepidation. Perhaps I had been living in a dream world for too long. If accepted, I would be put to the test. Alan had stuck his neck out for me and I was not planning to let him down.

Muntz must have been a very close friend of Alan's because he gave me a great deal of time and actually asked me what positions would interest me!

I said, "Mr. Muntz, I think that it is important that I be honest with you. This is the first job that I have ever applied for. I have been a performer my entire life and have never been exposed to answering to a boss. However, I can assure you that I will do the very best that I can."

"That's fine. I would like to call in Tod Faulkner, who is head of our Public Relations department. He will be the man that you will answer to." He placed the call and soon, a tall, nice looking gentleman with a pleasant smile, walked in. We were introduced and Muntz told Tod that he had hired me, and asked Tod to show me around and go over my job responsibilities.

I was given an office and a secretary! Tod suggested that I take a couple of days to acquaint myself with the company and its personnel and begin work the first of the week. He made me feel very comfortable and I did not sense any kind of tension. This was going to be easier and more pleasant than I had thought. The salary was pretty meager by show business standards but there seemed to be room to grow.

My first assignment was writing copy for three new car stereos that had just arrived from Japan. I was given specification sheets and was asked to describe the "wonderful" features of each model. I took the spec sheets home and studied them carefully. The following morning I began typing out my thoughts. When I had completed it, I showed it to Tod. He read it over carefully, smiled and took it right into Muntz. Muntz called me into his office and said, "Jerry, I think you are going to be an excellent asset to the company!"

I called Sylvia and told her the good news and she was ecstatic. My second call was to Alan and he was so happy for me. He wished me the best of luck and I was now on my way.

By chance, I joined the company just as they entered the new field of 4-Track stereo tapes. I was one of the first to become involved in the new product. We had added a music department and the executive in charge was responsible for making agreements with recording companies to duplicate the latest releases to 4-Track. I was the first to review the new releases, which was published in an in-house publication that was mailed to every car stereo dealer in the country. Ninety-eight percent of these tapes were Rock & Roll, which was totally foreign to me. I did a great deal of research and listening and finally knew enough to write with some semblance of authority. My reviews became so popular with the dealers and distributors, they were calling and writing in for reprints. Within a year, I became somewhat of a celebrity critic.

It was a huge challenge because I did not like the music, but of course all of my reviews had to be favorable. That is what I was being paid to do. What I had really done was to sell my integrity for the almighty buck. I was not particularly proud of myself at the time but I had a family to support.

> *I finally played this charade for as long as I could stand it...*

It became increasingly more difficult to write these reviews because R & R had a sameness that was driving me crazy. The one element that nearly pushed me over the edge was, "the beat". Everything was based on the volume of crashing drums, and the ear-splitting guitar chords.

One day, Earl (he insisted that I call him that) called me into his office. "Jerry, you have made wonderful strides. I would like you to consider becoming one of our Regional Sales Managers." I did not know the first thing about sales and was puzzled at this dramatic change. He soon cleared up the mystery. "I would still like you to continue reviewing our tapes." I was puzzled by this increase in responsibility. It also meant that I would be doing quite a bit of traveling with my regional salesmen. I accepted the challenge but worried about it all night. It finally rang a bell! I would become a figurehead Regional Sales Manager only because I had reached celebrity status as a critic. My presence in these stereo stores was meant to stimulate the sale of Muntz tapes. Each store took out ads in their local papers announcing my appearance! My assumptions were correct. The stores were jammed with people waiting to have their tapes autographed by me! I had gained unexpected notoriety and it caught me off guard. I was a professional musician and a music critic! I finally played this charade for as long as I could stand it, and told Earl that being a Regional Sales Manager was not for me. He didn't seem too surprised and immediately changed the subject. He said, "I have given much thought to placing you in charge of stereo in-store displays as well as our yearly trade show display when we attend the Consumer Electronics Show in Chicago. Would you like to tackle that?" I replied, "Earl, is there something wrong with my writing abilities that you seem determined to get me involved in other aspects of the company? I really don't know whether I am qualified. It's a huge responsibility and I have never had the experience."

"That's exactly why I think that it's for you. You will not start with any preconceived ideas. You're a very creative guy, Jerry. I can tell by the way that you write. How about giving it a shot? I will also add an extra hundred a week to your salary." I certainly liked that idea until he said, "Of course, I still want you to continue to write the reviews." Good ol' naive Adler. He did it again! It never occurred to me at the time that I was getting in way over my head.

I was off to my first Consumer Electronics Show, representing Muntz Car Stereo. We had an exceptionally large trade display which I had helped design, along with a team of electronics engineers.

I flew to Chicago in freezing February weather ahead of everyone else. I had never dealt with unions before and from what I could observe, it looked very distasteful. Arguments were common and the unions were making it nearly impossible to make any progress unless a payoff was involved.

It took approximately six hours to set up our booth. I had four carpenters, three electricians and four carpet layers. This being my first experience, I wanted everything to be perfect. Our display space was ten feet deep by one hundred and twenty-five feet long.

When it was finally completed, I stepped back to examine it. Everything seemed to be fine. I tested the various car stereos, and as I was doing that, I noticed a light was out on the display board. I twisted the bulb and it seemed to be secure. I traced the wire and discovered that it had not been plugged in. When I plugged it into the socket, I heard a gruff voice behind me. "Hey, whatcha think yer doin?"

I innocently replied, "The plug was out of the socket so I plugged it in."

"Dats da work of da lectricians. You don't touch no wires, y'unerstand?"

"I'm terribly sorry. I didn't know. I promise, it won't happen again."

"You betcher ass it won't happen again."

He walked off and I prayed that this slight infraction would not create a delay in my leaving so I could get some much needed rest. It was then 1:00 A.M.

I quickly closed my briefcase and was about to leave when a Neanderthal man drove up in an electric cart.

"Are you da guy what put the plug in da socket?"

"Yes, I guess I must plead guilty. I told the other man that I would not touch a wire again."

"Do you want electricity in your booth?"

I nervously replied, "Of course I do! You can't play stereo without electricity."

His face lit up but just for a brief second. "Oh, you're a real comic! Tell ya what. Tear your booth down and pack it up. When dat's finished, come to the electrician's desk and request an inspection. If you do as you're told, you can set it up again. OK?"

"You must be out of your mind You want me to have it torn down and packed up?"

"That's right, pal."

."Would you mind telling me why?"

"So when you come here next year, you'll remember to keep your hands off all wires."

I was furious. "I'll be damned if I'm going to tear this down."

He looked at me with amusement. "S'OK wit me. You jus won't get no electricity."

I said, "Can't I just pay a fine and let it go at that?"

"You tryin' to bribe an honest worker? Now tear it da hell down."

I realized that it was futile to argue. It was then 1:30 a.m. and I had to re-hire all of the workers and pay them double time to tear it all down and pack it up in its crates! I was furious but knew that I was fighting a losing battle. When that was finally completed at 3:30, I went to the desk and requested an inspection. The same man drove up in his little cart and gave his approval. "OK, now you can set it back up."

The workers proceeded to open the crates again and set the whole thing up once more. We were now into "golden time" which meant triple normal scale. When it was finished, I noticed that those bastards had deliberately left the same light unplugged just to see if I would dare plug it in. I went to the desk and told them about the plug. They said that they would send someone right over. Sure enough, another man arrived with a work order that I had to sign. He plugged it in. He was still there when I was about to leave. It was now 5:45 A.M. I looked at him.

"What?"

"Hey, I jus gave you real quick service! It should be worth a couple a extra bucks to you!"

I reached out and shook his hand. "Thank you sir, for your kindness."

He glared at me, turned to walk away and yelled, "You cheap sonofabitch!"

Suddenly, two men grabbed me from behind...

It was nearly 6:00 A.M. and it was semi-dark outside with a freezing rain to add to my bone-weary exhaustion. The Consumer Electronics Show was in the stockyard area in the South side of Chicago, a very rough section of town. I looked around for a cab. Suddenly, two men grabbed me from behind, pulled my raincoat down half way, pinning my arms to my sides, and proceeded to methodically beat me to a pulp. They broke my right arm in three places, fractured my jaw, broke three ribs and kicked me in the face and side. In my half-conscious stupor, I saw four blacks running toward me. I resigned myself to the fact that I was going to be killed. Frankly, all thoughts were simply a blur. To my amazement, the two men were pulled off of me and they took off! Two of the black men picked me up and steadied me on very wobbly feet. I winced when they touched my arm and ribs. I was bleeding in six or seven areas of my body. The spokesman of the four said, "Hey, man. What are you doin out here?" I tried to explain that I had just come out of the Convention Hall and was looking for a cab. He said, "You ain't going to find no cab around here! You wait here with my brothers and I'll get you a cab." In a very short time, a cab pulled up with him in it. They gently led me into the cab and told the cabby, "Take this man to the nearest emergency hospital!" I had a twenty dollar bill in my pocket but no money in my wallet. I tried to hand the money to him. He smiled and said, "Peace, brother. Take care of yourself." He refused the twenty.

When we reached the hospital, the driver rushed inside and two nurses pushed a gurney toward the cab. I was still clutching the twenty when they lifted me out of the cab and handed the driver the twenty. I was then wheeled into the hospital and do not remember much after that. They had to sedate me and I was not very coherent when I finally fell asleep.

When I awoke the next morning, I did not have any idea where I was. A nurse briefed me as much as possible. My arm was in a cast and my torso was tightly wrapped. I slowly began to recall the events of the night before. I felt that I knew who had mugged me but of course, I did not have proof. They did not try to rob me of my wallet or watch but apparently just wanted to beat me up. I filed a police report which was a useless study in futility. I was convinced that it was the work of someone from the electricians union but, of course, I did not have any proof.

I decided to call all of the Chicago papers to get them to print the story. I felt that it needed to be told because, frankly, I felt as guilty as anyone. I had simply assumed that the four men were there to add to my problems. I was terribly ashamed. I wanted so much for that story to appear in print but strangely, not one paper carried it!

I was in the hospital for two days. Earl was notified because he and his staff had already arrived in Chicago. Earl and Tod visited me along with two other salesmen. Earl told me that as soon as the hospital was ready to discharge me, to get on a plane and go home.

> *I remained at home...Two days later, I suffered a heart attack.*

I remained at home for one week and, despite Sylvia's objections, I went back to work. Two days later, I suffered a heart attack. One of the salesmen rushed me to my doctor. The office called Sylvia and she was waiting for me at the doctor's office. Of course, Sylvia was very worried but fortunately, the heart attack was mild. The doctor stabilized me and I rested for about an hour while he took an EKG. When the doctor checked the results, he said that it would be safe for me to return home but I should remain at home for at least ten days. Before Sylvia and I left the hospital, the doctor questioned me about my daily responsibilities at work. After I had described everything in detail, he became visibly concerned.

He said, "Jerry, it appears that you have a death wish! You are working a schedule that sounds like the work of three men. I don't wish to offend you but if you do not change your schedule drastically, I prefer that you find yourself another doctor. I cannot assume such a responsibility if you continue at this pace."

Sylvia said, "I want you to quit your job and I want you to do it NOW!"

"For God sake, Syl. I'm fifty years old! Who will hire me?"

"We'll discuss that when we get home."

Several days later, we had a serious discussion about our future. Sylvia was silent for a long time before she finally said, "Why don't you go back to doing what you enjoy most? What about show business?"

"Show business! There isn't any show business left!"

"Have you ever considered cruise ships?"

"I don't know anyone who books cruise ships."

Sylvia opened the Sunday Times travel section and showed me a complete list of cruise lines, their addresses and phone numbers.

Sylvia said, "Why don't you write to as many as you can and send them a resume. You're bound to hear from at least one!"

Jerry, his parents & his dog, Pal.

Jerry, age 10

Jerry's Mother

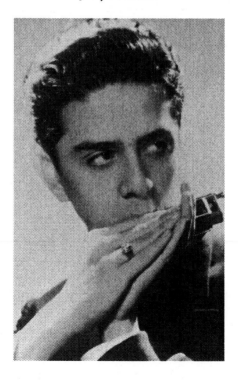

Jerry at 17

Jerry and Sylvia

Son, Michael

Daughter, Susan

Jerry and Larry with Margaret O'Brien on
MGM on set of "Music for Millions."

James Stewart on set of "Pot Of Gold"

Nawabzada Labal Muhammed Khan "James"

Tyrone Power and Jerry- WW II photo on the island of Saipan.

Jerry, Rita Hayworth, Dick Foran

Charles Laughton

Jerry and Sylvia, Mr. and Mrs. Cary Grant

Jean and Jerry

Cary Grant

Jackie Kennedy

(top row) Phil Regan, Desi Arnaz, Kay Kyser, Jerry
(bottom row) Jinny Sims, Lucille Ball, Marlene Dietrich, Linda Darnell

Vivian Leigh

Life After Fifty

On Stage and On Board

Sylvia was right on target. I heard from one cruise ship line. It was the Pacific Far East Line, based in San Francisco. They owned two ships: the Monterey and the Mariposa. I received a call from the head of the entertainment department, asking if I would be interested in taking a cruise from Honolulu to Los Angeles. I was thrilled! I asked him about my fee and he replied, "We don't pay any fee to an entertainer on their first cruise. This is like an audition and you get a free cruise with a nice passenger cabin."

This was not my idea of a blossoming profession. I thanked him for his call and politely said, "I'm sorry but that would not be acceptable."

"That's OK. However, if you change your mind, please get back to me."

We hung up and I then explained the conditions to Sylvia. She smiled knowingly and said, "Take it."

I replied, "Are you crazy? What do I do about making a living?"

"Take it." She repeated. "I have enough confidence in you to know that it will soon begin to pay off."

"I'm grateful for your confidence but you must remember, I have been away from show business for a long time. I simply don't know if I've still got it."

Sylvia smiled and simply pointed to the phone. Against my better judgment, I called back. He seemed pleased and said, "When can you leave?"

"When do you want me?"

"How about joining the Monterey in Honolulu, a week from this Sunday?"

"Fine. When will you send me my airline ticket?"

"That's up to you. We don't provide transportation to the ship."

I asked him to hold for a moment. I covered the phone mouthpiece. "He wants me to pay my own air fare!"

Sylvia said, "Do it."

I reluctantly accepted and I was told to report to the Monterey on the specified date.

I called Earl Muntz and told him that I had to resign. He seemed disappointed but added that there would always be a job waiting for me if I ever changed my mind. He wished me luck and I was back in show business.

♫

The Monterey

I arrived in Honolulu thinking that someone from the ship would meet me. Nobody. I took a cab and discovered that we were fairly close to the docks. When the Monterey came into view, I became excited. I had never been aboard a cruise ship and was looking forward to a new and exciting adventure. It was 1972 and the cruise business was at its peak.

I checked in at the reception desk and was shown to my cabin. The accommodations were pleasant with an outside double cabin, a comfortable bed, desk, couch plus a large manila envelope containing a letter of welcome from the Cruise Director and several sheets of information regarding time of performance, rehearsal, etc. I was surprised to learn that I was only scheduled to do two, forty-minute shows for the trip to Los Angeles.

This was the only time in my career that I was nervous. It had nothing to do with my upcoming performance. My anxiety was the horrible thought of failing, which meant that I would lose this exciting new career before it ever got off the ground. Fortunately, my concern was unfounded. The audiences could not have been better. They were extremely generous in their response and my show ended with a rousing standing ovation! The audience also demanded that I play more!

The main ballroom was packed for my second show and some of the passengers were upset because they could not get in! I was riding on a cloud and all of the credit goes to my wife who had the foresight to recognize the potential. Not for what the cruise business had to offer me but what I had to offer the cruise business. In my excitement, I threw financial caution to the wind and placed a radio call to Sylvia from the ship which cost me fifteen dollars per minute! She was thrilled that I had called and so pleased that I had left such a good impression. My phone bill came to sixty-five dollars but it was the most gratifying call that I had ever made.

> *...mingling with the audience after a performance...*
> *was an amazing experience...*

As an entertainer performing on land, the fulfillment is certainly there. However, the added dimension of mingling with the audience after a performance was an amazing experience that shot my ego heavenward.

We entertainers are show-offs. The secret, of course, is to keep it in perspective and never take yourself that seriously. I was invited to a private cocktail party aboard ship and the host and hostess treated me as the honored guest! I had found a new home but it would not mean a thing without my wife by my side.

Evaluation reports by passengers as well as individual reports from the Captain and the Cruise Director are sent ahead to the office in San Francisco. By the time that we docked in Los Angeles, all of the reports were in. The Entertainment Director flew to Los Angeles to board the ship when we arrived. He smiled and shook my hand warmly. "Congratulations, I understand that you did very well. How would you like to do a regular cruise for us?"

I replied, "I would love to but not at these prices."

He laughed and said, "Don't worry. This time, you will be paid. On the next cruise, you will receive three hundred dollars a week." I was shocked. I said to myself, My God, is that all they pay on cruise ships? I told him that he would be hearing from me.

Sylvia was at the dock to meet me and I described everything to her as we drove home. I also told her what they had offered me to do a complete cruise.

Sylvia said, "Take it."

"Is that all you can say is, Take it?"

"I have told you before that I have a strong intuition about the cruise business and I'm positive that the right salary will come to you in a short time."

I said, "That's fine, but what about you? I'm not going to go chasing all over the world and leave you and the kids at home!"

"Don't worry about us for now. Get yourself established with a good reputation and things will work out fine."

I waited a few days and thought about our future and what the cruise business had to offer. I did not have the slightest idea of what a decent salary was in that business. I wanted to avoid working through agents in the beginning so I began making phone calls to other performers who had worked on cruise ships. I found out that they were earning from four to five hundred a week which, to me, was still a pretty dismal fee.

I decided to call Pacific Far East and make a proposal without mentioning it to Sylvia. I reached the Entertainment Director, on the phone.

I said, "I have a counter proposal to make. I will work a cruise for five hundred dollars per week with two conditions. One, that I can bring my wife along as my guest and two, that your company pays for our transportation to and from the ship."

He began to laugh loudly and said, "Jerry, that is totally out of the question. Nobody pays that kind of money to an entertainer."

"Well, there's always a first time. Please call me if you change your mind."

I hung up feeling very proud of myself but I had a gnawing feeling that I had cut my own throat.

Three hours later, Bob called me back. "OK, I now have a counter offer for you. We will pay you four hundred dollars and will pay your transportation to and from the ship but we cannot pay for your wife's air fare."

I said, "I'll tell you what I'll do. I will pay for my wife's air fare but I want five hundred a week."

He paused for a few moments and said, "You've got yourself a deal."

I walked into the kitchen to tell Sylvia what I had done and she was overjoyed and threw her arms around me. She was very excited about the prospects of taking a cruise but, being an introvert, she felt terribly insecure. She did not have any problem advising me what to do when it was necessary. When it came to her own decisions, she became a basket case. "What will I wear? How much should I take? Will they like me? Will I fit in?" It is the height of irony that she immediately became the best asset that I could have had at my side. The passengers who met her, without exception, were quickly impressed by her warmth, charm and sincerity. The senior officers soon noticed the tremendous asset that they had in me as well as my wife on board. The biggest problem was convincing Sylvia!

One major difficulty was finding someone to work as a live-in helper to take care of our children. They weren't exactly children by then. Michael was 17 and Susan 16. Although our children insisted that they did not need a "nanny", Sylvia knew that they were not dependable enough to shift for themselves. Sylvia and I also felt that they needed an authority figure to maintain peace and dependability on a daily basis. We were fortunate enough to find an absolute gem and she remained with us for a number of years.

♫

I performed on my first three month World Cruise aboard the S.S. Monterey in July 1972. It was a momentous occasion because it was the first cruise ship to be granted permission to sail into Chinese waters as well as dock at their ports. The passengers were excited because it was unexpected. We had set sail for our world tour, with the first stop being Honolulu. Then it was on to Guam, followed by Hong Kong. We expected to visit Japan next. However, we received word through the ship's agent in Hong Kong that China had finally granted us permission to visit them. We had to call a meeting of all passengers and present the change of itinerary for their approval. It necessitated canceling Japan for China. They all agreed that it would be an adventure unparalleled in the history of cruise ships. However, there was one catch. The passengers had to agree in writing to disembark in Shanghai for three days and stay at their hotels. Again, all passengers excitedly agreed.

♫

Mao Tse Tung

The Captain then called a special meeting of the entertainment staff because Chairman Mao Tse Tung and his top government staff were to be invited to a special dinner aboard ship. A show had to be prepared to entertain them and a list of entertainers and their qualifications had to be submitted to the Chinese government for their approval. We had singers, dancers, comedians, orchestra and me. We then had to await their approval. We received an immediate reply saying that they were not interested in singers, dancers and comedians. However, they were interested in the orchestra and were enthusiastic about the harmonica player because they had recently opened a harmonica factory in Shanghai.

Our entertainers were not disappointed because they were all looking forward to time off to explore the exotic city of Shanghai. Our musicians were equally disappointed but they were stuck. I had mixed feelings but I resigned myself to the assignment. I had to carefully choose my program. After all, I was the only solo performer.

We finally docked in Shanghai Harbor and there was much ceremonial hoopla with the spreading out of red carpets, flower presentations, lots of bowing and hand shaking. A huge Chinese band played Chinese marching songs under a tremendous red banner with white lettering exclaiming "WELCOME TO S.S. MONTEREY - FIRST VISIT OF ANY PASSENGER SHIP TO CHINA." There were hordes of buses awaiting the passengers to be taken to the various hotels. Once the passengers had departed, everything calmed down considerably.

Promptly at 6:00 pm, the Captain was at the top of the gangway to greet Chairman Mao and his entourage of approximately forty people. Seventy-percent men and thirty-percent women. They were first given a tour of the ship and then escorted to the dining room. Our orchestra was in place and began playing. The ship had arranged three long tables to accommodate our guests. The menu featured broiled lobster, chicken Kiev, etc. plus a chocolate desert to die for. There were also countless bottles of gin, scotch and vodka on each table. I'm sure the Captain's heart was in the right place but the rich food plus the continuous flow of booze caused an immediate disaster. Everyone at their table quickly became intoxicated and the evening suddenly turned into a bunch of Chinese yelling, throwing up and passing out drunk. AND THIS WAS PRI0R TO MY SHOW!

I informed the Captain that it was hopeless for me to even attempt to perform. He looked at me imploringly and said with disgust, "Just cut the show to two numbers. They won't know the difference." And that is exactly what I did. The odor was unbearable and the poor waiters were fighting a losing battle to clean up the mess.

"The Chairman wants you to give him your harmonica."

I began to leave when the Chief Purser called me back.. He said, "The Captain wants to see you." I approached the Captain, "Jerry, I've got a serious problem and I need your help. The Chairman wants you to give him your harmonica." I stared at the Captain, "So what! He's not getting my harmonica, and that's final!" He pleaded, "Don't you have an old one in your cabin that you'd be willing to part with? Just name your price. The company will pay it." I said, "I'm sorry, Captain but I am not giving one of my harmonicas to that drunken slob!" Again he began to plead. He said that a lot depended on this first visit for future visits. I did give it some thought and suddenly realized that I did have a harmonica that was useless to me. I said, "I may be sorry for this but I think I have one." He got quite excited and said, "Whatever you charge will be OK." I replied, "Captain, I'm not charging for this but . . . . YOU OWE ME! He smiled, "Absolutely! I won't forget this."

I went to my cabin, brought the harmonica back and said, "Here, give it to him." He said, "Oh no, he wants you to give it to him!" I took it and walked toward the center of the floor. Mao stood up and nearly fell over. He righted himself and staggered to the microphone. I handed the harmonica to him. He gave me a toothy smile, took it, and so help me, this drunken idiot proceeded to play, *You Are My Sunshine*. I was offended by the fact that his rendition was received with much more enthusiasm than my act!

♬

Pacific Far East Line

I joined the Pacific Far East Line at the end of 1972 and remained with PFE for two years, performing eight to ten cruises a year. By the end of that period, my salary increased to one thousand dollars per week. Word about me quickly spread throughout the industry and I began receiving offers from competing lines with salary offers far exceeding PFE. Again, Sylvia was right in more ways than one. Through the years, I have worked for Sitmar, Royal Viking, Holland-America, Cunard, Crystal Harmony, Royal Caribbean and a few of the other leading cruise companies.

♬

During the latter part of my second year with PFE, a note was slipped under our cabin door. It read, "If you perform this evening, you die!" It was signed with a skull and crossbones. I brushed the whole thing off as someone trying to be "cute". Sylvia didn't read much humor into the note. She quickly took it to the Cruise Director and in a short period of time, it found its way to the Captain. I was summoned to his quarters and I could see immediately that he did not consider this a frivolous matter. He looked at me with deep concern. "We could have a maniacal nut aboard. As far as I'm concerned, you are not obligated to do the show."

I responded politely, "Captain, I do appreciate your concern but I honestly think that this was a childish prank and I refuse to be intimidated."

He said, "Well, the decision is yours to make. However, if you decide to do the show, I will post armed guards at both entrances to the ballroom."

"Mr. Adler, you have ignored my warning. You die tomorrow."

He did post the guards, I did my show. After the show, we returned to our cabin and found another note. "Mr. Adler, you have ignored my warning. You die tomorrow."

The Captain was again notified and he immediately assigned guards to us on a twenty-four hour basis! He also called the FBI in San Francisco. We were due to arrive there the next morning. They told the Captain that they would come aboard with the pilot boat and that all passengers were forbidden to leave the ship until they were cleared.

The FBI showed up with a handwriting expert. All of the passenger tickets were handed over to the FBI and, in an amazingly short period of time, the culprit was discovered by examining the handwriting on their tickets. It was a young lady in her twenties who was traveling with her parents. She explained that she had watched a film in the ship's theater showing a segment of Hawaii Five-O. The episode starred Bobby Darin as an entertainer aboard a cruise ship. His life was threatened in the same manner. She thought that it would be fun if she did the same thing to me! She continually repeated, "It was just a joke!"

Against screaming protests by her parents, she was taken into custody. We were never told whether she was prosecuted.

♫

Royal Viking Star

The following is just one of many strange anecdotes that I will be relating regarding cruise ships. Identical twin sisters in their eighties were sharing a table for two aboard the Royal Viking Star. Neither had ever been married and had lived together, conducting their lives as one. Every inch of clothing was identical including jewelry. Their general behavior was equally strange. Before taking their daily walks around the deck, they would first concentrate on their feet to be sure that they both stepped off on the same foot. When they ate, their forks went to their mouths at the same time and each forkful contained the same amount of food. When they were served coffee, the same thing happened. When they were ready to leave the dining room, their waiters were instructed to pull their chairs back at the same time and they arose together and walked out, side by side. They never spoke to anyone other than each other and were completely oblivious to the stares.

♫

The maitre d' had asked if I would be good enough to share a table for four. It was occupied by one couple plus a charming, elderly widow. The couple had the personality of two gold fish that had died in a fish tank. My dinner partner was very pleasant but I could see immediately that the couple was making her very uneasy. I did my best to strike up a friendly conversation without success. I could see why the maitre d' was using me as a buffer for the poor lady traveling alone.

When the main course was served, the wife would sniff her food and in a loud, obnoxious voice, say "I can't eat this! Take it away and bring me something else!" When the waiter returned with a different dish, the same thing happened. He was ready to destroy the old bitch.

One evening, the waiter had brought what she had ordered. She sniffed it, picked up the plate and turned it upside down on the tablecloth. The waiter finally complained to the head waiter. He came over, and politely as possible, told the lady that, in the future, she would not be permitted in the dining room and all of her meals would be served in her cabin. My table partner and I had two pleasant dinners together but on the third night, the couple returned. From that point on, she was a pussycat. During this entire episode, the husband remained silent.

♫

> *An elderly lady…was going through the drawers of my cabin!*

I had a habit, when traveling alone, to leave my cabin door unlocked. It was just a habit but as it turned out, a bad habit. It was 2:00 A.M. when I was suddenly awakened by all of my lights being turned on. An elderly lady, wearing a two piece suit and carrying a shoulder bag, was going through the drawers of my cabin!

I sat up and said, "Excuse me. Would you mind telling me what you're doing?"

"I'm looking for the blue thread that leads me to the Royal Viking."

"Blue thread?"

"I just told you. The blue thread that leads me to the Royal Viking."

I quickly realized that I was dealing with a lady that was not playing with a full deck.

"I'm sorry, but they removed it this evening."

"Removed it? Where did they take it?"

"It was taken to the reception desk."

"How very kind of you. Can you direct me to the reception desk?"

"Yes, you go out through that door, turn left and walk straight down the hallway. You can't miss it."

"Thank you so much. You have been very kind."

She left quietly and I sat on the edge of my bed wondering whether it was all a dream. They had served a Mexican dinner that night and I thought that the food had played a few tricks on me but was not convinced about anything, so I quickly got into some clothes and went to the reception desk. Yep, there she was, talking to the terrified girl on night duty. The poor girl was trembling from the woman's babbling. I cleared my throat and the woman turned to me. "Oh, hello, young man." She then pointed to a blank wall. "Did you see that?"

"See what?"

"Those strange things coming out of the wall. Aren't they ugly?"

I agreed that they were pretty ugly. I asked her to be seated on a nearby couch and said that I would try to find the blue thread for her.

"Oh, you are such a delightful, young man. Remind me to give you a tip."

I told the receptionist to call the doctor.

She replied, "No, he's sleeping."

"So was I!" Call the doctor !"

She finally phoned the doctor and I took the receiver. I quietly explained the situation and suggested that he come immediately with something to knock the lady out. He arrived a few minutes later carrying his black bag. When the lady saw the bag, she screamed loud enough to awaken every passenger on the ship. I asked the doctor to quickly give her a shot. I sat with her and calmed her down while the doctor was preparing the needle. I told her that we had ordered a complete search of the ship for her blue thread. It seemed to have a calming influence and while I held her attention, the doctor quickly gave her the shot. Within seconds, she was out cold. The Captain was notified and when he arrived, he went through the lady's shoulder bag and found her key plus a small address book. She was identified as Mrs. Harrison Holbrook of Los Angeles. The computer brought up her address and phone number plus her next of kin which was her daughter.

The Captain said, "Jerry, I think that you should call her daughter."

I was shocked. "Why me?"

"Well, you seem to have been involved from the beginning and I feel that you can explain it better to her daughter."

"OK, but what should I say?"

"We will be in Tahiti in three days. Call her daughter and explain everything and suggest to her that she fly to Tahiti to pick up her mother."

"Why don't we wait until morning?"

"No, I think it's best that you do it now."

The Captain called the radio room and authorized my call. I reached the daughter immediately and quickly assured her that her mother was fine. I explained everything and told her what the Captain had suggested. She agreed and said that she would put her own daughter on the next flight to Tahiti.

When the lady awoke in the infirmary the following morning, she was completely normal and had recalled everything that had happened on the previous night! The doctor finally found a small patch hidden under the lobe of her left ear to prevent seasickness. She obviously had experienced an allergic reaction. The granddaughter was waiting at the pier and the lady left but not before hugging me and thanking me for my help. She also remembered that she had promised me a tip. She reached in her purse and handed me fifty cents!

Brazilian Nightmare
Jane Cullen

I call this, The Brazilian Nightmare. I had been aboard the Royal Viking Sea for several weeks and we were about to arrive at one of the most beautiful cities in the world, Rio de Janeiro. It was the end of my contract and I was scheduled to fly home to Los Angeles via Miami, on Varig Airlines. It was not a scheduled disembarkation for passengers because the cruise was continuing to other ports. One passenger left at the same time simply because she was tired of cruising and wanted to go home. Her name was Jane Cullen and I was grateful to have someone from the ship fly to Miami on the same flight. She turned out to be great company!

Whenever employees leave a ship, they are always met by the ship's local agent who has the responsibility to take care of the usual needs like getting them to the airport. They are also responsible for passengers who happen to be leaving.

I had not met Jane during the cruise but we became acquainted very quickly. The agent helped her off with her luggage and then said to me, "Are you Mr. Adler?" I said, "Yes, I am."

"Are you going to the airport with Mrs. Cullen? Because if you are, please give me fifty dollars." I asked, "Why?"

"You want to get to the airport, don't you?"

"What's that got to do with it?"

"Never mind, Just give me fifty dollars."

I went to the Purser's office and told him what the agent wanted.

"What's this all about?"

"If you intend to make your flight, you had better give him the money."

On the Royal Viking Line, all employees are paid in cash. This was common knowledge to the ship's agents.

I walked back to the gangway and handed the creep fifty dollars.

We walked down the gangway and, to compound the unpleasant situation, it was raining. We then headed to the waiting taxi. The agent turned to me after Jane was safely in the cab and said, "Do you want to take the taxi with Mrs. Cullen?"

I replied, "Yes, I certainly do."

"Give me fifty dollars."

"I just gave you fifty dollars!"

"I want fifty more."

I looked at my watch and realized that valuable time was being wasted.

I gave him an additional fifty.

I had now doled out one hundred bucks to this thief and I had not left the dock!

As I entered the taxi. another man joined the agent in the front seat. He was a huge, barrel-chested gorilla with a crew cut and he remained silent during the entire trip to the airport. We were now on our way, driving along a wide, congested highway when the taxi suddenly had a blowout! All of the luggage had to be removed in the pouring rain, another taxi was hailed and then the luggage had to be loaded into the second cab. We were all drenched including our luggage. The two men loaded Jane's luggage and the agent said, "If you want this taxi, you will have to give me another fifty dollars!" I was furious but thought better than to argue the point, and gave him another fifty! Jane looked completely bewildered. Nobody asked her for a dime! She had witnessed the entire procedure but I just shrugged my shoulders and hoped that we had seen the last of this fiasco.

We finally arrived at the airport. The men removed Jane's luggage and again he turned to me. I said, "You're not going to ask what I think, are you?" Without a shred of emotion, he said, "You want your luggage, give me fifty dollars." I handed it to him and reached out to shake his hand. The sonofabitch had held me for ransom for TWO hundred dollars! He suddenly became a wind up toy. "Give me another fifty dollars."

"You can go straight to hell! I'm not giving you anymore money!"

"You want to board the plane, don't you?"

I gave him another fifty dollars and he finally disappeared. The other man, who looked as if he could break me in half with a stare, said, "You give me feefty dollah!" I shouted, "Go suck a worm, you miserable crook!" His face became a hideous mask and he clenched his fists, ready to strike. I held up my hand. "OK, ok Here's your Goddamned feefty dollahs!"

Jane and I were finally seated safely on the plane and I told her that I would scream my bloody head off to Royal Viking to get my money back.

Jane said, "If you need a witness, have them phone me." I thanked her and we then settled down for a nice flight to Miami.

As soon as I arrived home, I called Royal Viking and began to explain my hideous experience to Brian Beaton, when I was interrupted by loud laughter. I said, "Brian, you're a nice man but you do have a warped sense of humor. What in the hell is so funny?" Brian said, "Tell me what you paid him and we'll send you a check."

"Are you suggesting that you knew about this scam all the time?"

"Oh, sure. It happens to every employee who gets off in Brazil. The entire country is run by the Mafia. We pay dearly for the privilege of docking our ship in Rio. Had I warned you in advance, you would have refused to take the cruise.'"

♬

The SS Rotterdam

Whenever I board a ship, I bring my cassette tapes to be sold in the gift shop. Sylvia and I were aboard the S.S. Rotterdam together for a portion of the World Cruise. We joined the ship in Los Angeles and were scheduled to disembark in Fiji and fly home. I had performed my final show before arriving in Fiji. The following morning, a gentleman with whom I had sailed with many times before approached me and seemed disturbed. "You know, Jerry. I'm very upset."

"What are you upset about?"

"I saw your show last night and decided to bring my portable tape recorder with me and record it. When I played it in my cabin, it sounded so distorted that I could hardly hear you."

"You know, the gift shop sells my cassettes. Why don't you buy one of them?"

He looked at me in horror. "Did you see what they're asking for those tapes?"

"They are ten bucks, you cheap bastard! That's why you can afford to take so many World Cruises." Fortunately, we knew each other well enough for me to talk to him that way. The man was taking his twenty-third World Cruise at a cost of $75,000 per cruise!

♪

The Royal Viking Star

> *I spent every waking hour on my needlepoint!*

Barbara Mann, the wife of Cruise Director, Derek Mann, taught needlepoint aboard the Royal Viking Star. I had been looking for a hobby to occupy the many hours that I spent aboard ship when not performing. It was rare that I worked on cruises without Sylvia by my side. The few times that I did go alone, I found that time really dragged between performances, so I decided to take up a shipboard hobby, needlepoint. I enrolled in the beginner's class conducted by Derek's wife, and she was an excellent teacher. She taught me so well that it became a passion. I spent every waking hour working on my needlepoint! I have made dozens of them, some being quite intricate and I must admit that I am very proud of some of them. I usually give them away to friends as gifts because I no longer have any wall space to display them. I confess that since purchasing my computer, needlepoint has taken a back seat but I still take needlepoint with me when I take infrequent cruises. I say infrequent, because I have reached an age where joining a ship half way around the world or leaving them in far off lands has become a physical hardship. In time, my expertise in needlepoint was well-known and admired by the passengers. One evening, while working on my needlepoint on deck, the following happened:

Whenever I perform a show, I never eat dinner but wait until the midnight buffet to have some fruit and coffee. I was standing in line with the passengers and a fairly attractive lady was in front of me with a teen-age boy. She said, "Aren't you Mr. Adler?" I said that I was and she told me how much she had enjoyed the show. I politely thanked her and she said, "Are you planning to sit with anyone in particular? If not, would you care to join us?" I thanked her and we found a table nearby. The moment that we sat down, the young man said, "Mom, I'm going to the cabin to change. I want to go to the Disco." Off he went leaving his mother and me sitting opposite each other. We were due to end the cruise in Los Angeles the following morning.

She said, "Tell me something. Are there any eligible bachelors aboard?"

I was a bit shocked at the question, considering that we were concluding the cruise the following morning at 8:00 A.M.

I said, "I'm sorry but I don't have any idea."

"Oh, that's too bad. I just buried my third husband and I'm now looking for my fourth."

She said it so casually that it sounded as if she was looking for a fourth to play bridge.

"I wish that I could help you but I can't. I'm terribly sorry."

She paused for a few moments. "What are you doing tonight?"

Keep in mind that it is now 1:30 A.M. I realized that I was dealing with a very weird lady. However, I did not wish to offend her.

I said, "Why do you ask?"

"I just thought that you would like to come to my cabin with me."

I had to do some quick thinking and did not enjoy being placed on such a spot. I finally said, "It sounds like a very attractive offer but unfortunately, I can't make it."

She looked disappointed. "What could be so important?"

I placed my pinkie finger to the outside corner of my right eye and said, "I must finish my needlepoint before we arrive in Los Angeles."

She quickly disappeared from the table, never to be seen again.

S.S. Prinsendam

The Holland-America ship, S.S. Prinsendam was always one of my favorites. It was small, with a capacity of three hundred and twenty passengers. A five star ship from stem to stern. We were cruising the Southwest Pacific with a delightful series of stops in some of the most exotic and mysterious islands of Indonesia. One of them was the Island of Nias. This is probably the most primitive and the least visited of the many Indonesian islands. Due to the shallow waters that surround the island, very few ships can approach it without facing the danger of running aground. We managed to get in close enough to drop anchor and transport our passengers to the dock by tender.

♫

Indonesia, Island of Nias

The natives were probably as excited about seeing us as we were at seeing them. All of their supplies are transported to the island by fishing boats and canoes. Nias boasted one village which sat elegantly atop a steep mountain. To reach the village, it was necessary to be transported by ancient, open trucks straight up a one lane dirt road. I was wearing nothing but shorts and sneakers with my camera hanging from my neck. As we started climbing the hill, I said to the driver, "I was told that you have many crocodiles here."

"Oh, yes sar. Many crocodiles. They are in jungle on each side of this road, sar."

"Will you please stop when we are about half way up, and let me off?"

He looked frightened. "Why you want to get off here, sar?"

"I want to take some pictures of the crocodiles."

"Sar! Is very dangerous you go into jungle!"

"Don't worry, I'll be careful."

The passengers aboard the truck tried to dissuade me from making, what they all considered to be, a very foolish move. God, knows, I certainly was not dressed for the occasion. No shirt to protect me from the scorching sun nor insect repellent. The driver was only concerned about one thing. He was astounded that I was not carrying a gun! I insisted that I would be OK so he reluctantly stopped and I got off and waved to them as they continued up the mountain.

I proceeded into the jungle quickly and found myself ankle deep in swamp. As I continued further into the jungle, it suddenly became quite dark due to the high trees and tall undergrowth that obliterated most of the open sky. I tried to keep track of my direction but was ill-prepared to do it properly. I used the corner of my camera to force a cut into the trees, hoping that it would be sufficient.

I don't know how long I forced my way through the jungle but after approximately fifteen minutes of it, I realized how foolish I was not to bring additional articles for my own protection. I finally came to a large clearing and was startled to see a monstrous crocodile resting on a rock. It appeared to be sleeping but I was not about to find out. I quietly set my camera and snapped a couple of shots. The click startled the crocodile and it slowly raised itself on all fours, turned its ugly head toward me and I began to run. I wasn't exactly running. I was sloshing through the swamp which definitely impeded my attempt at speed. I could hear thrashing behind me and I did not dare turn to see if it was the croc. I was in a complete state of terror and did not have the slightest idea if I was running in the right direction. My clever idea of marking the trees was forgotten.

In my hysteria, I remembered someone telling me that a crocodile will not chase anything into an open area so all I could do was pray that I would come to the open road in time. I was running out of breath and afraid that I was about to meet a horrible death! Without warning, I broke out of the jungle to the open road. When I reached it, I continued running down the hill and turned to see if I was being chased. Thank God, he remained in the jungle! I fell down in the middle of the road, exhausted. All I could think of at the time was the truck. I prayed that it would appear soon. A few minutes later, the same truck was coming down the hill and I gratefully jumped aboard.

I must have been a dreadful sight with my body covered with mud and my legs bleeding from brushing against the sharp branches in the swamp.

The driver said, "Sar, did you really go into the jungle?"

I breathlessly described my experience and the driver said, "Sar, you not see snakes in swamp?"

"Snakes! What kind of snakes?"

"Sar, many cobras in jungle swamp!"

I didn't see one cobra. It would have made a great shot.

I was anxious to see the village of Nias before the ship was scheduled to leave. We returned to the ship and I took a much needed shower and dressed properly, wearing a shirt and boarded a truck with other passengers to the top of the mountain. The sight that greeted us was a magnificent panorama of a primitive village and its people. The men carried spears and wore loin cloth and their bodies were painted in various bright colors and all had beards. The women wore exotic designs of batik material and most of the children were totally nude.

The men of the tribe put on an exciting display of rock jumping and some of it was breathtaking. The point of it was that a man would take a running start, leap on top of a high rock and fly as far out as possible. Others tried to beat the competitor by running up higher rocks and flying through the air like birds. These were gentle, friendly people who went all out to please us. Nobody begged and nobody tried to sell us anything. I had the foresight to bring along some staples from the ship such as soap, tooth brushes, skin cream and cigarettes to distribute.

Their houses were typically thatched roof structures built on ten foot high bamboo poles, which, I was told were to keep the rats away. They used huge palm leaves for cooking inside their huts in a large hole in the middle of the floor. Roasted pig and crocodile meat was their delicacy but they also had an abundance of poultry that walked freely throughout the village. I became friendly with one family and they invited me to join them for a feast in their hut. They set up a ladder for me to climb and the inside was charming, with decorations of heads carved in stone plus many flowers. The women roasted a pig and it was delicious. They were extremely pleased with my compliments and then I presented them with my booty. They were too startled to utter a sound. They hesitantly touched all of the items but the cigarettes were immediately confiscated by the men. I had to explain in sign language what the other items represented and they giggled joyously and constantly bowed in appreciation.

I promised that on my next trip to Nias, I would bring them a bolt of Batik from Bali for the ladies. They were overwhelmed with joy and some began to cry. The chief of the hut presented me with some stone carvings. In sign language, I asked how they were able to get drinking water. They showed me a most intricate series of bamboo poles that had been cut in half the long way, forming a gutter effect. They were uniquely tied together in various stages of height and angles which caught the water running down from the mountain and directed to every hut in the village. An engineering miracle.

We were in Indonesia and had visited Bali and Sumatra. I remembered to purchase a bolt of Batik material because we were scheduled to visit Nias once again and I wanted to keep my promise to my lovely hosts. Our last stop in Indonesia was Nias, and I was very excited about the reunion with my friends at the top of the mountain. The bolt of Batik was fairly heavy but I managed to get it loaded onto the truck. I explained to the passengers on the truck about my last visit and my promise to bring back the Batik to this particular family. They were fascinated and wanted to see me present it to them. I told them that it might not be a good idea because I wanted to avoid it becoming a spectacle. They were kind enough to respect my wishes.

We arrived at the village and it felt as if I had never left. I spotted my host immediately and proudly carried the Batik to his hut. Practically everyone in the village surrounded me in excited delight. The chief's wife came out of the hut and when she saw me holding the Batik, she burst into tears. She gently lowered herself to the ground and with tears still rolling down her cheeks, she bowed and knelt to the ground. I motioned to the chief to ask her to stand up. I laid the Batik at her feet and bowed. Two of her daughters carried the bolt of material up the ladder and I was invited to join the family in the hut. The girls began preparing a feast in my honor. This time, it was baked fish with sweet potatoes and wild rice. The gentleness of these primitive people was so touching that I was reluctant to leave. They presented me with additional gifts and the chief's wife conveyed to me that she wished to make a dress for my wife. I managed to get my message across that the material was for her and her family.

It was now time to depart and return to the ship. I climbed down the ladder and was about to shake hands with the chief and bow to his wife and children when the chief gently placed his hand on my shoulder urging me to wait. I didn't know what he meant until four young boys appeared carrying a chair mounted on two bamboo poles. They motioned for me to get into the chair which I did. I was then lifted up and carried to the truck while most of the women in the village danced in a circle as we moved forward. The sight of me being carried left quite an impression on the passengers sitting in the truck. I was then lowered to the ground and bid farewell to all of the villagers. Especially my good friends. I miss them very much.

♫

> *…Holland America Line…had been negotiating with the Chinese government for three years…*

I had been to Mainland China one time before. The first was aboard the Monterey. Cruise ships were not allowed into Chinese waters as mentioned previously noting our performance for Mao Tse-Tung. This time Holland-America Line, owners of the Prinsendam, had been negotiating with the Chinese government for three years for permission to visit their ports. The ship received a Telex from the Holland-America office that they had reached an agreement with China. Due to the fact that we were so close to China, we received permission to sail to Shanghai. However, it created a complication. We had been scheduled to visit two ports in Japan. To allow us time to visit China, we had to eliminate Japan from our schedule once again. That necessitated a vote by all of the passengers and it had to be one hundred percent in favor of China or we would not be able to go. The Captain called a special meeting in the ballroom and the vote was taken. It was fortunate that everyone agreed that this could be a historical breakthrough.

The agreement was that our first stop would be Shanghai for three days. The passengers had to leave the ship and stay at hotels. They were issued a list of things that were forbidden, such as removing anything from the hotel rooms as souvenirs. These included matchboxes, soap, towels, ash trays, etc. The passengers were also warned in advance that an inspection of all hotel rooms would be made. If one item was missing from any room, the ship would be delayed until the items were returned!

Passengers were advised to take their own soap, cosmetics, toilet paper, Kleenex, non-electric razors, etc. They would not be permitted to leave the hotel on their own but would be taken on a guided tour of the city and surrounding areas for three days. Everyone was anticipating a thrilling adventure of the unexpected.

We arrived at the mouth of the Ya-Lu River that led directly to the heart of Shanghai. A Chinese boat pilot boarded the ship, accompanied by six armed Chinese soldiers. The guards were placed at strategic spots around the ship and the passengers had a frenzied field day snapping pictures. Many of them had their pictures taken with the soldiers who were very cooperative.

The Ya-Lu River narrowed dramatically to the width of a canal so winding our way to the dock became a hazard for the ship as well as the hundreds of small fishing boats trying to get a closer look at the ship and the passengers on deck. The Chinese on shore as well as those in the boats stared at us with their mouths open. They had never seen anything like the size of our ship and they were mesmerized.

We passed many factories which could be seen from both sides of the ship. On the roof of each factory, was a huge horn blasting Chinese music in addition to propaganda between each song. I tried to listen closely to the music in an attempt to define the pattern and musical construction but it was very difficult. It took nearly six hours to reach our dock where we were greeted by a huge welcoming committee with a large, red banner in the background that stretched the entire width of one of the factories reading, "WELCOME S.S. PRINSENDAM TO THE PEOPLE'S REPUBLIC OF CHINA". They had also spread a mammoth, red carpet on the ground next to the gangway. Of course, the compulsory welcoming speeches were made in Chinese and then translated by a man who spoke little or no English.

The Captain was the first one off the ship and went through the formal ceremonies of handshakes as well as receiving the traditional bouquets of flowers from young children. Gifts were exchanged and then it was finally time for the passengers to disembark. Many buses were at the dock and the passengers eagerly rushed off and were directed to specific buses.

Once the passengers had left, the officials came aboard for a special luncheon. The leader of the Chinese contingent advised the Captain that the crew and staff were free to go ashore and walk the streets of Shanghai without restrictions. After all, we were the workers!

We were overjoyed because we did not have any idea about our status or if we would be allowed to go ashore at all! We left as quickly as possible and were strictly on our own.

I noticed a group of Chinese in blue uniforms standing around watching us. I walked up to one of them and asked if he spoke English. He spoke it beautifully! I asked him if he could be my guide which he gleefully accepted. He told me to wait and he soon returned with a car.

The passengers were not due back to the ship for three days so I intended to make as much of my freedom as possible. My guide must have held a pretty high position to have a car at his disposal but I did not question him. He first introduced himself as Cheng Fu, then bombarded me with questions about the U.S. and was vitally interested in my "duties" aboard ship and how many hours per day I worked. I explained that I was an entertainer and performed one night per week and did not have additional duties. His reaction did not surprise me. I get the same response from family and friends at home! He simply could not conjure up in his mind that anyone would be hired to provide services which required one hour per week!

The car clearly belonged to the Army but I chose not to comment on it. We took off and his descriptions were methodical in his explanation about life in China and its customs. I suddenly got a bright idea. I had heard many stories about the Children's Palace. I did not know what it meant so he explained that it was like a day care center while their parents worked in the factories. He said that the word, "Palace" was a misnomer but he was unable to provide me with its origin. I finally said, "Is there a chance that I could perform for the children at the Palace?" He became extremely excited. "Would you really do that?"

"Of course," I replied.

He stopped the car to make a phone call and returned to say that they would be ready in two hours. I didn't have the slightest idea what I would play for them. They were not familiar with music from the West. I then recalled listening to the Chinese music as the ship approached the harbor. After listening to it for several hours, I was able to form a pattern in my mind that seemed to make some musical sense. I made a bold decision and decided that I would do an entire program of ad-lib Chinese music.

When we arrived at the Children's Palace, I was stunned to view a sea of children's faces seated on the huge lawn of the Palace. Someone had told me that there were over five thousand children in attendance. Most had been trucked in from other Children's Palaces all over Shanghai. They had constructed a stage, installed a sound system plus a giant backdrop with my name in English and Chinese. All of this was accomplished in less than two hours! The Children's Palace was a drab three story building that looked like any other building in Shanghai.

The children were very well behaved and it was abundantly clear to me that the Chinese people adored their children. Just before being introduced, a beautiful four-year old child who looked more like a porcelain doll, presented me with flowers. I bowed and then leaned down and kissed her on the cheek. The teachers standing by seemed very pleased as they smiled and applauded. The Chinese applaud a great deal for anything that pleases them. If a car rides down the street, people leaning out of their windows applaud!

I was introduced and started for the stage when I felt two small arms wrap around my leg. I looked down to see this exquisite face staring up at me refusing to let go. I looked at the teachers for guidance and they said that it was perfectly all right to take her on stage with me if I didn't mind. I took her hand and we both walked on stage to the squealing delight of the children. She leaned against me for the entire thirty minutes of my show. I played, what I hoped would be something that they might relate to. When I had finished, they all stood up and cheered and clapped their little hands together. It was a very emotional moment for me. After leaving the stage with my "partner" one of the teachers asked how I learned to play Chinese music and also wanted to know the titles! I tried to explain that I had made it up as I went along but she was unable to comprehend what I was saying.

I was now ready to leave with my guide, Cheng Fu. My dear little girl friend refused to let me go. When I looked down at her, huge tears were rolling down her cheeks. I have always been a pushover by such expressions of emotion so I also broke into tears and leaned down and hugged her. Photographers began shooting pictures of the whole scene. I asked if I could have a set of prints mailed to me and was promised that I would receive a full set. I thanked everyone for their hospitality and promised to return. I never did receive the photographs.

I was told that there was a harmonica factory on the outskirts of Shanghai so I asked if I could see it. Arrangements were made and a formal inspection visit was planned for me the following day. Cheng Fu was at the dock waiting for me and said that it would take about an hour to get there. It gave me the opportunity to view the countryside as we passed peasant farmers plowing their fields with oxen, using the most primitive of field equipment The car attracted their attention and when they saw a foreigner in the passenger seat, they applauded!

> *I was amazed to see the man...enter his shack and return with a bottle of Coke.*

It was an unusually hot day and Cheng Fu asked if I was thirsty. I said that I was but what was available in the countryside? We stopped at an old blacksmith shop and Cheng Fu asked the owner for water. They conversed a few minutes and the old man pointed to a pump. Cheng Fu pumped water into a rusty ladle and brought it to me. I said, "I do not wish to be rude but we were warned aboard ship to avoid drinking water in China. He understood perfectly and asked the man if he had Coca Cola. I was amazed to see the man stand up, enter his shack and return with a bottle of Coke. I gratefully thanked him and wanted to pay but he held up his hand and smiled. It was warm but it was wet! After we left, Cheng Fu explained that the blacksmith felt that he was being honored by offering a Coke to an American visitor.

I tried to picture the harmonica factory. I had anticipated a small, run-down building with five or six people working at wooden benches. Instead, it was a four-story, modern building with several satellite buildings encircling the main hub. When we arrived, we were greeted at the entrance by the foreman plus the entire working staff which appeared to be about two hundred people! The foreman did not speak English so Cheng Fu became my translator. Before we entered, two girls came out carrying bouquets of flowers for me. It is a delightful custom that provides a warm feeling of sensitivity and charm. We were escorted into a lovely dining room where a lavish tea had been prepared. After tea, we were escorted to the heart of the main factory.

Everywhere I looked, I could see hundreds of people working on various stages of harmonica construction. We were shown an impressive display case of various models. I spotted one that was identical to the Hohner that I used. They removed it and handed it to me, indicating that they wanted me to play it. I was amazed at the power and clarity of the instrument and the construction appeared to be top grade. I played a few runs and everyone stopped working to hear me. When I had concluded everyone applauded and that it appeared to be an excellent instrument. I was informed that they had a total of twenty-five hundred employees which included other factories in Shanghai.

The foreman was keenly interested in my evaluation and presented me with a box of six harmonicas. They asked me to put them through a rigid test in my performance and to please let them know how they held up under stress. They invited us to remain for lunch but I apologized by saying that I had to return to the ship, which was a lie. I had tasted Chinese food in China and had difficulty in keeping it down. I did not wish to embarrass my hosts by not eating what I would have been served. There is no relationship between Chinese food in China and what we consume in the U.S. as Chinese food.

Before we left, the foreman said, "If you find that these instruments meet with your approval, would you consider endorsing our product for export?" I tried to be as diplomatic as possible. I replied, "Why don't we wait until I put them through a rigid test?" They politely agreed.

I did use them on my first show after we left Shanghai but they did not hold up. The brass reeds were too thin and they cracked so I had to switch back to my Hohners. I wrote to them and explained the problem and promised to keep in touch in anticipation of my next trip to China.

We returned to Shanghai and drove to the ship in hopes of getting authorization to bring Cheng Fu aboard. The Chinese guards posted at the gangway flatly refused to allow it and nothing that I could do could change their minds. The Chinese military are completely different in personality and attitude than the average Chinese. I surmised that the government, which included the military, were despised and feared by the vast majority of Chinese.

I asked Cheng Fu to stand by while I went aboard to get something. I gathered up a plastic bag of goodies such as cookies, soap. Kleenex, toothpaste, disposable razors, shampoo, fountain pens, scratch pads, etc. I handed the bag to Cheng Fu and he responded as if he had won the Florida lottery! He could not wait to show it to his wife.

> *I hold the unofficial title of the only person to ride a bike from Shanghai to Los Angeles.*

He asked what else I would like to see. I replied that I would leave it to him but would like to visit a Friendship Store. This is a store open to foreigners only and they accepted American money. I purchased a few gift items plus a hand carved cedar chest plus a bicycle for myself. In those days, the ship returned to its original port. In my case, it was Los Angeles. I hold the unofficial title of the only person to ride a bike from Shanghai to Los Angeles. I did this by riding every morning on the top deck where very few people congregated. The Captain heard about my bike and asked if he could also ride it.

Cheng Fu next asked me if I would be interested in observing how a typical Chinese family lived. I thought that it would be a great idea. However, I am ashamed to admit that my first thought was, "Oh, boy. he has set me up with a prearranged apartment for propaganda purposes." He said, "As we drove along, please point to any apartment at random and I will ask for permission to bring you inside." I was mortified.

All of the buildings looked alike but I chose one on the second floor. He left the car and returned shortly to say that I would be most welcome.

We walked up one flight and were greeted by an elderly couple. I would guess that they were both in their eighties, very short and were smiling happily. They were obviously overjoyed to have an American visitor. The wife brewed some tea and they did everything to make us feel at home. It was a two room apartment unlike anything that I had ever seen. Six individuals lived there. Their son, the son's wife, and their two, small grandchildren. The grandparents slept in the bedroom with the children. The youngsters slept in sleeping bags on the floor. The bedroom also had a large, round hole with an enameled pan inside that was used as their toilet. I did not ask where they disposed of the waste. The "living room" was also the bedroom for their son and his wife. It also contained a stove and a small sink. They seemed to be very happy with what they had and the grandparents proceeded to describe what it was like in the evening when they were all together. The children played games together or with their parents. Sometimes, the parents and grandparents read books. On other occasions, they sang songs together. A very important lesson could be learned from this form of Chinese togetherness. Grandma set the table for tea and cookies and I was offered raw octopus, a rare delicacy for them. I gently declined the offer.

They were too shy to ask questions so all of the dialogue came from us and they answered all of our questions. Before we left, they insisted on giving me a pair of beautiful Chinese porcelain figures. The only thing that I had to offer in return was a couple of Holland-America key chains with the ship's logo. I handed it to them and they were thrilled! They gently stroked the leather attachment to the rings and obviously admired the picture of the ship stamped in gold leaf. The visit was a touching as well as a revealing experience. We finally returned to the ship and we both felt saddened by the fact that neither one of us knew if we would ever see each other again. We exchanged addresses and promised to write. I felt that I had made a genuine friend in Cheng Fu. He was very reluctant to see me go. I asked him to wait because I wanted to give him a personal remembrance. When I returned, I handed him one of my harmonicas. Tears came to his eyes and he grabbed my shoulders and rested his head on my chest as he wept. I wasn't exactly dry-eyed myself. We did write to each other for over two years but suddenly my letters were returned, unopened. I have always wondered what had happened to him and if our association had caused trouble. I will never know.

When the passengers finally returned, I could tell by their excitement that they loved every moment of the experience. We were soon ready to cast off and all of the passengers were on deck in a festive mood and were joyfully waving to the crowd on shore. I searched the faces for Cheng Fu without success. It was one terrific experience and emotions were running high.

We had already raised the gangway and had released the docking ropes, when we heard a loud blare of a car horn. We saw a car driving toward the ship at a dizzying speed, kicking up a great deal of dust. A soldier in the back seat had his head and one arm out of the window, waving frantically for us to stop! Our first reaction was that one of our passengers had broken the rules and had removed something from their hotel room. The ship had to back up, tie up again and lower the gangway. A costly and time consuming procedure. By the time the Captain had arrived at the gangway, the soldier had raced up to the deck. The soldier handed an item to the Captain, saluted and left the ship. The Captain held it up for all to see. Someone had left a bar of soap and he was returning it! The Captain had the soap mounted in a glass display case with a brass plate on the front describing the incident and the date.

> *...he ran us up on a sand bar and we were stuck!*

We finally left with a Chinese boat pilot aboard to guide us down the Ya Lu river. Unfortunately, it was a different pilot and he was not familiar with the size of our ship. One hour later, he ran us up on a sand bar and we were stuck! In attempting to move the ship, the pilot ordered the engines to be reversed, causing the sand to be sucked up into the ship's plumbing and air conditioning system! All of the plumbing was shut down and we sat on that sand bar for three days while the crew worked feverishly to flush the dreadful mess from the ship. Miraculously, they finally got everything working properly but the three day delay was pure hell. No running water, no toilets and no air conditioning. We were finally pulled off the sand bar by three tugboats. The best thing that can be said about that experience is that it was the topic of conversation for the rest of the cruise.

♫

Royal Viking Star

Having spent twenty-four years in the cruise business, I feel that I am somewhat of an authority on practically every kind of situation from serious to humorous.

A lady once asked, "How do they get electricity aboard ship?"

Thinking that she was pulling my leg, I replied, "You will be pleased to know that Royal Viking owns the longest extension cord in the entire world."

She gave me a threatening glare. "I didn't ask for a smart ass answer! I really want to know!"

I said, "I didn't mean to offend you because I thought that you were joking. Now I will ask you a question. How do you get electricity in your car?"

She quickly realized how foolish she must have sounded but I hastened to assure her that it was OK. To put her at ease, I told her a true story of a gentleman who asked, "Where do they take the crew at night?"

He had assumed that they were all taken off the ship by helicopter at night when everyone was asleep and then returned in the morning.

She laughed heartily and said, "Oh, dear. I must have sounded so foolish and I do apologize for being so rude. I gave her a hug saying, "It's part of the territory."

♫

Sylvia and I had met a remarkable lady aboard the Royal Viking Star. She was ninety-three, traveled alone, had a ramrod posture, white hair piled high on her head and dressed exquisitely. She was impeccably groomed down to her bright red toenails. It was obvious that she had been blessed with excellent health. She did not wear glasses and did not require a hearing aid! She preferred to be alone but had mysteriously taken a liking to us. As a result, we spent many wonderful hours with her. She was a great conversationalist with a biting wit.

One morning, Sylvia and I were having breakfast in the Lido Lounge when our dear friend asked if she could join us. She was like a little kid. Her eyes were sparkling with excitement. It was obvious that she was anxious to talk. Sure enough, she said, "I've got something that I must tell you. I was sitting in the Main Lounge last night, watching the couples dancing when two gentlemen approached and asked if they could buy me a drink! I was a bit skeptical but decided to invite them to join me. Well, we chatted aimlessly for a while, had our drinks and then I told them that they would have to excuse me as I was feeling a bit tired. They insisted on escorting me to my cabin. I protested but they insisted. As we neared my cabin, I became a bit nervous but then I suddenly realized that I should not have been so concerned. When I boarded the ship, I remembered to bring the pill!"

♫

...a most <u>un</u>remarkable individual...

We were seated in the dining room at a table for eight. The husband of one couple (a most unremarkable individual) was an electronics engineer and he was about to astonish us with his engineering genius. He claimed to have developed a remarkable invention which was destined to revolutionize the electronics industry. His major problem was finding the proper service personnel with enough electronics background and expertise to ensure its continuous operation. I have just related the entire story. It took him twenty-five minutes to tell the same story. His constant repetition was driving everyone at the table into a catatonic state. Some began to doze off and one couple abruptly left the table without saying a word. The engineer's final words were, "So you see, if I had the proper personnel, I would be a rich man today." Sylvia had not said a word all during dinner. She leaned across the table, resting her chin in her hands and quietly said, "Have you tried looking in the Yellow Pages?" In one brilliant line, she had destroyed this crashing bore who left in a huff with his wife timidly following behind. Sylvia received a standing ovation!

It is compulsory when visiting countries like Russia and China, to bring a special visa that the passengers must obtain from their respective consulates. The passengers are warned in advance, before boarding to be sure to bring the visa with them. If not, they would not be permitted to leave the ship when we arrived at those ports.

When we were on our way to China during my second trip, I met two couples from Los Angeles, who were quite excited about the prospects of going to Communist China. I told them that I had been there twice before and they bombarded me with typical tourist questions. "Where's the best place to shop?" I asked if they had the necessary visas and one of the men laughed. "That visa crap doesn't mean a thing! What they want to see is American greenbacks! That's visa enough for them." Here was the classic example of the "Ugly American". I tried to explain to them that they had better be prepared to remain aboard ship for eight days because the Chinese officials do not bend the rules. They did everything but laugh in my face so I dropped the subject and excused myself.

When we arrived in Shanghai, I made a point of looking for the two couples just so I could gleefully observe the drama about to unfold. The passengers started down the gangway and there were two Chinese guards carefully examining passports and visas. When it was finally their turn, they handed the guards their passports and the guards examined them, looking for their visas. Neither guard spoke English but they made themselves understood by pointing to the ship, shaking their heads, "no" and ordering them back! One of the men pulled out a huge roll of money from his pocket and shoved it under one of the guard's nose. Again they were ordered back to the ship. All four were in a state of shock at such behavior and returned aboard ship, screaming their heads off and demanding to see the Captain. The Captain finally came to the gangway and the spokesman of the four began shouting, "Captain, we paid a hell of a lot of money to visit this God-damned Commie country and if we are not permitted off the ship, we demand a full refund!" The Captain performed a remarkable display of self control. "I'm very sorry about this but the Royal Viking Line warned you about this on three different occasions before you boarded the ship. There is nothing that I can do." The loud one continued to rave but the Captain held up his hand. "Sir, I don't believe that you understand that we are in a foreign country and we are their guests. You obviously chose to ignore our warnings so I suggest that you make yourselves as comfortable as possible aboard ship for the next eight days." They all nervously paced the deck, pounding their fists together but nothing helped. I was yearning to sing like a little kid, "You're not going to Chi-na.

I was standing at the reception desk when one of the wives meekly walked up and said to the receptionist, "Look, we feel so stupid! We have come all this way to see China and realize that it's all our fault and we're sorry. We didn't bring our VISA but we do have our AMERICAN EXPRESS. Will that do?"

♫

Danny Leone

> *Cruise Directors have an obligation directly related to the success or failure of all cruise ships.*

Given the longevity of my association with cruise ships, it also indicates the large variety of Cruise Directors with whom I have worked. Cruise Directors have an obligation directly related to the success or failure of all cruise ships. Its success represents hundreds of thousands of dollars in repeat business. Once a passenger leaves a ship with a negative attitude, it's a pretty safe bet that the line has lost him or her for good. It is sad that the majority of passengers do not appreciate the efficiency, professional know-how and administrative talent that it takes to be a successful Cruise Director. When it appears to be easy, that is when he has utilized his talents well. Two who stand head and shoulders above the rest are Derek Mann and Danny Leone. Derek was the Cruise Director for the Royal Viking Line when we met, and Danny was with the Cunard Line. My first experience with Danny was aboard the Sagafjord. It is strange how vicious rumors spread. I was warned that Danny was tough as nails to work with and that he browbeat his staff and was a thoroughly distasteful individual. What I found instead, was a sincere, compassionate and generous person who was every inch a professional and knew more about cruise ships than most Captains. He had remarkable respect for anyone whom he thought had exceptional talent and he did everything possible to make that performer look good. He is loved and respected by practically all passengers and he gives back one thousand percent of his efforts in return. The ugly rumors about Danny were based on his low tolerance toward anyone on his staff who gives less than their best in their performances as well as general behavior amongst the passengers. It is to his credit that he was and still is a perfectionist.

Derek Mann

The Royal Viking Line was rated Five Star, which is as high as ratings can get. When we checked into our cabin, we found a personal note from Derek Mann inviting us to join him for cocktails after the ship had left port. I called him at his office and we arranged to meet at

7:30 P.M. Derek was everything that I had anticipated. He was also a professional through and through. He wanted to discuss my act and decide on the best night to present me, and, in general, made Sylvia and me feel very much at home. He was warm and charming and I knew that I was dealing with a man who was dedicated to his profession. What a refreshing change! He also asked if we were comfortable in our cabin and urged me to contact him if I needed help of any kind. Derek and I worked on a fairly steady basis for over ten years and he and his wife, Barbara, remained two of our dearest friends. We even worked out a comedy routine that we presented as a late night show in the nightclub. This became a tradition whenever we worked together. We usually packed the room and we had as much fun doing the show as the passengers had in watching us make fun-loving fools of ourselves.

…my favorite port…Alaska

I have cruised around the world five times and although I have enjoyed it ninety percent of the time, anything can become boring after many years of cruising. I have been asked about my favorite port in the entire world. I usually shock people with my reply. Alaska is the big winner for me. I love the ever-changing, exquisite scenery, the tranquility and peace that seems to slow down the world. It is not that my age is showing. I have felt the same way since my first visit to Alaska, twenty-four years ago. I know that it is hard to believe but I have taken the Alaska cruise with various cruise lines for a total of sixty-seven times and never tire of it! I have been through the Panama Canal forty-two times and I confess that twice was enough for me. I now confine my cruising activities to one or possibly two per year and keep them within the North American continent.

Russia and the Royal Viking

During the first seven years of cruising, I was never offered the opportunity to visit Russia. My chance finally came when Royal Viking offered me a contract to cruise all of the Scandinavian countries including a stop at what was then Leningrad. This took us half way around the world and my contract was for one month. An unusually long contract for me but the thought of visiting Russia was overwhelming.

We left Los Angeles, stopped at three ports in Mexico, went through the Panama Canal to Ft. Lauderdale, New York and then made the Atlantic crossing to Oslo and the Norwegian Fjords which are awesome in the splendor of their spectacular beauty. We then continued to Amsterdam, Stockholm, Helsinki and finally, Leningrad! As we entered this historical port, the channel became quite narrow, allowing us to view both sides of the city clearly at close range. The streets and buildings were shockingly drab. The amazing contrast between Leningrad and the Scandinavian countries which were so close and far more dramatic than I had anticipated. Everything seemed depressingly dirty and terribly run down. Many of the buildings were empty with huge gaping shell holes as a constant reminder of World War II. It was a frightening example of the futility of war. The streets were empty as if a government edict had been issued prior to our arrival to keep off the streets! The year was 1980, a period of turbulence and tension between the U.S. and the U.S.S.R.

The soldiers guarding the dock made it very clear, in their hostile stares, that we were not welcome. In marked contrast, was the Soviet Police Band, assembled on the second tier of the dock. They struck up some very exciting Russian marches as they musically welcomed us to their country. All of the passengers were on deck and the excitement was catching to everyone including the Soviet musicians. At the conclusion of the brief concert, a wild roar of approval came from our passengers as well as enthusiastic applause. The conductor smiled broadly, made a sweeping bow and applauded the passengers.

We were docked in front of a recently built, modern hotel. To enter the city, one had to walk through a gauntlet of heavy-handed officials, finally entering the hotel lobby. The walls and floor were pure marble which offered a massive elegance to the eye. We then walked out to the street where taxis and buses were waiting.

I had recently purchased a video camera and was anxious to put it to the test. As I walked through security, one of the stone-faced soldiers stopped me and ordered me to leave the video camera with them and pick it up on my return. Fortunately, an officer was standing nearby and asked to see my identification. When he saw my crew pass, he smiled and handed the camera back. I took the bus into the center of town and noticed immediately that the city was spectacular. What we had viewed on our way up the channel was the seamy side of the city and obviously not very inviting. I took far more video footage than necessary but did get some exciting shots of the Russian people as well as the famous Hermitage Art Museum. Sylvia was not feeling well so she chose to remain on board and hoped that she would feel well enough to see the city the next day. We were scheduled to remain in Leningrad for three days.

...I heard exciting music coming from the third floor...

On my way back to the ship, I heard exciting music coming from the third floor of the hotel lobby. I quickly made my way up to the source and discovered a marvelous, private party in full swing. Most were dancing to the music of a trio and everyone seemed to be having a glorious time. Instead of a door, the entrance was covered by a thin curtain. The windows in the room were open on the opposite side creating a draft outwards toward me, allowing a perfect view of the festivities. Throwing my usual caution to the wind without considering the fact that I could be shooting something forbidden by the KGB, I thrust my camera past the curtain and hoped that I was getting some decent shots. I did not have the slightest idea what the reason was for the party. Suddenly, a deep voice behind me said, "Vat you do?"

I turned to see two burly gentlemen. I was not about to mess with the KGB! I sensed that I was in very deep trouble. "I'm very sorry. I know that it was rude of me to but . . . excuse me, do you gentlemen speak English?"

"Da . . . I mean, yes. A leetle bit."

I said, "I was so excited, hearing the wonderful music and the dancing that I wanted my friends at home to see how happy the Russian people are." My God, what a con job! Could I actually get away with it?

He smiled and said, "Dot's OK." I heaved a deep sigh of relief. I told him that I worked on the ship as an entertainer. He was suddenly very interested.

"You entertainer?"

I said, "Yes. I play the harmonica."

"A harmonika! You have harmonika?"

"Yes, I do but it is on the ship."

He began jumping up and down like an overgrown kid. "You go beck end gat harmonika end bring beck to play for pipple!"

"Really? You want me to play for them?"

"Da, da! You go now end gat harmonika, yes?"

I said, "Yes! Can you tell me why they are having the party?" He hesitated and I could see that he was having difficulty explaining the purpose of the party.

"Is salibration for twenty-five years for doctors."

"You mean that it's a 25th Anniversary celebration for the doctors who graduated medical school?"

"Da, Da! Eniwersary salibration." I told them that I would return as quickly as possible. I nearly fell down the stairs in my eagerness to get to the ship. When I boarded, I saw a fellow entertainer and told him what I was about to do. He said, "Wow! Is there any chance that I could go with you?"

"Yes, but you've got to do me a favor. I want you to shoot some video of me playing for the people but be sure to shoot mostly local color of the party participants." I grabbed a harmonica and off we went. The Russians had obviously paved the way for our return because when we walked in, they all stood up and cheered! I was introduced by one of the women doctors while I struggled to figure out what I was going to play with the trio. The first thing that came to mind was *Midnight in Moscow*, which was a universal favorite, and of course, they knew it. I began to play and everyone in the room began clapping in tempo, as they all burst into song! It was very exciting for me and I encouraged them to come out on the floor and dance. At the end of the number, they all leaped up and threw glasses at the wall! It was obvious that the vodka had served its purpose. It startled me for a moment but then I realized that they were all happily loaded and were expressing their enthusiasm.

A man yelled, "You play Amerikan moosic!"

I said, "Fine, what would you like to hear?"

He yelled back, "You play *Chatanooga Choo Choo*."

I turned to the musicians and they nodded their approval. We started to play and practically everyone got up and began to jitterbug. At that point, I sensed that I was over-staying my welcome. I thanked them and was about to leave but they all roared for me to come back.

"What else do you want me to play?"

A man jumped on top of his table and yelled, "You play, *Sain Louie Bluz*!"

We played it, and again, they all came out and danced their little Russian hearts out. Everyone was having such a marvelous time but I reluctantly said to the lady doctor in charge that I had to return to the ship. I asked her to please express my heartfelt thanks for allowing me to crash their private party. In addition, I added that if all of our differences could be resolved with music and dancing, the world would be a much better planet. At the conclusion of the translation, everyone stood up, cheered and gave me a V sign.

Before we left, the doctor asked me to wait for a moment. She said something to someone and in a short time, a gentleman returned carrying a small, handsome gift box. I opened it to find a beautiful silver medallion. The doctor explained that everyone in the room had received one as a remembrance of their 25th year in medicine. They wished to make me an honorary doctor in their graduating class! It was a touching gesture as I thanked them, saluted and left with my friend.

> *Sylvia…had a natural charisma that everyone recognized.*

Being aboard ship with a spouse who is a successful entertainer, was a difficult role to fill – or so Sylvia thought. As I have stated before, Sylvia was an introvert despite her amazing ability to endear herself to anyone with whom she had met. She had a natural charisma that everyone recognized. It was so genuine that she did not recognize this attribute. She had been living in the shadow of my notoriety and was constantly bombarded with comments and questions about me. She accepted it with grace and charm, but I'm sure that there were times when she wished that she would be treated as Sylvia Adler, instead of Sylvia, Jerry Adler's wife, which probably made her feel that we were joined at the hip! If our roles had been reversed, I am certain that I would have had major difficulties dealing with it.

I was standing on pool deck, leaning against the rail, chatting with a gentleman. Sylvia was standing about eight feet away, conversing with a lady. I was close enough to hear most of their conversation and was so pleased, for Sylvia's sake, that they were discussing the beauty of the ship. While they were engrossed in conversation, two elderly English ladies approached them. One said, "Please excuse our interruption for just a moment." I glanced at Sylvia and saw a look that I had never seen before. It told me, "Oh, God, here we go again!"

The English lady continued, "Mrs. Adler, we saw your husband's performance last night and we must tell you that he was marvelous!"

Sylvia graciously thanked them and added, "I'm so pleased that you enjoyed it."

"It must be so wonderful to be married to such a . . ."

Sylvia stopped her in mid-sentence. "I hope that you do not think me rude, but do you have any idea what it is like to be married to an egotistical ass?"

The ladies were jolted and walked away in a daze. I laughed so hard that I lost my balance and fell to the deck. The nice gentleman helped me up but couldn't understand why I was laughing. I had to explain it to him. I then walked over to Sylvia, gave her a tight hug and kissed her. Typically, Sylvia looked at me, turned to see if anyone had seen this affectionate display and said, "Stop that."

It felt so good to see and hear Sylvia assert herself. What I was most pleased about was that she did it with such style.

♫

Cary Grant

In the history of the motion picture business, one man stands out as the undisputed, classy gentleman. I sense that you already know to whom I am referring. Of course, it is Cary Grant. Cary had the kind of magical charisma and charm that was the most remarkable in the history of films. We had been friends for a number of years until his untimely death. I had worked on three of his pictures, the most recent being, "Houseboat". We shared the same kind of humor, we enjoyed the same music and we always had a great deal to talk about. I was aboard the Royal Viking Star with Sylvia on a World Cruise. The Cruise Director received a Telex, saying that Cary, and his beautiful wife, Barbara, were coming aboard as guests of the line. The ship went mad with excitement. Sylvia knew that Cary and I had been friends and she was shaking with excitement at the prospect of meeting him. Sylvia did not sleep that night and when she got out of bed, she began going through her wardrobe to figure out what she would wear for dinner!

"Honey, it's only Cary Grant!"

Cary and his wife boarded in Hong Kong the following morning and, as usual, he looked fabulous. They were escorted to one of the Penthouse suites and remained there until dinner. When they entered the dining room, he in his tuxedo and she in a black taffeta gown, it took everyone's breath away. They were shown to a table for four but just the two of them occupied it. By chance, Sylvia and I were seated at the next table with two other couples. Cary and I looked at each other and he shouted, "Jerry!" My God, what are you doing here?" He stood up and so did I as Cary walked over and we both embraced warmly. I introduced him to Sylvia and the other couples. We arranged to have drinks at the piano bar after dinner. When he returned to his table, I looked at Sylvia and she had a wide, blank stare on her face. I said, "Honey, it's only Cary Grant!" She looked at me as if I should be caged. Sylvia was unable to eat her dinner in anticipation of having drinks with the Grants at the piano bar.

The passengers finally settled down to a reasonable degree of normalcy but continued to stare at him at every opportunity. When passengers were ready to leave the dining room, most of them took the long way around just to pass his table. He was remarkable. As each couple passed, he stood up and bowed a greeting to all of them!

We finally met with the Grants at the piano bar where Page Cavanaugh was holding forth at the piano. We sat around the piano and Page played all of our favorites. Sylvia was in seventh heaven. If that wasn't enough, Cary leaned over and said, "Jerry, is it possible to arrange for you and Sylvia to join us permanently at our table? We hate sitting alone but we prefer to sit with someone who speaks our language, if you know what I mean. If you feel that you will offend your current table partners, we'll simply forget it." I said that I would speak to the maitre d' and was sure that he would take care of it.

I checked with the maitre d' and he assured me that it would be fine. I found our table partners and as diplomatically as possible, explained the situation. They were very understanding about it and assured us that if positions were reversed, they would do the same thing.

I have worked with many famous personalities but Sylvia never got used to the idea of meeting them in person. She was an outrageous dessert eater and I had asked her to please cut down because I didn't want to see her gain weight. My request was not necessary. She hardly ate anything when we dined with the Grants. She didn't even touch her dessert! Thanks to them, she lost eight pounds!

♫

Malcolm Atterbury

Sylvia and I had met a great couple aboard the Royal Viking Star. Their names were Ellen and Malcom Atterbury. Malcolm was a character actor in films and both of them had been stage actors in New York in their younger days. It was love at first sight for all four of us. Every time we met on the ship, it was laughter from beginning to end.

They lived in Beverly Hills, and one day, he said to me, "How would you like to do a concert in Hollywood when we get home?" I said that I would love to. He then said, "Here's my proposal. I will advance the money and it will be a benefit performance for the City of Hope, the marvelous cancer research hospital in Duarte, California."

I said, "I'll do it on one condition. That you will be reimbursed before the hospital gets the rest." He said, "We'll worry about that later."

We performed the concert at the Wilshire-Ebell Theater with a great nine piece orchestra and had a surprisingly healthy turnout. The concert was a success and the hospital received ten thousand dollars. Malcom decided to match that figure so the City of Hope did quite well.

The Atterburys and the Adlers remained very close friends for a number of years and we were deeply saddened when we heard that dear Mac had died, after a long illness. The best tribute that I can pay him is the fact that his marvelous sense of humor never wavered, and his goodness shall shine forever. Like so many who have shared their lives for so many years, Ellen seemed to lose all hope and incentive when she lost Mac. Her health deteriorated rapidly and she required twenty four hour nursing care for many months before her tragic death in 1994. Their daughter, Jill was the one person in their lives who provided the love, warmth and understanding. She was an extremely devoted daughter and she and her husband, Carroll were responsible for making the remaining months of Jill's parent's lives worth living. Jill is one of three children and she is the one who carries on the tradition of kindness and goodness that made the Atterburys such special people.

♬

Royal Viking Sea

Experiences aboard ship come in a variety of packages, from the hilarious to the macabre. We were aboard the Royal Viking Sea, returning to San Francisco from the South Pacific and were scheduled to arrive in two days. Like their other ships, the Sea offers nine Penthouse Suites with a price (at that time) of $3,500 per day, double occupancy. One of the suites was occupied by an eighty-five year old lady and her male traveling companion, aged forty.

One afternoon, a terrible fight broke out between them and the butler, who serviced all nine suites heard screaming coming from suite number six and called the Hotel Manager. He arrived immediately and knocked on the door but the screams were so loud that his knocking was drowned out. A pass key was finally used and what faced them was something out of a horror film. The walls, carpet, furniture, drapes and clothing strewn about were covered with blood. The man sat in a chair in a daze, holding a broken whiskey bottle. He did not respond to questioning so they searched the suite and finally found the dead body of the lady, sprawled face down on the lanai. Security was called and the man was handcuffed and placed in custody.

> *...they searched the suite and finally found the dead body...*

247

The San Francisco police were notified and the Captain was ordered to seal the suite and they would come aboard with the pilot before we docked. It was obvious that word would be leaked to the press so when the ship finally docked, it was suddenly swarming with reporters, police and FBI agents. The passengers were forbidden to disembark, causing major headaches. Most of them had flights to catch and it was obvious that they would have to make other plans. The men and women of the press were not making it any easier with some carrying bulky video equipment and all of them fighting to be the first ones to get pictures of the body. Tempers were flaring and Royal Viking was facing a major public relations problem. They wanted to soothe the passengers but were also walking a fine line in trying to accommodate the press. From what I could determine, it was a no win situation.

The additional problem was getting the ship ready for the next cruise, due to leave in five hours! All cabins and public rooms had to be thoroughly cleaned in preparation for the new passengers. Every passageway was crowded with press, police and angry, shouting passengers who wanted nothing more than to get off the ship.

That afternoon, the papers had the entire story on the front page. "MURDER ABOARD CRUISE SHIP!" Restoring that suite to normal was a gigantic headache. It had to be repainted, new carpet, furniture and drapes had to be replaced.

The body was finally removed and the prisoner was taken off the ship. After much pleading by the Hotel Manager in charge of the accommodations aboard ship, the ship was finally granted permission to allow the passengers to leave and to start work immediately on restoring the suite. The new passengers who were scheduled to occupy that infamous suite had to be living in outer space not to have heard or read about the murder. When the suite was completely refurbished, the new passengers came aboard. The passengers for that suite went directly to the Hotel Manager's office and demanded a refund.

The Hotel Manager said, "Please, let us discuss this calmly."

The husband replied, "I'm perfectly calm and there is nothing to discuss other than a refund."

"Please give me the opportunity to explain. We realize what you have been thinking. However, I can guarantee you unequivocally that the suite is perfect in every detail."

"We still don't want it."

"I'll tell you what I will do. I will take you both to the suite and if you find anything that even suggests this unfortunate incident, the suite is yours at no charge!"

That seemed to change their attitude considerably. After all, it cost $3,500 a day for fourteen days. A tidy $49,000! They entered the suite like Sherlock Holmes and Dr. Watson. They went through everything in minute detail. It all looked perfect and they appeared to be satisfied. The wife decided to walk out on the lanai and discovered the chalk outline of the body that had been made by the police. The cleanup crew missed it, which cost the company dearly.

We were on a ship heading for Los Angeles when an eighteen year old girl was observed racing all over the ship calling for her mother. Being an unusually large ship, the staff tried to calm her down by explaining the size of the ship and how easy it was to lose someone for a while.

She cried, "For a while! I haven't seen my mother in two days!"

This caused considerable alarm so one of the staff called the Captain in his quarters. The Captain instructed him to speak to the Hotel Manager immediately and conduct a thorough search. The lady had vanished and we were due to arrive in Los Angeles the following morning. The young lady had to be sedated and now the entire ship was aware of the problem. The Chief Purser had hundreds of copies of the mother's passport photograph copied and distributed to passengers and crew.

At 8:00 A.M. the following morning, the mother magically appeared in her stateroom. She seemed to be unharmed and in excellent spirits. She was questioned by two senior officers but refused to say where she had been. After considerable questioning, she finally broke down and admitted that she had been in the Captain's quarters the whole time and was enjoying herself so much that she forgot to notify her daughter. When we docked, the Captain was fired on the spot and was taken into custody by the Long Beach police and charged with kidnapping. The mother and daughter disembarked into the loving arms of Daddy.

♫

Royal Viking Sky

It is amazing how quickly one becomes accustomed to the sounds of a ship. Any deviation is usually cause for at least natural curiosity. I was aboard the Royal Viking Sky and was sound asleep. I awoke at 2:00 A.M. and knew that something was wrong. The ship had stopped and the silence was deafening. I tried to turn on the light but the power was out. I quickly dressed, grabbed my flashlight and worked my way up to Promenade Deck. I found six passengers pacing back and forth in concerned confusion. There were no lights burning throughout the entire ship. Fortunately, we were in an unusually calm sea and a full moon was out. It is surprising how much light a full moon projects at sea. We were three days out of Tahiti but we were dead in the water. Shortly, several of the ship's crew appeared and began working on the back-up generator that was mounted on the bulkhead above one of the doors. I overheard one of the crew mention that the main generator had blown and the back-up had also stopped. This meant that everything had shut down including the ability to steer the ship! They did have fully charged batteries enabling them to send an S.O.S. if necessary. It also meant no air conditioning and no refrigeration for the galley.

> *We were three days out of Tahiti but we were dead in the water.*

Rumors spread quickly and within a half hour a large number of passengers were on deck with some wearing night clothing, others fully dressed carrying small pieces of luggage. No announcements could be made due to power loss. In retrospect, God was surely watching over us. If we had been in any kind of significant sea movement, the ship would have bounced around out of control and would have presented the very real danger of capsizing! The rumors were now spreading in a dangerous manner and officers walked around assuring everyone that everything was under control and we would soon be on our way. An S.O.S. had been sent and two Russian freighters responded that they were on their way at full speed.

I walked to the back of the ship and noticed three young couples huddled together in conversation. I heard what sounded like hysterical laughter so I walked over to investigate. I pointed my flashlight at a woman sitting on the deck, hugging her knees to her chest, laughing uncontrollably. I asked if she was the wife of one of them and the husband stepped forward.

I said, "Do you realize that your wife is hysterical?"

He replied, "Yes, I know but I don't know what to do."

"The only way to stop her is to slap her hard across the face!" I moved toward his wife but he stopped me. "Please, don't do that."

"But she needs to be jolted out of it."

"Yes, I know. I'll do it."

He gently lifted his wife to her feet and with a tightly clenched fist, threw a beautiful right cross to her chin. This caused her to drop back to the deck, glaring at her husband while crying and rubbing her chin.

She was out of danger but I wasn't too sure about him!

The ship had been sitting for five hours. The first indication of daylight was just beginning to show its welcome light. Suddenly, we heard the coughing of an engine that seemed to be gasping for breath. Lights began to flicker and everyone on deck began to cheer when we all heard the glorious sound of a humming generator. A radio message was quickly dispatched to the freighters that we were finally out of danger.

The Captain came on the speakers while everyone was having breakfast. He announced that he was inviting all passengers to a special cocktail party in the Ballroom at 7:00 P.M. Drinks would be on the house and a full explanation of the problem would be presented.

Everyone showed up, anxious to hear the Captain. When he was introduced by the Cruise Director, a thunderous cheer exploded from everyone. The Captain was marvelous because he did not make light of the emergency but simply stated the facts. He said, "First, let me express my thanks on behalf of my entire crew and myself for your outstanding conduct in the face of this serious problem. Your calm, understanding behavior allowed us to perform our duties as swiftly as possible." He then explained the technical problems and what it took to correct everything. He continued, "It now gives me great pride and pleasure to introduce these hard working crewmen and engineers who were responsible for our safety and the safety of everyone aboard."

When the crew filed in, the passengers leaped to their feet screaming, "Bravo!" They gave these men the longest and loudest standing ovation that I have ever witnessed. On the following night, the Captain declared the Ballroom off-limits to passengers and the entire crew was treated to a lavish buffet and party that lasted through the night.

One question that is often asked, "What are the potential problems in riding out a vicious storm?" The worst storm that I can recall was aboard the Queen Elizabeth II making the Atlantic crossing from New York to Southampton, England. The month was April and we were two days out of New York when radar showed that we were headed into a full-blown hurricane. It was so widespread that it was physically impossible to avoid it so we met the storm head on. We plunged ahead, sailing directly into the wind. The crew quickly set up the necessary safety ropes and other safety precautions. An announcement was made by the Captain, urging everyone to remain indoors and do as little walking as possible. He also announced that the dining rooms would be closed until further notice. Sandwiches and fruit would be delivered to the cabins. We were soon crashing into sixty foot waves!

It was my good fortune to be scheduled to perform that night so I felt pretty confident that it would be canceled. No such luck. It was scheduled for 9:30 P.M. and I received a call from the Cruise Director at 9:15 saying, "I hate to tell you this but we have nearly three hundred people waiting to see your show!" Dammit, where did that old bromide originate, "The show must go on!"

I staggered and stumbled on my way to the ballroom, holding on to ropes and safety bars. I could not imagine why people would wish to sit in the Ballroom to watch something that was bound to be a professional disaster. In retrospect, I can now appreciate why they were there. Remaining in one's cabin in that kind of tossing around was much worse than being in a much larger room. They also wished to have their minds diverted to something other than worrying about the hurricane.

The orchestra was in place, trying valiantly to hold on to their instruments and their stomachs at the same time. I was introduced with much emphasis on my "bravery" for doing the show. Bravery! I was scared out of my wits. I was greeted with wild cheers of encouragement as if I was a circus performer preparing for a death defying leap! That analogy was not far from the truth! I could have refused to do the show for reasons of personal safety because I did not have anything to hold on to. I need two hands to play the harmonica. At least a singer or comic can hold on to the microphone stand for support! I managed to get past the first number by spreading my legs far apart. The ship continued on its roller coaster direction and it became a matter of who would win the fight. I was out-muscled by the raging seas but was determined to get through my show as quickly and as safely as possible.

> *I quickly stepped aside like a matador fighting a bull, just in time to see it (the baby Grand piano) fly by...*

Violent seas are completely unpredictable. They do not have a set pattern to provide advanced warning of a particularly huge wave. It can suddenly strike the ship from any direction. I was into my second number when I heard two simultaneous sounds: one was the screams of women and the other was the baby grand piano breaking loose from its anchor blocks, heading directly toward me! I quickly stepped aside like a matador fighting a bull, just in time to see it fly by as if it had been fired from a cannon! It crashed on to the dance floor and turned upside down. The waiters had to struggle to get it right side up and then hoist it back on to the bandstand where it was secured. Not an easy job under the best of circumstances. This difficult and awkward process took thirty minutes but nobody left. I then resumed my performance and soon heard a different sound behind me. I turned to watch in fascination as all of the music stands fell forward in unison as if the stands were all taking a bow! My music went flying into the air like so much confetti and the musicians were not about to scramble on to the dance floor to retrieve it. The waiters were, once again, pressed into service. They gathered up all of my music and handed it to the leader who then had to sort out the parts for each instrument. This took an additional forty-five minutes. The passengers just sat there cheering us on. What the hell, they didn't have anything better to do. Trying to return to their cabins would have constituted running an obstacle course that could have proved to be disastrous.

With two interruptions, my show did not finish until 11:45! I received a great ovation but nobody stood up! The storm slowly subsided by 2:45 A.M. and things gradually returned to normal.

Cunart Sagafjord

One of my favorite ships is the Cunard Sagafjord. I have always felt comfortable aboard this elegant lady and the work schedule was considerably less than most other ships. This is a one-sitting dinner instead of the usual two sittings. The majority of the ships have two sittings because of the number of passengers that they carry.

The first sitting dinner usually starts at 6:30 and the second sitting begins at 8:00. While the first sitting passengers are having their dinner, the second sitting is watching our first show. When it is time for the second sitting, the first sitting passengers see our second show. I know that this may sound confusing but I cannot describe it any other way. That is one of the reasons why I love the Sagafjord. I am only required to do one show instead of two on the evening that I am scheduled to perform.

Danny Leone was the Cruise Director and he was instrumental in making me feel as if the ship was my second home. I also knew that I would never be confronted with unprofessional problems and would receive the kind of respect that is usually shown to a seasoned performer.

♫

Royal Viking

I received a call from Royal Viking, asking if I was available for another cruise to China. This would be my third trip there, and I immediately wrote to the officials at the harmonica factory, when we would be arriving. When the ship had reached the half way point, I received a call asking me to please come to the Chief Purser's office. When I walked in, he said, "I don't know how to tell you this, but through an obvious lack of communication in our office in San Francisco, they forgot to order your special visa for China." I was not that concerned because I assumed that they could make the necessary corrections through the U.S. Embassy in Shanghai because I was a crew member. I asked if it could be worked out that way and he said, "I'm terribly sorry, Jerry, but you know how the Chinese are about such things. They simply do not bend. I'm afraid that you are stuck aboard ship for our eight day stay."

I protested, "But I have already made arrangements to meet with some very important people from the harmonica factory!"

I was angry and recalled a similar situation when passengers were refused entry on a previous cruise. Regardless of the unfairness - nothing helped.

Two Chinese passengers, who lived in Hong Kong, were quite distressed when they heard about my problem. We had become friends during the cruise and they were going to Shanghai on business. This couple had considerable influence in Mainland China and promised to do everything possible to resolve the problem.

When we finally arrived in Shanghai, I watched my friends conversing with the officials on the dock. There was much arm waving and shouting in Chinese and finally the wife came aboard to break the sad news that nothing could be done. The problem was compounded by telling me that the officials from the factory were bitterly disappointed. They had arranged a huge banquet in my honor that evening plus an appearance with the Shanghai Symphony Orchestra! They had to cancel the banquet and concert and send everyone home! It seemed impossible that the Chinese officials were not aware of these special activities. They were also told that on a previous visit, I had performed a one man concert at the Children's Palace. But even that didn't help.

Bali

On one of the six cruises that I had taken to Indonesia, an incident occurred that was traumatic as well as frightening. We had dropped anchor in the waters off Bali and were tendered in to the dock. We were greeted by the colorfully dressed Balinese dancers and musicians who performed beautifully as we approached the dock. It was the first taste of Balinese culture for most of the passengers and everyone was very impressed.

Buses were waiting to take us on a guided tour of the island so I decided to go along, although I had been through it a number of times. We drove through many villages and large numbers of children ran alongside the bus as we slowed down, begging for coins or attempting to sell souvenirs. A young German passenger was on our bus plus a large contingent of older German passengers. The young German suddenly thrust his arm out of the window in a Nazi salute and yelled, "Heil Hitler!" We were shocked at this strange behavior and simply chalked it up to a young man trying to be "cute". When we reached the next village, the same thing happened. This time, several of the passengers became angry and proceeded to scold the young man for his disgusting behavior. He simply laughed and said something in German, waving them away.

When we returned to the ship, I reported the incident to the Cruise Director. He didn't seem too disturbed until I said, "I'm supposed to be doing a show this evening. If that man appears in the show room, I will refuse to do the show."

He said, "Are you crazy? You've GOT to do the show!"

"I'm sorry but I flatly refuse to do it if he is there so I suggest that you have another act standing by."

He had no choice but to report it to the Captain. I was shocked at the Captain's response. "If it were me, I would also refuse to do the show. As far as I am concerned, Jerry is within his rights under these circumstances."

Apparently, word had spread throughout the ship about the unpleasant incident. Fifteen minutes before show time, I walked through the crowded room looking for that Nazi sonofabitch but he was not there. When I was introduced, I received a standing ovation with shouts of, "Bravo"! They were obviously expressing their approval of my position on this unpleasant matter. It was very gratifying to receive such recognition from the audience. Especially from the many Germans who were there.

♪

Rescue At Sea, S.S. Monterey

I was aboard the S.S. Monterey when the ship received an S.O.S. from a Japanese freighter. They were forty nautical miles south of us and the message said that one of their crew had fallen three decks in the engine room and was impaled on a steel rod! We radioed back, giving our position and said that we were on our way at full speed. It took us approximately three hours to reach the freighter. It was 9:30

P.M. and the seas were calm. Our ship's doctor was in constant radio contact with their Captain, explaining what to do until we arrived. Our doctor was told that the man was unconscious, which was, as we were told later, a blessing. We came as close to the freighter as possible and lowered a lifeboat with our doctor and nurse aboard as they headed toward the freighter.

It took the doctor two hours to remove the crewman from the steel rod. Having completed the necessary first aid, they transferred him to our ship as quickly as possible and took him to our hospital facilities. The patient was fortunate that we had an extremely efficient surgeon aboard. The sailor was in surgery for four hours and the doctor felt that he had been stabilized and, all things considered, felt that everything went well. We radioed the freighter that we would care for the patient and when he was strong enough to travel, he would be taken off at the nearest Japanese port. The freighter radioed their thanks and we both took off as both ships exchanged ships horn acknowledgment.

The passengers were anxious to take up a collection for the sailor but our Captain had to gently explain to everyone that this was a very private, tradition between the crews of all ships in distress. Our crew took up a collection that totaled over one thousand dollars. We reached Yokohama and had him picked up by ambulance and transferred to a hospital. They carried him off on a stretcher and the injured seaman waved to everyone aboard. There wasn't a dry eye on the entire deck.

On a nice, sunny day at sea, I like nothing better than to have my buffet lunch outdoors around the pool area. I had filled my tray and found a nice table. As I was eating, I noticed a gentleman holding his tray, obviously looking for a place to sit. I invited him to join me. We introduced ourselves and proceeded to eat our lunch. He was the first to speak. "Did you see the show last night?" He had seen my show but obviously didn't recognize me.

I replied, "Yes, I saw it and thought that it was terrible!"

He was astonished. "You thought WHAT?"

"I thought that it was awful."

"Did you see the harmonica player?"

"Yes, I did and I thought that he was lousy."

"I don't know what show you saw but the audience gave him a standing ovation!"

"Yes, I know that. I still thought that he was terrible."

Right after that, a lady approached the table. "Excuse me, Mr. Adler. I don't mean to disturb your lunch but I wanted to tell you how much I enjoyed your performance."

I thanked her and she left.

My luncheon partner looked at me and said, "So tell me. What didn't you like about him?"

Sitmar Fairsky

We were aboard the Sitmar Fairsky going through the Panama Canal on our way to Los Angeles, which was to be our final port. The day after leaving Acapulco, we were hit by a hurricane unlike any that I had seen since the QE-2 crossing from New York to Southampton. Every social activity came to a screaming halt. Safety ropes and barf bags were strung strategically around the ship as we were being tossed violently in every direction. We had an all Italian crew and soon, the Captain came on the loudspeaker. "Ladies and uh gentle-a-men. Please, you no walk around de deck outside or in-a-de-ship because you break-a-you leg! The dining room will be-a-closed until further notice. Waiters will-a-come around to you state-a-room and-a bring you a basket of fruit. Ladies and-a gentle-men, we wish you bon-apetito!"

Larry Adler, the Later Years

In 1986, my brother Larry called me from London so say that he had just completed his autobiography and wanted to know what I thought about the title, "It Ain't Necessarily So". I hesitated a moment and finally mentioned that the title leads one to believe that parts of the book would be "lies". The title of the book actually is supported by one of his first stories recounting an incident in which several soldiers came away with very different accounts. But I didn't know that at the time. He responded, "Well?" I replied, "If you must choose to steal from Gershwin, you are stealing from the best. However, if it must be Gershwin, why don't you pick a title much more appropriate?"

"Like what?" he asked.

"Why don't you call the book "The Man I Love". To confirm to everyone who knew of his ego, he excitedly replied, "That's GREAT!" I will speak with the publisher in the morning." Of course his publisher thought he was out of his mind and refused to change it.

♫

Ronald Reagan

I have had many passengers, friends and family ask if I had ever met Ronald Reagan. It turned out we worked on two films at Warner Bros. studio, a film company that turned out movies with tremendous popular appeal in the 1960's.

Ronald Reagan was an affable gentleman, cordial, good-natured and charming. He was hard-working and a fair actor who obviously knew his own limitations. His strength lay in his desire to please and this made him popular with the cast and crew. He was ambitious, and in a relatively short period of time became president of the Screen Actors Guild. He too was caught up in the McCarthy era scandal and sided with the House Committee on Un-American Activities. We never discussed politics and our relationship remained pleasant.

He often asked me to play the harmonica. That was the limit of my relationship with this very well-liked gentleman.

In 1988, I was devastated with the news that Sylvia had terminal cancer! She had seen her doctor regularly, had proper check-ups and this suddenly exploded into our lives like a thunderbolt. Obviously, we did not know how to deal with it and we stared at each other in silence and then embraced, clinging to each other in desperation. I don't know what I can attribute it to but shock. Sylvia seemed to take the news very calmly. She immediately went into the traditional chemotherapy and although I knew that she was in great pain, she never complained and seemed to accept her fate in quiet dignity. I was not that stoic. It hit me with the force of colliding meteors. The horrible knowledge that she was destined to die in a short period of time was more than I could bear. Sylvia's doctor informed me as gently as he could that it was malignant and his prognosis was that she could die as early as two months. It was during this time that Larry, who was not one to show warmth or human affection, called and asked me to join him in San Diego. He was to fly from England to appear as guest soloist with the San Diego Symphony Orchestra. He asked me to appear with him on stage as a surprise guest. He said, "Jerry, I feel what you are experiencing with Sylvia. Please find someone to be with her for one night so you can be with me on stage at the concert." I joined him at his hotel and immediately called home to check on Sylvia. I spoke to the nurse and was told that the end was near but she felt secure in saying that Sylvia would still be alive when I returned home. I dissolved into tears. When I looked up, my brother was approaching me with outstretched arms. I was shocked. I had never seen this side of my brother before. I finally realized how deeply and warmly Larry felt about me, and I certainly felt the same about him. At the concert, Larry introduced me and he sat at the piano. Larry not only taught himself to play the harmonica, but the piano as well. He accompanied me on Gershwin's, *The Man I Love.* It was an evening that filled a lifetime for me. Sylvia survived for two more years and endured great pain and suffering until the end. She died August 6, 1990.

> *Having lost my partner, I felt that there was nothing left to live for.*

I was devastated and quickly slipped into an acute depression. Having lost my partner, I felt that there was nothing left to live for. I brooded for four or five weeks and refused to leave the house. One day, I received a call from Sylvia's oncologist asking me to come to his office. With much reluctance, I agreed to see him. When I entered his office, he told his nurse that he did not wish to be disturbed. He gently proceeded to discuss Sylvia and her remarkably heroic attitude about her malignancy. It was not too difficult for him to recognize that I was having great difficulty with this conversation. His obvious concern for my grief was truly touching. He urged me to contact my agent and get back to work as quickly as possible. His theory being that mourning the death of a beloved spouse is perfectly natural, but the sooner I started concentrating on my own life, the better off I would be. A difficult theory to live by, considering the fact that we had been married for forty-five years!

♫

Sagafjord

Four months later, with great trepidation, I boarded the Sagafjord in Acapulco. It seemed so strange to be doing this with the realization that Sylvia would never be with me again. Perhaps I had made a dreadful mistake in accepting this cruise so soon after Sylvia's death. However, I thought about those four hellish weeks sitting alone in our home for hours at a time, just staring at the walls, wishing that it was all a nightmare and Sylvia would be walking into the room any second.

Sometimes I would get in my car and drive aimlessly around the city. I am not a loner and could not see myself spending the rest of my life in this manner. I took stock of my options and knew that I could always fall back into working cruise ships. Other than that, my future looked pretty bleak. I hated Los Angeles and had planned to discuss a major move with Sylvia before she became ill. I had to get out of that home and I had to leave the city.

Being aboard the Sagafjord, allowed me the time to do a great deal of soul searching. I knew I would never find anyone who could even come close to how I felt about Sylvia and I certainly had not made any plans to start "looking". I was extremely apprehensive aboard ship and that, in itself, was a new and horrifying experience. I tried valiantly to be my usual, gregarious self and was determined to throw myself into the happy-go-lucky den of fun. It was far more difficult than I had imagined, and for a brief time, I was seriously tempted to have the Cruise Director contact the New York office and ask to be released from my contract. I went so far as to take Danny into my confidence. I asked him to join me in the North Cape Lounge for a drink where we could talk privately. He was my contemporary and I felt that he would be a compassionate listener. I poured my heart out to him in detail and he listened without interrupting. When I had finished, he said, "Jerry, don't even think about throwing in the towel. Your life is now your music and you have so much to offer. Please make it count for something. Do you think that Sylvia would approve especially after all of her work to get you into the cruise business?" Of course, he was right and I thanked him for listening, but my emotions were so deep seated that it obstructed my sense of reality. Sylvia and I had been married for so long that I felt that somebody had sliced me in half. It had a nightmarish quality and I did a lot of private crying.

My efforts to meet people aboard ship began to work and I started to believe that all was not lost. One day, a woman spotted me on deck, rushed over with her arms outstretched, squealing with delight. I did not remember her name but knew that we had sailed together before. "Jerry, it's so good to see you again. Gosh, I haven't seen you since the trip to Australia on the Royal Viking Star. Is Sylvia with you?" I felt that I had been slugged in the stomach with a baseball bat. This was the first of many incidents like that. The little "reunion" had set me back a few days.

All things considered, I slept well that night which I attribute to emotional exhaustion. I awoke feeling refreshed and after showering and shaving, I went up to the Lido Lounge where most people have their buffet breakfast. I filled my tray but wished to eat alone. I took my tray outdoors near the pool and after breakfast, struck up a conversation with a gentleman. As we chatted, I noticed a lady sitting with a couple and she was working on her needlepoint. Needlepoint being one of my favorite hobbies, I was curious as to what she was working on. I excused myself and walked over to their table. I told her that I also do needlepoint and was curious about hers. She held it up for me and it was beautiful. I complimented her on her neat work and then introduced myself, explaining that I was an entertainer and had just boarded in Acapulco. When I mentioned my name, she nearly jumped out of her chair. "So you're Jerry Adler.!" I didn't know what she meant but she then explained her excitement. She had boarded the ship in Los Angeles and, by coincidence, we had a mutual friend. She was visiting her brother and sister-in-law and some friends had been invited for coffee and one of the guests said, "I understand that you do a lot of cruising. Have you ever sailed with an entertainer named, Jerry Adler? I told her that I had heard of you but we had never sailed together. She said that she knew you very well and I should look for you in the future because you are supposed to be an excellent performer. It's strange that you should be aboard at this time."

Jean Ruppa

She then introduced me to her friends and invited me to join them. Her name was Jean Ruppa and the lady with whom she was traveling, was Fran Gustavson. The gentleman's name was Bob Fray, who was traveling alone. She asked if I had brought my needlepoint and when I nodded yes, she insisted that I bring it up on deck so she could see it. All three had made me feel very comfortable and I was grateful for the company. I brought the needlepoint back and they politely told me how lovely it was. Jean asked me about my family so I had to tell her about Sylvia and that I had two married children but no grandchildren.

Again, I was not looking and neither was Jean. She had been a widow for eighteen years so it seemed pretty obvious that she wasn't looking around for a husband at that stage of her life. We did spend an inordinate amount of time together as a foursome just because we were comfortable with each other. I made the comment to Jean that I felt that I had known her for years, which startled her. "You're going to think that I'm putting you on but I have been feeling the same way."

My contract began in Acapulco and ended in Aruba. We went through the Panama Canal and stopped at several Caribbean ports. I disembarked in Aruba and Jean, Fran and Bob continued on to other ports. I felt a strange depression when I disembarked. At first, I thought that it was because I was disappointed in leaving the Sagafjord. However, it wasn't the ship. It was Jean! That threw me into a mental turmoil so I knew that I had to get my thoughts and priorities in order. I said goodbye to all of them and left the ship to fly to Ft. Lauderdale to spend a week layover before joining the Regent Sea in Barbados.

I stayed with Sylvia's aunt, Eve Rintzler, and enjoyed a very relaxing week. The longer that I was away from Jean, the more I missed her. I did not know how to deal with this new feeling and the more I thought about it, the more confused I became. I did not dare reveal these feeling to Eve because I was not sure what my feelings were! My God, this was the first woman that I had met since Sylvia died! I just hoped that the next cruise would give me the chance to straighten out an already confused state of mind. I was thrilled and terrified at the same time.

Spending one week with Eve was the best therapy for me. She has always been a delightful lady with a positive attitude and was one of the family favorites. She adored Sylvia and I was afraid to say anything to her about my emotional problems.

One evening, I finally gathered up enough courage to tell Eve about Jean. She dealt with the news beautifully and her advice was as straightforward and honest as she always had been. She said, "The lady sounds too good to be true, but I would urge you to consider your own life and try to visualize your life with her. Please give yourself a little more time before you make such an important decision. However, if you continue to have these same, strong feelings about Jean, my advice is, don't let her get away." I hugged her tightly and thanked her for not coming on too strong in either direction. I could not resist throwing in what was obviously on her mind. "And she's Jewish, too!" As if that would have made any difference to me. She seemed pleased but said, "Her name is Jean Ruppa? What kind of a Jewish name is Ruppa?"

I knew that I had to make a decision and it had to be soon. Eve said, "By the way, how does she feel about you?"

Oh my God, that thought had never entered my mind! In retrospect, it was just as well that I didn't know at that particular time.

On the second day, I told Eve that I was going to their community swimming pool for a swim. She said, "Fine. Go ahead and enjoy yourself but look out for the barracudas."

I innocently asked, "What do you mean?"

She smiled and said, "You'll find out."

On the east coast of Florida, the population is predominantly Jewish and it is an area unlike any other place in the world. Some of the greatest comedy situations in theater were derived from life on the east coast of Florida. Most of the population originated in the Bronx and Brooklyn and eventually transplanted themselves to Florida. When I entered the pool gate, I quickly counted about twenty-five to thirty people in the pool area. Four ladies were sitting on the pool steps. One of them moved over to make a path for me. She looked at me coyly and said, "You're new here?"

I told her that I was visiting my aunt, Mrs. Rintzler.

"Oh, you're de nephew!" I nodded, yes. The next question caught me by surprise.

"So tell me. You're married?"

"No, I'm not. Why do you ask?"

She smiled and winked. "Nuttin' . . . jost esking."

Some were in the pool and some were in deck chairs soaking up the sun on the pool perimeter. I swam a couple of laps and heard a man who was also in the pool call out in a loud voice to a man who was sunning himself in a deck chair. "Hey, Irving! You'll cover up, fer God sake! I can see your jock strap!"

That evening, I invited Eve out for dinner. Being unfamiliar with the area, I asked her where she would like to go. She said, "How about Pumperniks?"

"Is the food good?"

"It's probably the best Jewish deli-restaurant in town."

A good bowl of bean and barley soup plus an order of stuffed cabbage started my juices flowing. I had rented a car so we drove to Pumperniks. There were three lines of people standing outside and it looked as if we would never be served.

I said, "Maybe we should find another restaurant. This looks as if it's going to take forever."

She assured me, "Don't worry about it. Each line is for different sized parties. One is for singles, the middle one is for parties of two and the other is for parties for three or more. The lines move very fast."

I sensed that this was going to be a memorable experience.

"I'm from CBS and we're here doing a special...

As soon as we were seated, I had a bright idea but first I had to get my video camera out of the car. I had not seen such a gathering since

I worked in the Catskills when I was a kid. None of them seemed to have changed! They all looked like the same people! My camera was one of the old type RCAs which was large by today's standards and looked much like a professional studio camera. Eve took one look and said, "Oh, God! You're you going to use that thing in here?" I promised that I would not embarrass her. I walked up to the Manager, holding my camera and said, "I'm from CBS and we're here doing a special to show how the Jewish community lives in Florida. Would you mind if I took a few shots in your restaurant?" I could see that he was delighted to get the free publicity on national TV.

"Sure, go ahead and take all you want."

Before I had the chance to take my first shot, rumors quickly spread that there was a cameraman from "60 Minutes" in the restaurant to shoot video. As I glanced around, women were frantically going through their purses for brush, comb, mirror and lipstick. Other women were pulling down on their blouses, revealing more cleavage than I cared to see. Men were pushing their hair back and removing their glasses.

I announced in a fairly loud voice that I was about to shoot some video and asked everyone to please act natural, converse with each other like always but under no circumstances, look directly into the camera. I turned the camera on and slowly began to move down one aisle. The first lady looked directly into the lens and said, "You from "60 Minutes?" I nodded, yes. "S'funny, you don't look like Mike Villiss." At another table, a woman expressed her disappointment. "So why didn't I know you was comin? I jus bought a gawjus outfit, on sale! How long you gonna be here? I jus live around de corner. I'll go home and change and I'll be right back." Another lady yelled to me from the other side of the restaurant. "Hey, Mr. CBS! You'll come over an take a pitcher of me!" I walked over to her table and she whispered, "I jus had ah face lift and I want all mine friends to see how gawjus I look." A man yelled, (Jewish people in Florida don't talk. They yell.) "Hey, when we gonna see us on TV?"

I filmed a number of other tables and in twenty minutes, I had enough material for another Jackie Mason concert. One man thought that he had it all figured out. He looked at me wisely and said, "Listen, young fella. You realize dot you kent take mine pitcher on your TV show without foist I'm signink ah waiver."

"I'm sorry sir, but that is no longer required. If you do not wish to be in the shot, I will respect your wishes."

"Dot's OK. Go ahead and shoot me."

I finally finished and sat down with Eve. She was fuming. People kept coming over to our table to give me their names, addresses and phone numbers to be notified when the show would be on. When everyone had left, Eve looked at me scornfully. "How could you do such a thing? Remember, I live here." I apologized and promised that I would not show her on video unless she signed a waiver!

♬

Jewish humor must be enjoyed and digested like a hot bowl of chicken soup. It's too easy to cross the line between good and bad taste. In many respects, we refer to it as a unique art form. I have never seen a non-Jewish comedian do funny Jewish comedy. If the material is funny and is told by a Jewish comedian, Jews will laugh even if it pokes good-natured fun at them. It is also very rare for a comedy writer to write Jewish humor unless he is Jewish. Neil Simon is the undisputed king. Running a close second is Woody Allen.

Jewish humor surfaces without warning, which is part of the magic that separates it from any other comedic form. I have seen many Jewish people who are hysterically funny without realizing it. Here's a good example. I had decided to go to a Jewish deli for lunch. I was standing in line and there were seven people ahead of me. The female manager came to the front of the line holding a bundle of menus. "How many in yer party?" A woman replied, "Five."

"Dis vay, plizz."

This left one lady in front of me. The manager returned, "Party of two?"

The woman said, "No, just one."

She looked at both of us. "You ain't togedder?"

"No," replied the woman. The manager looked sadly at us. "Dot's too bad. You look like soch a nice copple."

♫

> *If you love what you do, it is the best of both worlds.*

I have been asked many questions about cruising and what it feels like to be an entertainer aboard ship. My answer has always been the same. "If you love what you do, it is the best of both worlds." The first priority is professional acceptance. However, unlike any other form of entertainment, the responsibility aboard ship does not stop there. Being gregarious helps considerably and a natural, genuine desire to meet new people is a very important attribute. For the record, none of the additional responsibilities are contractually necessary. They are all done on a voluntary basis as part of an overall public relations contribution to enhance the ship's image as well as your own. I have strong opinions on how we, as entertainers, conduct ourselves publicly aboard ship. More than in any other phase of show business, public relations plays a major role. Most passengers are fascinated with an entertainer's life and they appreciated an easy line of communication with them. I take exception to performers who choose to remain isolated from passengers. They are only visible when they do their shows or when they appear for meals. Their leisure time is usually spent in their cabins or they hide themselves away in a corner of the top deck, rarely used by passengers, to read a book or sun themselves.

I was astonished the first time that I heard passengers discuss a particular entertainer with the added comment, "But we never see him around." Of course, amongst the passengers, one will always find a small percentage of bores, but an effort should be made to find out what makes them tick but still understand the fact that they are interested in meeting you, the entertainer. I am fortunate in that I enjoy meeting everyone. When I form friendships aboard ship it is because I quickly discover that we have much in common. One of the major assets that I look for is someone with a keen mind and a good sense of humor. That is how I met my second wife, Jean.

♫

Regent Sea
Jim Russell

When I boarded the Regent Sea, it was my debut on that ship. My head was swimming in many directions and I knew that I had to concentrate on this new engagement. My dear friend, Derek Mann, former Cruise Director with Royal Viking was now the Cruise Director on this ship and I could not have been happier. I had invited one of my best friends from California, Jim Russell, to join me as my guest. We had shared so many of our personal problems together and he was very much a part of our lives before Sylvia's death. He was more like a brother than just a friend and has always been great company. He promised me that he would not allow me to lapse into a depression. He flew to Miami where we met at the airport and we flew together to join the ship in Barbados.

Jim and I had a great time aboard ship. He is an extremely gregarious individual, and when he smiles, he lights up the entire room. Things were going well and it gave me an opportunity to think about Jean and consider the possibility that she could be the one to fill a gaping void in my life. As I continued to think more about her, the word "love" began creeping into my head. My God, could I actually be in love with Jean while still mourning the death of Sylvia? Perhaps I was heading for a tremendous fall. What if Jean was not interested in marrying me?

271

While aboard the Regent Sea, I made a point of going out on deck at night to find a private spot along the rail to "talk to Sylvia." My conversation with her may sound bizarre but it gave me great peace of mind. (Sylvia, at her request, was cremated and her ashes had been put into the Pacific Ocean.) I would lean against the rail and talk softly to her for about an hour. I told her about Jean and asked her what she thought about it. I needed answers but more important, I needed approval from Sylvia that I was doing the right thing. I knew in my heart that I had received the right answers. It felt as if a heavy load had been lifted from my shoulders.

We were due to arrive in Ft. Lauderdale in three days. Two days before docking, I began to have severe chest pains. As a matter of fact, I had had similar pains while aboard the Sagafjord but not as severe. I chalked it up to mental stress. I had a show to do that night and Jim urged me to call Derek and arrange for a replacement. He also wanted me to see the ship's doctor immediately.

I refused both suggestions. I had pain medication with me and took it before doing the show. I did not sense any difficulty during the show and talked myself into the fact that it was probably gas! When I came off stage, I broke into a cold sweat and went directly to my cabin and flopped on my bed. I took another pain pill and Jim sat next to me looking very worried but quite angry at my stubborn attitude.

He said, "You are the most frustrating, stubborn sonofabitch I have ever known!"

The pill was doing its job and I began to smile which only made him more angry. He said, "You are going to see a doctor as soon as we dock! Will you promise me that you will?"

At that point, I knew that something serious was wrong and I did promise.

Hannah Owen

My agent, Hannah Owen was there to meet me because I had planned to be her house guest for a couple of days before flying to California. Jim was flying right back. When I walked down the gangway, Hanna took one look at me and knew that something was wrong. I asked her if she could drive me right to her doctor's office, which she did. The doctor gave me an EKG immediately and then scheduled me for an angiogram at the hospital. I was awake during the procedure and there was a TV screen above my head to show what they were doing. He pointed out that two of my arteries were completely blocked and the third had ninety percent blockage. He said that he was scheduling me for open heart by-pass surgery in the morning.

I yelled, "Are you crazy! I'm not going anywhere but home!"

> "...if you move from this table, you will never survive beyond that door!"

The doctor said, "Mr. Adler, if you move from this table, you will never survive beyond that door!"

Now that I had the diagnosis, I was more determined than ever to go home and have the surgery performed there. I was not about to place my life in the hands of strangers without the comfort of love and sense of security from family and good friends. I told the doctor what I wanted to do and he quietly said, "If you decide to fly home in your condition, it is my opinion that you will never survive the flight." Strangely enough, I was willing to take that chance. I had lived a full, wonderful life and if it was my fate to die at that time, so be it. The doctor said, "I'm sorry but I cannot assume that responsibility if you leave here without my permission."

I said, "Can you please call my doctor in Los Angeles and explain the situation?" He agreed and made the call. When he described the diagnosis and the prognosis, I could hear my doctor shouting through the phone. He turned and said, "Your doctor wants to talk to you."

My doctor said, "Are you out of your mind? You cannot fly anywhere in your condition! I insist that you have the surgery performed there."

"Doctor, I apologize for sounding like a stubborn mule but nothing will keep me here and all of the cajoling and threats will not change my mind."

He heaved a sigh of despair. "OK, you idiot. However, I insist that you follow my orders to the letter with a promise from you that you will do it."

I meekly replied, "OK, doctor. Whatever you say."

"I want you transported to the airport by ambulance, placed in a wheelchair and wheeled aboard the plane all the way to your seat! Understand, so far?"

"Yes, I understand perfectly."

"You will remain in that seat unless you need to go to the bathroom. The stewardess will take you there and bring you back. When you arrive in Los Angeles, there will be an ambulance for you, and your son will also be there. You will be taken directly to Good Samaritan Hospital and will be scheduled for surgery."

I thanked him and said that I would see him in Los Angles. Well, it was finally settled.

The Florida doctor had his nurse call Delta Airlines to inform them of the emergency. It was December 23rd and everything was booked solid so someone had to be bumped to accommodate me. I was wheeled out to the ambulance and taken immediately to Delta departure. A wheelchair was waiting for me at the curb. Hanna, my agent had followed the ambulance to the airport. The departure schedule indicated that our flight was on time.

Hanna was quite worried. "Jerry, are you OK? I hate to say this but I have an important appointment and must leave."

I said, "Don't worry. I have been sedated and I'm feeling comfortable. The plane leaves in forty-five minutes so please go to your appointment. Thank you so much for your help. I could not have made it without you."

She leaned down and kissed me and squeezed my hand and whispered, "Good luck. I will be praying for you."

One minute after Hanna left, a change was made on the departure schedule. Our flight would be delayed for four hours due to adverse weather conditions. Our plane was coming in from Chicago. Someone from Delta said to me, "I am taking you to the Club Lounge where you can stretch out on a couch until flight time." Those were very happy words to hear. I actually fell asleep and was gently awakened to be told that the flight would be ready for boarding very soon.

They wheeled me aboard and lifted me from the chair to my aisle seat. The woman next to me weighed in excess of two hundred pounds and was already falling asleep on my shoulder and we were still on the ground! The Chief Stewardess noticed it and moved the lady's head in the other direction without awakening her!

Shortly after takeoff, the Stewardess said, "Sir, you are not looking well. May I place an oxygen mask on you?" I nodded, yes and must admit that it did make me feel better. The mask was finally removed and, all things considered, I was feeling comfortable. We were now about two hours into the flight when the Stewardess approached me once more.

"I do not wish to alarm you sir, but you are not looking well. I am going to ask the pilot to please land at the nearest airfield or turn back." I feebly answered, "If you do, I will cause a great deal of trouble. I appreciate your concern but I am determined to make it to Los Angeles and that is that." She recognized that I meant it so she shrugged her shoulders and walked away.

We arrived in Los Angeles at 9:10 P.M. and I was not feeling that great. I was actually looking forward to the ambulance so I could lie down. The Chief Stewardess announced that the emergency patient would be removed from the plane before anyone else disembarked. My son Michael was there and he obviously looked distressed although it was heart-warming to see his face. They brought a wheelchair aboard and I was lifted into it and quickly wheeled me out. I was placed on a gurney and rushed to the ambulance. I was promptly transported to Good Samaritan Hospital. Michael magically appeared which automatically gave me a great comfort.

That is the last thing that I remember until I half awoke in Intensive Care with a tube down my throat, thoroughly confused. I vaguely recalled hearing voices saying Merry Christmas to each other but at that time, none of it made any sense.

I then heard a familiar voice say, "You're OK, now. The surgery was successful and you're going to be fine." It was the voice of one of my dearest friends, Irma Mitchell. I could not make the connection until much later when she and her husband, Ben visited me in my regular room. Irma had told the nurse that she was my sister. That is why she was allowed in Intensive Care.

It is strange how Jean found out about my surgery. Jean lived in Sarasota and knew that I was planning to stay with my agent, Hanna Owen and her husband, Dag, for a couple of days. Jean called and Dag answered. She asked to speak to me and he had to tell her that I was back in California and had undergone triple by-pass surgery after suffering a heart attack aboard the Regent Sea.

Jean screamed, "My God, is he all right?"

"As far as I know, he's fine. The surgery was successful. As a matter of fact, I can give you the phone number of his room."

Jean called me immediately and when I answered, she said, "Good God, you sound as if nothing was wrong!" The strange part is that I do not remember her calling me!

Jean and I did not see each other for two months, but we spoke to each other often. She wanted to come to Los Angeles immediately but I insisted that she remain in Sarasota until I was in better shape and could move around on my own. It was obvious that we were serious about each other.

After two months of rest, the doctor said that, if I was feeling up to it, I could go back to work. Although I did not admit it to Jean, I was apprehensive about returning to cruising so soon. One of my problems, if you can call it a problem, is that I always give one hundred percent of my energy to my performances. I called my good friend,

Brian Beaton at Cunard and asked what was available. He said that he had a five day Atlantic crossing on the QE-2 from Southampton to New York. I accepted.

♫

QE-2

I called Jean to tell her what I was about to do and she seemed very concerned that I was pushing too fast. I assured her that if I was not feeling well enough, I wouldn't do it. I promised to keep in close touch with her and she reluctantly accepted my decision. I called my agent, Hanna and told her that I had spoken to Brian so she made all of the necessary arrangements. My brother lived in London and we were anxious to see each other. Shortly after my surgery, Larry and I had a brief but pleasant few days together before I joined the ship. When I performed my first show, I knew that my fears were groundless. I felt and played better than before!

The QE-2 was the clincher insofar as reaching a conclusion about Jean. I knew then that I was in love with her but was not sure that she was ready to make the traumatic move to marriage again. I was seventy two and did not have the luxury of biding my time. I remembered what Sylvia's aunt had said. "If you really love her, don't let her get away." My age was, in one sense, a blessing. Had I procrastinated before asking Jean to marry me, there was always the chance that I might lose her. I still didn't know how she felt about getting married. I flew home after the cruise on the first week of April 1991. I called her as soon as I got home and bravely discarded the preliminaries, told her that I loved her, and she, just as quickly said that she loved me. We talked of many things concerning our future.

I finally said, "Well, what do you think?" There was a pause that scared the hell out of me. I waited for her reply, holding my breath.

She finally said, "Don't you want to ask me something?"

Stupid me didn't know what she was talking about. "Ask you what?"

She stopped again because I had obviously thrown her one hell of a curve. She must have felt that I knew what she meant so she was at a loss as to what to say next. It is a tribute to her enormous insight that she suddenly realized that I did not have the slightest idea of what she was talking about.

She finally said, "Are you proposing to me?"

I was shocked! What did she think that I meant? I said, "Yes! I'm asking you to marry me!"

> *"…I'm not a mind reader! Of course I'll marry you!"*

She replied, "Well, for God sake, I'm not a mind reader! Of course I'll marry you!"

Jean said, excitedly, that she had much to do at home in preparation for our new life and would fly to Los Angeles in the middle of May. We decided to be married on June 27th. No special reason for the date. It just sounded good. I asked her to send me a photo of herself for my wallet which she did. She had written October 30th on the back which I had assumed was the date that it was taken.

When I spoke to her that night, I asked if it had been taken on October 30th and she said, "Yes, that's my birthday." I was amazed! I said, "That's MY birthday!"

I made a regrettable decision. What I did, I did without thinking it through. Sylvia and I had lived in our North Hollywood home for twenty eight years. The last months of her life were spent in a hospital bed that we had set up in our den, after we had brought her home from the hospital. I know that my decision to have the wedding ceremony there was resented by many family members and friends, but I was so happy about the future that I failed to give myself time to reflect on the past before making that decision. My two children were bitter about it at first and I could not blame them. However, they seemed to understand me better than I understood myself and eventually did forgive me for my impropriety, generously attributing it to my enthusiasm for the future. Fortunately, it was only a handful of people who felt bitter. I knew who they were but never discussed it with them because, frankly, it was none of their business, nor did I wish to go through a dissertation on how to run my life. One of my best friends, Moe Rothman, who was also my best man, admitted to me that he was skeptical and concerned about my planned marriage. I did not resent it coming from Moe because we were such good friends and his only concern was whether I would be happy.

Moe Rothman

One day, Moe came to my home to meet Jean. Although he was meeting her for the first time, I was not in the least concerned. I was convinced that he would immediately recognize her wonderful qualities. By chance, I had an important errand to run so after quickly introducing them, I left, saying that I would only be gone for a short time. When I returned, Moe heard my car in the driveway and he came running out and threw his arms around me. His first words were, "Jerry, you are one lucky guy! I must admit that I had my doubts before meeting Jean, but dammit, you have found yourself a winner!" We hugged each other and he wished us much happiness. That meant a great deal to me because Moe knew me better than anyone. I regret to say that Moe died a year after Jean and I were married.

Our next decision was where we would live. Jean didn't know it but I was determined to leave Los Angeles. I was fed up with that city long before Sylvia became ill. We had even discussed making a move but never got around to deciding where to go. The city was becoming a shooting gallery and, in addition, the smog was killing us. Jean fully expected that we were going to reside in Los Angeles but what I didn't know was that she never liked LA but was still willing to live anywhere with me. One day, I said, "How would you like to move back to

Sarasota?" Jean was overjoyed! She had lived there for the past ten years and loved it. She quickly assured me that I would love it as much as she did. I was ready to give it a fair shot.

The real estate market in California was at its lowest ebb but I put my home up for sale and turned the details over to a very dear friend, Marge Court, who was a real estate agent. We packed everything and had it shipped to Sarasota.

> *...I never wanted to see California again...*

When Jean and I boarded the plane for Florida, I refused to look out of the window. As far as I was concerned, I never wanted to see California again although I knew that I would miss seeing my kids, plus a few very dear friends. I simply hoped that, in time, my kids would manage to visit us. They both promised that they would.

We did not have any idea how long it would take to sell my home but I honestly didn't care. After we had landed and retrieved our luggage, we took a cab to Jean's home. It was quite nice but I felt it to be too confining. We didn't discuss it until the following day. I told her that I wanted to buy a new home with a completely new start for both of us. She agreed but it also created additional problems. We then had to sell Jean's home but we were both on such a high, that we were behaving like young newlyweds. We immediately went house hunting and Jean's real estate agent found us a beautiful home that was exactly what we had in mind, including a screened in pool which added to the wonderful aura of Florida living. Being accustomed to California's amazingly inflated prices, I could not believe how reasonable real estate prices were in Florida. I signed the papers on the same day and was told that it would be available in two weeks. On that same evening, I received a call from my real estate friend in California saying that she had a reasonable offer for my home and I said, "Take it!" We purchased one home and sold another within twenty-four hours which probably sets some kind of record.

We had lived in our new home for five years and still behaving like kids enjoying the fun of owning our first place together. I was still actively performing on the east and west coasts of Florida on weekends. Our main topic of conversation whenever we were on the east coast was, "God, I can't wait until we get back to our own home."

Working the Condos

When word reached the many Florida agents that I now lived in the same state, I was bombarded with offers of work. I was eighty-two and still going strong.

I had worked the condominium circuit before and knew what to expect. Condominium dates were set with forty-five minutes for each show and a fifteen minute intermission in-between. Performing before a senior citizen audience makes the intermission a physical necessity. In my younger days, I hadn't realized how important intermission was. Now I did and being a senior citizen, I could relate much more readily to my audience. I was now one of them.

Traditionally, senior citizens have an amazing love for live entertainment and they become involved as if the acts and the audience were one happy family. If they are encouraged, they like nothing better than to sing along with the performer. There have been times when the audience sang so loud, I couldn't hear myself play! In many cases, they will sing, even if they are not encouraged to do so. One of the selections that I play is Liszt's *2nd Hungarian Rhapsody*. One night, I jokingly suggested that if they knew the words, to please sing along. Damned if they didn't sing, "De de . . . di di dee dee, etc."

Benny Shields

The residents accept certain responsibilities on a voluntary basis. One of them being to M.C. the shows. From a performers standpoint, it works out fairly well, but most of the time, it is a disaster. We usually write out what we would like to have them say about us and we deliberately keep it as brief as possible, but many of them become tongue-tied and screw up the entire introduction. My introduction is usually, "And now, ladies and gentlemen, the harmonica artistry of Jerry Adler." Some will say, The harmonica "artsy" and others say, "The harmonica player of artistically." I try not to listen.

♫

I was working with a marvelous comedian named Benny Shields. Rehearsals are held one hour before show time, which doesn't give a musical performer much time to explain tempos, etc. Somehow, we get through it but it becomes an open invitation for an ulcer.

An elderly man came backstage and it was apparent that he was not in a very good mood. "Awright, so who's de comic?"

Benny said, "That's me. I'm Benny Shields."

"Hokay, so who's gonna open de show?"

Benny and I looked at each other. Closing the show is always the traditional spot for the headliner. I knew Benny very well and was aware that he hated to open a show.

I said, "I'll open the show tonight." Benny looked gratefully at me and nodded.

I know that a comic can be deadly to follow, especially if they are doing well because they are inclined to run far beyond their allotted time.

The M.C. turned to me. "Hokay, so you're gonna hopen de show, right?" I nodded, yes.

He looked menacingly at Benny. "I gots to varn you about suppin'. Dis whole show hincludink announcements and hintermission is gonna run a hundred and tventy minutes. Ve end exactly at ten! Not nine fifty nine. Not ten Oh one. Ten o'clock exactly, Hokay?"

Benny agreed but we were puzzled about the precise time.

I performed for forty-five minutes and was off. I was now fascinated with the mystery of "10 P.M. exactly."

> *The entire audience leaped up as if their seats had been hot wired...*

I made my way to the back of the auditorium to watch Benny. He was on a roll and the people were dissolved in tears of laughter. I looked up at the wall clock and it read, 9:58. It was difficult to hold my breath for two minutes but that is what I felt myself doing. At 9:59, Benny started another story. As the second hand moved around, it finally hit 10:00! I was nearly scared out of my wits. The entire audience leaped up as if their seats had been hot-wired and they all rushed out of the auditorium. Benny was within thirty seconds of the punch line but he was delivering it to an empty house! I stood in the center aisle, dumfounded. Benny yelled, "Jerry! What the hell happened? Where'd everybody go?"

The M.C. ran up to the edge of the stage and looked up, shaking his finger at poor Benny.

"I tuld you, dammit! I varned you, dummy! Dun't go pest ten!"

I ran to the back to see where everyone had gone. I found them in another huge room, all seated at tables, eating grapefruit. I saw the custodian leaning against the wall and asked him to explain the bizarre behavior.

He said, "Simple. Lemmie tell ya. We serve a free half a grapefruit at 10:00 P.M. Each grapefruit has a cherry on top. If the people don't get to their proper seats on time, somebody is always stealing the cherry off their grapefruit!" Makes sense!

No Regrets

Crystal Harmony

Jean and I were aboard one of the most beautiful ships in the cruise industry, the Crystal Harmony. It is Japanese owned but run by Norwegians. It became obvious to me as soon as we boarded that this ship was going to be something very special. The exquisite detail and the planning of the ship in terms of ambience and plush comfort, proved to me that they had left nothing to chance.

Besides the usual pluses made available on most of the newer luxury ships, such as gourmet food, beautiful gift shops, magnificent exercise facilities, etc. they had, in the Main Ballroom, facilities unheard of on any other ship. The huge, theater size stage, top quality lighting and state of the art sound system were enhanced by professionally equipped dressing rooms backstage. It was a dream come true!

One area in particular that was my favorite during the day was the Club Lido. This is where the marvelous buffet breakfasts and lunches were served. I was particularly fascinated to watch the passengers cue up for the buffets. One day, I was sitting at a table close to the beginning of the line. A woman had taken a front position fifteen minutes before the buffet was open. Quickly, a line began to form and at 12:30, they opened it up for lunch. As the line started forward, the lady in front yelled, "Murray! They've got your favorite, spaghetti and meat balls." She was yelling to her husband who was also in line but ten people back. A short time later, she shouted, "Murray, don't forget to take plenty of green vegetables. They're good for you, Murray." As the line moved along, she again yelled, "Murray! Guess what! They've got your favorite cheese cake, Murray." As the lady left the line, she screamed, "Murray, I'm gonna save a table by the window, Murray."

I watched them both with fascination. As soon as he had set his tray down, he left to go to the men's room. I jumped up and approached his wife.

"Excuse me for interrupting, but may I ask you a question?"

She looked up with her mouth full of spaghetti. "Sure. What is it?"

I said, "Well, I play a little game with myself. I love to watch people and try to guess their first names. I was watching your husband and I said to myself, "That man is a Murray. Am I correct?"

She let a meatball fall out of her mouth. "Oh my God! That's amazing! Yes, you're right! His name is Murray! Wait until he gets back. He won't believe it!" I made a hasty retreat.

♫

Abilene Philharmonic Orchestra

I have always yearned to be a guest soloist with a first rate Pops Symphony orchestra. I was offered that opportunity when my agent booked me with the Abilene Philharmonic in Abilene, Texas in March of 1992. Abilene is a medium sized Texas town with a large number of loyal supporters for the arts. I felt that I would not be working with the kind of orchestra that I had hoped for. How wrong I was! When I arrived at the airport, the conductor, George Yaeger and his wife plus several people from the press and TV were there to greet me.

George and his wife drove me to the hotel. He said that he would be rehearsing the orchestra in the morning and didn't need me until after lunch. The auditorium was located opposite the hotel. The following afternoon, I made my appearance and was introduced to the eighty piece orchestra. The auditorium was first rate and beautifully built which seated two thousand. I was told that the concert was sold out! As soon as the orchestra played the first few bars of music, I knew that I was in the company of first class musicians. I can say, without reservation, that it was a thrilling musical experience. I was truly inspired and played better than I had ever played. The audience responded with a thrilling, spontaneous standing ovation. Once the concert was over, I was told that a cocktail party was being held in my honor at George Yaeger's home. The house was filled with the important patrons of the season.

I have devoted the last sixty-six years of my life to nearly every phase of show business from night clubs to motion pictures, television, recordings, condominiums, cruise ships, concerts and yes, even a circus! The entertainment business has been very good to me and at the risk of sounding immodest, I feel that I have been good for show business.

There is an amazing, ironic twist to the inevitable end of my professional career. I found myself being more in demand than I had been in the past. Perhaps maturity has much to do with it as well as the fact that I can more closely relate to my audiences. I am still fiercely proud of what I do and am appalled at younger performers who feel that they know it all and resent good advice, mistaking it for jealous interference. I will always be grateful to Red Skelton and Jimmy Durante, who unselfishly took the time and trouble to teach me things that would normally have taken years to learn. Show business is one of the most fascinating and gratifying professions and I am very proud to be a member of a business that places great emphasis on originality, creativity, and, last but certainly not least, talent. It is unique in one other way. I do have a tendency, at times, to be impatient with performers who are so spoiled by venues like cruise ships that they whine and complain if they are asked to work an extra show. These people were never exposed to the days of vaudeville when it was natural to work four and five shows a day!

I will always be grateful to the audiences who responded to my performances with such enthusiasm. Applause is the icing as well as the cake. Being an entertainer has kept me young in health and spirit despite my by-pass heart surgery. I continued performing as long as God gave me the strength and stamina to do it.

I have a loving wife as well as a new life. My children are happy and we continue to have a close relationship despite the miles that separate us.

Moving to Sarasota, Florida proved to be a professional windfall. I never anticipated that I would find a new venue for musical expression in this city. I was encouraged by Jean to join the Sarasota Jazz Club. I soon discovered that the membership was loaded with top level musicians from New York, Chicago and Los Angeles who, like myself, moved to Sarasota to retire. I became very active and performed three successful jazz concerts. I had always yearned to perform jazz in front of an audience and this was a new challenge to an entirely new form of music for me. It was a marvelous revelation to a kind of music that I never thought that I was capable of performing on a professional level.

I began writing this memoir in February 1994. It is now May 2005. I will be 87 in October and, all things considered, feel relatively good. I have been retired from show business for over two years. Of course, people ask, "Do you miss it?" Of course I do but I also had the sense to quit while I was ahead.

Jean and I now live in Milwaukee, Wisconsin to be close to her family. Her son, Paul Ruppa and his beautiful wife, Pam and their two marvelous children, JoAnna and Anderson. We are now living the glorious feeling of being active grandparents, a gift that I never expected to enjoy as much as I do.

"Living From Hand To Mouth" has been my life in the nicest sense of this popular expression.

♫

Index

Printed in the United States
56710LVS00005B/1-96

9 781420 861228